MznLnx

Missing Links Exam Preps

Exam Prep for

Physical Geology

Plummer, McGeary, & Carlson, 9th Edition

The MznLnx Exam Prep is your link from the texbook and lecture to your exams.
The MznLnx Exam Preps are unauthorized and comprehensive reviews of your textbooks.

All material provided by MznLnx and Rico Publications (c) 2010
Textbook publishers and textbook authors do not particpate in or contribute to these reviews.

MznLnx

Rico
Publications

Exam Prep for Physical Geology
9th Edition
Plummer, McGeary, & Carlson

Publisher: Raymond Houge
Assistant Editor: Michael Rouger
Text and Cover Designer: Lisa Buckner
Marketing Manager: Sara Swagger
Project Manager, Editorial Production: Jerry Emerson
Art Director: Vernon Lowerui

Product Manager: Dave Mason
Editorial Assitant: Rachel Guzmanji
Pedagogy: Debra Long
Cover Image: Jim Reed/Getty Images
Text and Cover Printer: City Printing, Inc.
Compositor: Media Mix, Inc.

(c) 2010 Rico Publications
ALL RIGHTS RESERVED. No part of this work
covered by the copyright may be reproduced or
used in any form or by an means--graphic, electronic,
or mechanical, including photocopying, recording,
taping, Web distribution, information storage, and
retrieval systems, or in any other manner--without the
written permission of the publisher.

Printed in the United States
ISBN:

For more information about our products, contact us at:
Dave.Mason@RicoPublications.com

For permission to use material from this text or
product, submit a request online to:
Dave.Mason@RicoPublications.com

Contents

CHAPTER 1
Introduction to Physical Geology — 1

CHAPTER 2
Atoms, Elements, and Minerals — 10

CHAPTER 3
Igneous Rocks, Intrusive Activity, and the Origin of Igneous Rocks — 18

CHAPTER 4
Volcanism and Extrusive Rocks — 29

CHAPTER 5
Weathering and Soil — 38

CHAPTER 6
Sediments and Sedimentary Rocks — 48

CHAPTER 7
Metamorphism, Metamorphic Rocks, and Hydrothermal Rocks — 61

CHAPTER 8
Time and Geology — 73

CHAPTER 9
Mass Wasting — 83

CHAPTER 10
Streams and Floods — 90

CHAPTER 11
Ground Water — 100

CHAPTER 12
Glaciers and Glaciation — 111

CHAPTER 13
Deserts and Wind Action — 121

CHAPTER 14
Waves, Beaches and Coasts — 130

CHAPTER 15
Geologic Structures — 137

CHAPTER 16
Earthquakes — 143

CHAPTER 17
Earth's Interior and Geophysical Properties — 151

CHAPTER 18
The Sea Floor — 162

CHAPTER 19
Plate Tectonics — 173

CHAPTER 20
Mountain Belts and the Continental Crust — 187

Contents (Cont.)

CHAPTER 21
   Geologic Resources   197
ANSWER KEY   210

TO THE STUDENT

COMPREHENSIVE

The *MznLnx* Exam Prep series is designed to help you pass your exams. Editors at MznLnx review your textbooks and then prepare these practice exams to help you master the textbook material. Unlike study guides, workbooks, and practice tests provided by the texbook publisher and textbook authors, *MznLnx* gives you **all** of the material in each chapter in exam form, not just samples, so you can be sure to nail your exam.

MECHANICAL

The MznLnx Exam Prep series creates exams that will help you learn the subject matter as well as test you on your understanding. Each question is designed to help you master the concept. Just working through the exams, you gain an understanding of the subject--its a simple mechanical process that produces success.

INTEGRATED STUDY GUIDE AND REVIEW

MznLnx is not just a set of exams designed to test you, its also a comprehensive review of the subject content. Each exam question is also a review of the concept, making sure that you will get the answer correct without having to go to other sources of material. You learn as you go! Its the easiest way to pass an exam.

HUMOR

Studying can be tedious and dry. MznLnx's instructional design includes moderate humor within the exam questions on occassion, to break the tedium and revitalize the brain

Chapter 1. Introduction to Physical Geology 1

1. An _____ is the result from the sudden release of stored energy in the Earth's crust that creates seismic waves. At the Earth's surface, earthquakes may manifest themselves by a shaking or displacement of the ground. An _____ is caused by tectonic plates getting stuck and putting a strain on the ground. The strain becomes so great that rocks give way by breaking and sliding along fault planes.
   - a. Earthquake0
   - b. Thing
   - c. Undefined
   - d. Undefined

2. _____ is the native consolidated rock underlying the Earth's surface. Above the _____ is usually an area of broken and weathered unconsolidated rock in the basal subsoil.
   - a. Thing
   - b. Bedrock0
   - c. Undefined
   - d. Undefined

3. _____ are earthquakes in the same region of the central shock but of smaller magnitude and which occur with a pattern that follows Omori's law.
   - a. Aftershocks0
   - b. Thing
   - c. Undefined
   - d. Undefined

4. The _____ is defined as the part of the land adjoining or near the ocean. A coastline is properly a line on a map indicating the disposition of a _____, but the word is often used to refer to the _____ itself. The adjective coastal describes something as being on, near to, or associated with a _____.
   - a. Place
   - b. Coast0
   - c. Undefined
   - d. Undefined

5. _____ is a field of study within geology concerned generally with the structures within the crust of the Earth, or other planets, and particularly with the forces and movements that have operated in a region to create these structures.
   - a. Thing
   - b. Tectonics0
   - c. Undefined
   - d. Undefined

6. _____ is a theory of geology that has been developed to explain the observed evidence for large scale motions of the Earth's lithosphere. The theory encompassed and superseded the older theory of continental drift.
   - a. Thing
   - b. Plate tectonics0
   - c. Undefined
   - d. Undefined

7. Faults are planar rock fractures, which show evidence of relative movement. Large faults within the Earth's crust are the result of shear motion and active _____ zones are the causal locations of most earthquakes. Earthquakes are caused by energy release during rapid slippage along faults. The largest examples are at tectonic plate boundaries but many faults occur far from active plate boundaries. Since faults do not usually consist of a single, clean fracture, the term _____ zone is used when referring to the zone of complex deformation that is associated with the _____ plane.
   - a. Thing
   - b. Fault0
   - c. Undefined
   - d. Undefined

8. A _____ is a landform that extends above the surrounding terrain in a limited area. A _____ is generally steeper than a hill, but there is no universally accepted standard definition for the height of a _____ or a hill although a _____ usually has an identifiable summit.
   - a. Mountain0
   - b. Place
   - c. Undefined
   - d. Undefined

Chapter 1. Introduction to Physical Geology

9. _____ is the science and study of the solid matter that constitute the Earth. Encompassing such things as rocks, soil, and gemstones, _____ studies the composition, structure, physical properties, history, and the processes that shape Earth's components.
   a. Geology0
   b. Thing
   c. Undefined
   d. Undefined

10. _____ is molten rock expelled by a volcano during an eruption. When first extruded from a volcanic vent, it is a liquid at temperatures from 700 °C to 1,200 °C.
    a. Lava0
    b. Thing
    c. Undefined
    d. Undefined

11. _____ are clastic rocks composed solely or primarily of volcanic materials.
    a. Pyroclastics0
    b. Thing
    c. Undefined
    d. Undefined

12. A _____ is an opening, or rupture, in the Earth's surface or crust, which allows hot, molten rock, ash and gases to escape from deep below the surface.
    a. Volcano0
    b. Thing
    c. Undefined
    d. Undefined

13. A _____ is a common and devastating result of some volcanic eruptions. The flows are fast-moving fluidized bodies of hot gas, ash and rock. The flows normally hug the ground and travel downhill under gravity, their speed depending upon the gradient of the slope and the size of the flow.
    a. Thing
    b. Pyroclastic flow0
    c. Undefined
    d. Undefined

14. _____ consists of very fine rock and mineral particles less than 2 mm in diameter that are ejected from a volcanic vent. The very fine particles may be carried for many miles, settling out as a dust-like layer across the landscape
    a. Thing
    b. Ash fall0
    c. Undefined
    d. Undefined

15. A _____ is the most rapid up to 80 km/h and fluid type of downhill mass wasting.
    a. Thing
    b. Mudflow0
    c. Undefined
    d. Undefined

16. A _____ is a body of water with a current, confined within a bed and banks. Streams are important as conduits in the water cycle, instruments in aquifer recharge, and corridors for fish and wildlife migration.
    a. Stream0
    b. Thing
    c. Undefined
    d. Undefined

17. _____ is displacement of solids by the agents of ocean currents, wind, water, or ice by downward or down-slope movement in response to gravity or by living organisms.
    a. Erosion0
    b. Thing
    c. Undefined
    d. Undefined

Chapter 1. Introduction to Physical Geology 3

18. _____ is rock that is of a certain particle size range. In geology, _____ is any loose rock that is at least two millimeters in its largest dimension and no more than 75 millimeters.
   a. Thing
   b. Gravel0
   c. Undefined
   d. Undefined

19. _____ is a naturally occurring liquid found in formations in the Earth consisting of a complex mixture of hydrocarbons of various lengths.
   a. Petroleum0
   b. Thing
   c. Undefined
   d. Undefined

20. _____ is a fossil fuel formed in swamp ecosystems where plant remains were saved by water and mud from oxidization and biodegradation. It is a sedimentary rock, but the harder forms, such as anthracite _____, can be regarded as metamorphic rocks because of later exposure to elevated temperature and pressure. It is composed primarily of carbon along with assorted other elements, including sulfur.
   a. Thing
   b. Coal0
   c. Undefined
   d. Undefined

21. A _____ is a natural resource that cannot be re-made, re-grown or regenerated on a scale comparative to its consumption. It exists in a fixed amount that is used up faster than it can be made by nature.
   a. Non-renewable resources0
   b. Thing
   c. Undefined
   d. Undefined

22. A _____ is a naturally occurring substance formed through geological processes that has a characteristic chemical composition, a highly ordered atomic structure and specific physical properties. A rock, by comparison, is an aggregate of minerals and need not have a specific chemical composition. Minerals range in composition from pure elements and simple salts to very complex silicates with thousands of known forms.
   a. Thing
   b. Mineral0
   c. Undefined
   d. Undefined

23. _____ is a sedimentary rock composed largely of the mineral calcite. _____ often contains variable amounts of silica in the form of chert or flint, as well as varying amounts of clay, silt and sand as disseminations, nodules, or layers within the rock. The primary source of the calcite in _____ is most commonly marine organisms. These organisms secrete shells that settle out of the water column and are deposited on ocean floors as pelagic ooze or alternatively is conglomerated in a coral reef.
   a. Thing
   b. Limestone0
   c. Undefined
   d. Undefined

24. _____ is a gaseous fossil fuel consisting primarily of methane but including significant quantities of ethane, butane, propane, carbon dioxide, nitrogen, helium and hydrogen sulfide.
   a. Thing
   b. Natural gas0
   c. Undefined
   d. Undefined

25. A _____ is a large, slow moving river of ice, formed from compacted layers of snow, that slowly deforms and flows in response to gravity. _____ ice is the largest reservoir of fresh water on Earth, and second only to oceans as the largest reservoir of total water. Glaciers cover vast areas of polar regions but are restricted to the highest mountains in the tropics.

4 **Chapter 1. Introduction to Physical Geology**

  a. Glacier0
  b. Thing
  c. Undefined
  d. Undefined

26. In geology, a _____ is a depression with predominant extent in one direction. The terms U-shaped and V-shaped are descriptive terms of geography to characterize the form of valleys. Most valleys belong to one of these two main types or a mixture of them, at least with respect of the cross section of the slopes or hillsides.
  a. Valley0
  b. Thing
  c. Undefined
  d. Undefined

27. An _____ is a layer of gases that may surround a material body of sufficient mass. The gases are attracted by the gravity of the body, and are retained for a longer duration if gravity is high and the _____'s temperature is low. Some planets consist mainly of various gases, and thus have very deep atmospheres.
  a. Atmosphere0
  b. Place
  c. Undefined
  d. Undefined

28. Earth's _____ is a ~2,900 km thick rocky shell comprizing approximately 70% of Earth's volume. It is predominantly solid and overlies the Earth's iron-rich core, which occupies about 30% of Earth's volume. Past episodes of melting and volcanism at the shallower levels of the _____ have produced a very thin crust of crystallized melt products near the surface, upon which we live.
  a. Mantle0
  b. Thing
  c. Undefined
  d. Undefined

29. In geology, a _____ is the outermost layer of a planet, part of its lithosphere. They are generally composed of a less dense material than its deeper layers.Earths' is composed mainly of basalt and granite. It is cooler and more rigid than the deeper layers of the mantle and core.
  a. Crust0
  b. Thing
  c. Undefined
  d. Undefined

30. _____ is the part of Earth's lithosphere that surfaces in the ocean basins. _____ is primarily composed of mafic rocks, or sima. It is thinner than continental crust, or sial, generally less than 10 kilometers thick, however it is more dense, having a mean density of about 3.3 grams per cubic centimeter.
  a. Oceanic crust0
  b. Thing
  c. Undefined
  d. Undefined

31. The _____ is the layer of granitic, sedimentary, and metamorphic rocks which form the continents and the areas of shallow seabed close to their shores, known as continental shelves. It is less dense than the material of the Earth's mantle and thus "floats" on top of it. _____ is also less dense than oceanic crust, though it is considerably thicker. About 40% of the Earth's surface is now underlain by _____.
  a. Thing
  b. Continental crust0
  c. Undefined
  d. Undefined

32. The _____ is the solid outermost shell of a rocky planet. On the Earth, the _____ includes the crust and the uppermost mantle which is joined to the crust across the Mohorovièiæ discontinuity. _____ is underlain by asthenosphere, the weaker, hotter, and deeper part of the upper mantle.

Chapter 1. Introduction to Physical Geology   5

    a. Lithosphere0
    b. Thing
    c. Undefined
    d. Undefined

33. The _____ is the region of the Earth between 100-200 km below the surface that is the weak or "soft" zone in the upper mantle. It lies just below the lithosphere, which is involved in plate movements and isostatic adjustments. In spite of its heat, pressures keep it plastic, and it has a relatively low density. Seismic waves pass relatively slowly through the _____.
    a. Thing
    b. Asthenosphere0
    c. Undefined
    d. Undefined

34. A _____ is a geological feature that is also known as a Rip in the earth causing magma to flow out and forming an undersea volcano, it also has geological features, a continuous elevational crest for some distance. Ridges are usually termed hills or mountains as well, depending on size.
    a. Ridge0
    b. Thing
    c. Undefined
    d. Undefined

35. _____ refers to the movement of the Earth's continents relative to each other. _____ is a concept that said the shapes of continents on either side of the Atlantic Ocean seem to fit together and the similarity of southern continent fossil faunae could mean that all the continents had once been joined into a supercontinent. It was suggested that the continents had been pulled apart by the centrifugal pseudoforce of the Earth's rotation.
    a. Thing
    b. Continental drift0
    c. Undefined
    d. Undefined

36. _____ is the result of the transformation of a pre-existing rock type, the protolith, in a process called metamorphism, which means "change in form". The protolith is subjected to heat and extreme pressure causing profound physical and/or chemical change. The protolith may be sedimentary rock, igneous rock or another older rock.
    a. Metamorphic rock0
    b. Thing
    c. Undefined
    d. Undefined

37. Metamorphic rock is the result of the transformation of a pre-existing rock type, the protolith, in a process called metamorphism. The protolith is subjected to heat and extreme pressure causing profound physical and/or chemical change. _____ make up a large part of the Earth's crust. They are formed deep beneath the Earth's surface by great stresses from rocks above and high pressures and temperatures.
    a. Thing
    b. Metamorphic rocks0
    c. Undefined
    d. Undefined

38. _____ can be defined as the solid state recrystallisation of pre-existing rocks due to changes in heat and/or pressure and/or introduction of fluids. There will be mineralogical, chemical and crystallographic changes. _____ produced with increasing pressure and temperature conditions is known as prograde _____. Conversely, decreasing temperatures and pressure characterize retrograde _____.
    a. Thing
    b. Metamorphism0
    c. Undefined
    d. Undefined

39. In geology, a _____ is a place where the Earth's crust and lithosphere are being pulled apart.

a. Rift0
b. Thing
c. Undefined
d. Undefined

40. A _____ in geology is a valley created by the formation of a rift.
   a. Thing
   b. Rift valley0
   c. Undefined
   d. Undefined

41. _____ is molten rock located beneath the surface of the Earth, and which often collects in a _____ chamber. _____ is a complex high-temperature fluid substance. Most are silicate solutions. It is capable of intrusion into adjacent rocks or of extrusion onto the surface as lava or ejected explosively as tephra to form pyroclastic rock. Environments of _____ formation include subduction zones, continental rift zones, mid-oceanic ridges, and hotspots, some of which are interpreted as mantle plumes.
   a. Magma0
   b. Thing
   c. Undefined
   d. Undefined

42. _____ is the process of heating a solid substance to a point where it turns into a liquid. An object that has melted is molten.
   a. Melting0
   b. Thing
   c. Undefined
   d. Undefined

43. A _____ is a large underground pool of molten rock lying under the surface of the earth's crust. The molten rock in such a chamber is under great pressure, and given enough time and pressure can gradually fracture the rock around it creating outlets for the magma.
   a. Thing
   b. Magma chamber0
   c. Undefined
   d. Undefined

44. In plate tectonics, a _____ a linear feature that exists between two tectonic plates that are moving away from each other. These areas can form in the middle of continents but eventually form ocean basins.
   a. Divergent plate boundary0
   b. Thing
   c. Undefined
   d. Undefined

45. In plate tectonics, a _____ is said to occur when tectonic plates slide and grind against each other along a transform fault. The relative motion of such plates is horizontal in either sinistral or dextral direction. Many transform boundaries are locked in tension before suddenly releasing, and causing earthquakes.
   a. Transform boundary0
   b. Thing
   c. Undefined
   d. Undefined

46. In plate tectonics, a _____ is an actively deforming region where two tectonic plates or fragments of lithosphere move towards one another. When two plates move toward one another, they form either a subduction zone or a continental collision.
   a. Convergent boundary0
   b. Thing
   c. Undefined
   d. Undefined

Chapter 1. Introduction to Physical Geology 7

47. In geology, a _____ zone is an area on Earth where two tectonic plates meet and move towards one another, with one sliding underneath the other and moving down into the mantle, at rates typically measured in centimeters per year. An oceanic plate ordinarily slides underneath a continental plate; this often creates an orogenic zone with many volcanoes and earthquakes.
- a. Thing
- b. Subduction0
- c. Undefined
- d. Undefined

48. A _____ is an area on Earth where two tectonic plates meet and move towards one another, with one sliding underneath the other and moving down into the mantle, at rates typically measured in centimeters per year. In a sense, subduction zones are the opposite of divergent boundaries, areas where material rises up from the mantle and plates are moving apart.
- a. Subduction zone0
- b. Thing
- c. Undefined
- d. Undefined

49. _____ refers to the mode of igneous volcanic rock formation in which hot magma from inside the Earth flows out onto the surface as lava or explodes violently into the atmosphere to fall back as pyroclastics or tuff.
- a. Extrusive0
- b. Thing
- c. Undefined
- d. Undefined

50. _____ rocks form when molten rock, magma, cools and solidifies, with or without crystallization, either below the surface as intrusive, plutonic rocks or on the surface as extrusive, volcanic, rocks.
- a. Thing
- b. Igneous0
- c. Undefined
- d. Undefined

51. _____ forms when rock cools and solidifies either below the surface as intrusive rocks or on the surface as extrusive rocks. This magma can be derived from partial melts of pre-existing rocks in either the Earth's mantle or crust. Typically, the melting is caused by one or more of the following processes -- an increase in temperature, a decrease in pressure, or a change in composition.
- a. Thing
- b. Igneous rock0
- c. Undefined
- d. Undefined

52. An _____ is a body of igneous rock that has crystallized from a molten magma below the surface of the Earth.
- a. Intrusion0
- b. Thing
- c. Undefined
- d. Undefined

53. _____ rock is one of the three main rock groups. Rock formed from these covers 75% of the Earth's land area, and includes common types such as chalk, limestone, dolomite, sandstone, and shale.
- a. Sedimentary0
- b. Thing
- c. Undefined
- d. Undefined

54. _____ is one of the three main rock groups. _____ covers 75% of the Earth's land area. Four basic processes are involved in the formation of a clastic _____: weathering caused mainly by friction of waves, transportation where the sediment is carried along by a current, deposition and compaction where the sediment is squashed together to form a rock of this kind.

a. Sedimentary rock0
b. Thing
c. Undefined
d. Undefined

55. Mean _____ is the average height of the sea, with reference to a suitable reference surface.
  a. Sea level0
  b. Thing
  c. Undefined
  d. Undefined

56. A _____ is a group of mountains bordered by lowlands or separated from other mountain ranges by passes or rivers. Individual mountains within the same _____ do not necessarily have the same geology; they may be a mix of different orogeny, for example volcanoes, uplifted mountains or fold mountains and may, therefore, be of different rock.
  a. Thing
  b. Mountain range0
  c. Undefined
  d. Undefined

57. _____ is a body of techniques for investigating phenomena and acquiring new knowledge, as well as for correcting and integrating previous knowledge. It is based on gathering observable, empirical and measurable evidence subject to specific principles of reasoning,
  a. Thing
  b. Scientific method0
  c. Undefined
  d. Undefined

58. _____ is the rise of land masses that were depressed by the huge weight of ice sheets during the last ice age, through a process known as isostatic depression. It affects northern Europe, especially Scotland and Scandinavia, Siberia, Canada, and the Great Lakes of Canada and the United States.
  a. Thing
  b. Post glacial rebound0
  c. Undefined
  d. Undefined

59. _____ is the rise of land masses that were depressed by the huge weight of ice sheets during the last ice age, through a process known as isostatic depression.
  a. Thing
  b. Post-glacial rebound0
  c. Undefined
  d. Undefined

60. _____, in everyday life, is most familiar as the agency that endows objects with weight. _____ is responsible for keeping the Earth and the other planets in their orbits around the Sun; for the formation of tides; and for various other phenomena that we observe. _____ is also the reason for the very existence of the Earth, the Sun, and most macroscopic objects in the universe; without it, matter would not have coalesced into these large masses, and life, as we know it, would not exist.
  a. Gravitation0
  b. Thing
  c. Undefined
  d. Undefined

61. _____ is the condition of a system in which competing influences are balanced.
  a. Thing
  b. Equilibrium0
  c. Undefined
  d. Undefined

62. _____ is a common and widely occurring type of intrusive, felsic, igneous rock. Granites are usually medium to coarsely crystalline, occasionally with some individual crystals larger than the groundmass forming a rock known as porphyry. Granites can be pink to dark gray or even black, depending on their chemistry and mineralogy.

Chapter 1. Introduction to Physical Geology 9

a. Granite0
c. Undefined
b. Thing
d. Undefined

63. _____ is any particulate matter that can be transported by fluid flow and which eventually is deposited as a layer of solid particles on the bed or bottom of a body of water or other liquid.
    a. Thing
    b. Sediment0
    c. Undefined
    d. Undefined

64. _____ is the process of deposition of dissolved mineral components in the interstices of sediments. It is an important factor in the consolidation of coarse-grained clastic sedimentary rocks such as sandstones, conglomerates, or breccias during diagenesis or lithification. Cementing materials may include silica, carbonates, iron oxides, or clay minerals.
    a. Thing
    b. Cementation0
    c. Undefined
    d. Undefined

65. The _____ is used by geologists and other scientists to describe the timing and relationships between events that have occurred during the history of Earth.
    a. Geological time scale0
    b. Thing
    c. Undefined
    d. Undefined

66. A _____ is a process that results in the interconversion of chemical substances. The substance or substances initially involved in a _____ are called reactants. Chemical reactions are characterized by a chemical change, and they yield one or more products which are, in general, different from the reactants.
    a. Chemical reaction0
    b. Thing
    c. Undefined
    d. Undefined

Chapter 2. Atoms, Elements, and Minerals

1. _____ is molten rock located beneath the surface of the Earth, and which often collects in a _____ chamber. _____ is a complex high-temperature fluid substance. Most are silicate solutions. It is capable of intrusion into adjacent rocks or of extrusion onto the surface as lava or ejected explosively as tephra to form pyroclastic rock. Environments of _____ formation include subduction zones, continental rift zones, mid-oceanic ridges, and hotspots, some of which are interpreted as mantle plumes.
   - a. Thing
   - b. Magma0
   - c. Undefined
   - d. Undefined

2. In geology, a _____ is the outermost layer of a planet, part of its lithosphere. They are generally composed of a less dense material than its deeper layers. Earths' is composed mainly of basalt and granite. It is cooler and more rigid than the deeper layers of the mantle and core.
   - a. Crust0
   - b. Thing
   - c. Undefined
   - d. Undefined

3. _____ is a common and widely occurring type of intrusive, felsic, igneous rock. Granites are usually medium to coarsely crystalline, occasionally with some individual crystals larger than the groundmass forming a rock known as porphyry. Granites can be pink to dark gray or even black, depending on their chemistry and mineralogy.
   - a. Granite0
   - b. Thing
   - c. Undefined
   - d. Undefined

4. _____ is the second most common mineral in the Earth's continental crust. It is made up of a lattice of silica tetrahedra. _____ belongs to the rhombohedral crystal system. In nature _____ crystals are often twinned, distorted, or so intergrown with adjacent crystals of _____ or other minerals as to only show part of this shape, or to lack obvious crystal faces altogether and appear massive.
   - a. Quartz0
   - b. Thing
   - c. Undefined
   - d. Undefined

5. A _____ is a naturally occurring substance formed through geological processes that has a characteristic chemical composition, a highly ordered atomic structure and specific physical properties. A rock, by comparison, is an aggregate of minerals and need not have a specific chemical composition. Minerals range in composition from pure elements and simple salts to very complex silicates with thousands of known forms.
   - a. Thing
   - b. Mineral0
   - c. Undefined
   - d. Undefined

6. _____ is the mineral form of sodium chloride. _____ forms isometric crystals. It commonly occurs with other evaporite deposit minerals such as several of the sulfates, halides and borates. _____ occurs in vast lakes of sedimentary evaporite minerals that result from the drying up of enclosed beds, playas, and seas.
   - a. Halite0
   - b. Thing
   - c. Undefined
   - d. Undefined

7. A _____ is a solid in which the constituent atoms, molecules, or ions are packed in a regularly ordered, repeating pattern extending in all three spatial dimensions. Most metals encountered in everyday life are polycrystals. Crystals are often symmetrically intergrown to form _____ twins.
   - a. Crystal0
   - b. Thing
   - c. Undefined
   - d. Undefined

8. An _____ is a type of atom that is defined by its atomic number; that is, by the number of protons in its nucleus.

Chapter 2. Atoms, Elements, and Minerals

a. Thing
b. Element0
c. Undefined
d. Undefined

9. In chemistry, a _____ is defined as a sufficiently stable electrically neutral group of at least two atoms in a definite arrangement held together by strong chemical bonds.
   a. Thing
   b. Molecule0
   c. Undefined
   d. Undefined

10. In physics, the _____ is a subatomic particle with an electric charge of one positive fundamental unit a diameter of about 1.5×10^{-15} m, and a mass of 938.27231(28) MeV/c2 (1.6726×10^{-27} kg), 1.007 276 466 88(13) u or about 1836 times the mass of an electron.
    a. Proton0
    b. Thing
    c. Undefined
    d. Undefined

11. In physics, the _____ is a subatomic particle with no net electric charge.
    a. Thing
    b. Neutron0
    c. Undefined
    d. Undefined

12. The _____ is a fundamental subatomic particle that carries a negative electric charge.
    a. Electron0
    b. Thing
    c. Undefined
    d. Undefined

13. The _____ is the mass of an atom at rest, most often expressed in unified _____ units.[
    a. Atomic mass0
    b. Thing
    c. Undefined
    d. Undefined

14. In chemistry and physics, the _____ is the number of protons found in the nucleus of an atom. It is traditionally represented by the symbol Z.
    a. Atomic number0
    b. Thing
    c. Undefined
    d. Undefined

15. _____ are any of the several different forms of an element each having different atomic mass. _____ of an element have nuclei with the same number of protons but different numbers of neutrons.
    a. Isotopes0
    b. Thing
    c. Undefined
    d. Undefined

16. _____ is the science and study of the solid matter that constitute the Earth. Encompassing such things as rocks, soil, and gemstones, _____ studies the composition, structure, physical properties, history, and the processes that shape Earth's components.
    a. Thing
    b. Geology0
    c. Undefined
    d. Undefined

17. The _____ is used by geologists and other scientists to describe the timing and relationships between events that have occurred during the history of Earth.

Chapter 2. Atoms, Elements, and Minerals

    a. Thing
    b. Geological time scale0
    c. Undefined
    d. Undefined

18. The _____ A, also called atomic _____ or nucleon number, is the number of nucleons in an atomic nucleus. The _____ is unique for each isotope of an element and is written either after the element name or as a superscript to the left of an element's symbol. For example, carbon-12 has 6 protons and 6 neutrons.
    a. Thing
    b. Mass number0
    c. Undefined
    d. Undefined

19. _____ is the process of breaking down rocks, soils and their minerals through direct contact with the atmosphere. _____ occurs without movement. Two main classifications of _____ processes exist. Mechanical or physical _____ involves the breakdown of rocks and soils through direct contact with atmospheric conditions. The second classification, chemical _____, involves the direct effect of atmospheric chemicals in the breakdown of rocks, soils and minerals.
    a. Weathering0
    b. Thing
    c. Undefined
    d. Undefined

20. An _____ is an atom or group of atoms which have lost or gained one or more electrons, making them negatively or positively charged.
    a. Thing
    b. Ion0
    c. Undefined
    d. Undefined

21. Earth's _____ is a ~2,900 km thick rocky shell comprizing approximately 70% of Earth's volume. It is predominantly solid and overlies the Earth's iron-rich core, which occupies about 30% of Earth's volume. Past episodes of melting and volcanism at the shallower levels of the _____ have produced a very thin crust of crystallized melt products near the surface, upon which we live.
    a. Mantle0
    b. Thing
    c. Undefined
    d. Undefined

22. _____ is the oxide of silicon, chemical formula SiO_2, and is known for its hardness as early as the 16th century. It is a principle component in most types of glass and substances such as concrete.
    a. Silica0
    b. Thing
    c. Undefined
    d. Undefined

23. In geology and astronomy, the term _____ is used to denote types of rock that consist predominantly of _____ minerals. Such rocks include a wide range of igneous, metamorphic and sedimentary types. Most of the Earth's mantle and crust are made up of _____ rocks. The same is true of the Moon and the other rocky planets.
    a. Thing
    b. Silicate0
    c. Undefined
    d. Undefined

24. An _____ is a volume of rock containing components or minerals in a mode of occurrence that renders it valuable for mining.
    a. Thing
    b. Ore0
    c. Undefined
    d. Undefined

Chapter 2. Atoms, Elements, and Minerals

25. A _____ is a unique arrangement of atoms in a crystal. It is composed of a unit cell, a set of atoms arranged in a particular way, which is periodically repeated in three dimensions on a lattice. The spacing between unit cells in various directions is called its lattice parameters. The symmetry properties of the crystal are embodied in its space group.
    a. Thing
    b. Crystal structure0
    c. Undefined
    d. Undefined

26. _____ in meteorology are large scale patterns in the atmospheric pressure field that are nearly stationary, effectively "blocking" or redirecting migratory cyclones. These _____ can remain in place for several days or even weeks, causing the areas affected by them to have the same kind of weather for an extended period of time.
    a. Thing
    b. Blocks0
    c. Undefined
    d. Undefined

27. The mineral _____ is a magnesium iron silicate. It is one of the most common minerals on Earth, and has also been identified on the Moon, Mars, and comet Wild 2.
    a. Olivine0
    b. Thing
    c. Undefined
    d. Undefined

28. The _____ are a group of important rock-forming silicate minerals found in many igneous and metamorphic rocks. They share a common structure comprised of single chains of silica tetrahedra and they crystalise in the monoclinic and orthorhombic system.
    a. Thing
    b. Pyroxenes0
    c. Undefined
    d. Undefined

29. _____ rocks form when molten rock, magma, cools and solidifies, with or without crystallization, either below the surface as intrusive, plutonic rocks or on the surface as extrusive, volcanic, rocks.
    a. Thing
    b. Igneous0
    c. Undefined
    d. Undefined

30. _____ forms when rock cools and solidifies either below the surface as intrusive rocks or on the surface as extrusive rocks. This magma can be derived from partial melts of pre-existing rocks in either the Earth's mantle or crust. Typically, the melting is caused by one or more of the following processes -- an increase in temperature, a decrease in pressure, or a change in composition.
    a. Thing
    b. Igneous rock0
    c. Undefined
    d. Undefined

31. _____ defines an important group of generally dark-colored rock-forming inosilicate minerals linked at the vertices and generally containing ions of iron and/or magnesium in their structures. Amphiboles crystallize into two crystal systems, monoclinic and orthorhombic.
    a. Amphibole0
    b. Thing
    c. Undefined
    d. Undefined

32. The _____ group of sheet silicate minerals includes several closely related materials having highly perfect basal cleavage. All are monoclinic with a tendency towards pseudo-hexagonal crystals and are similar in chemical composition. The highly perfect cleavage, which is the most prominent characteristic of _____, is explained by the hexagonal sheet-like arrangement of its atoms.

Chapter 2. Atoms, Elements, and Minerals

a. Mica0
b. Thing
c. Undefined
d. Undefined

33. _____ is a very important series of tectosilicate minerals within the feldspar family. Rather than referring to a particular mineral with a specific chemical composition, it is a solid solution series.
    a. Thing
    b. Plagioclase0
    c. Undefined
    d. Undefined

34. _____ is the name of a group of rock-forming minerals which make up as much as sixty percent of the Earth's crust. Feldspars crystallize from magma in both intrusive and extrusive rocks, and they can also occur as compact minerals, as veins, and are also present in many types of metamorphic rock.
    a. Thing
    b. Feldspar0
    c. Undefined
    d. Undefined

35. _____ is the process of formation of solid crystals from a uniform solution. It is also a chemical solid-liquid separation technique, in which mass transfer of a solute from the liquid solution to a pure solid crystalline phase occurs.
    a. Thing
    b. Crystallization0
    c. Undefined
    d. Undefined

36. _____ is a single chain inosilicate mineral described chemically as $|Ca,Mg,Fe|SiO_3$ or calcium magnesium iron silicate. The crystals are monoclinic and prismatic. _____ has two prominent prismatic cleavages, meeting at angles near 90°.
    a. Thing
    b. Augite0
    c. Undefined
    d. Undefined

37. _____ is a complex inosilicate series of minerals. _____ is not a recognized mineral, in its own right but the name is used as a general or field term, to refer to a dark amphibole. It is an isomorphous mixture of three molecules; a calcium-iron-magnesium silicate, an aluminium-iron-magnesium silicate and an iron-magnesium silicate.
    a. Hornblende0
    b. Thing
    c. Undefined
    d. Undefined

38. _____ is a common phyllosilicate mineral within the mica group. Primarily a solid-solution series between the iron-endmember annite, and the magnesium-endmember phlogopite; more aluminous endmembers include siderophyllite.
    a. Thing
    b. Biotite0
    c. Undefined
    d. Undefined

39. _____ is a phyllosilicate mineral of aluminium and potassium. It has a highly perfect basal cleavage yielding remarkably thin laminae, which are often highly elastic. Sheets of _____ 5 metres by 3 metres have been found in Nellore, India.
    a. Muscovite0
    b. Thing
    c. Undefined
    d. Undefined

40. _____ is a term used to describe a group of hydrous aluminium phyllosilicate minerals, that are typically less than 2 micrometres in diameter. _____ consists of a variety of phyllosilicate minerals rich in silicon and aluminium oxides and hydroxides which include variable amounts of structural water. Clays are generally formed by the chemical weathering of silicate-bearing rocks by carbonic acid but some are formed by hydrothermal activity.

Chapter 2. Atoms, Elements, and Minerals

   a. Thing   b. Clay0
   c. Undefined   d. Undefined

41. _____ rock is one of the three main rock groups. Rock formed from these covers 75% of the Earth's land area, and includes common types such as chalk, limestone, dolomite, sandstone, and shale.
   a. Thing   b. Sedimentary0
   c. Undefined   d. Undefined

42. _____ is one of the three main rock groups. _____ covers 75% of the Earth's land area. Four basic processes are involved in the formation of a clastic _____: weathering caused mainly by friction of waves, transportation where the sediment is carried along by a current, deposition and compaction where the sediment is squashed together to form a rock of this kind.
   a. Sedimentary rock0   b. Thing
   c. Undefined   d. Undefined

43. In organic chemistry, a _____ is a salt of carbonic acid.
   a. Carbonate0   b. Thing
   c. Undefined   d. Undefined

44. _____ is a sedimentary rock composed largely of the mineral calcite. _____ often contains variable amounts of silica in the form of chert or flint, as well as varying amounts of clay, silt and sand as disseminations, nodules, or layers within the rock. The primary source of the calcite in _____ is most commonly marine organisms. These organisms secrete shells that settle out of the water column and are deposited on ocean floors as pelagic ooze or alternatively is conglomerated in a coral reef.
   a. Limestone0   b. Thing
   c. Undefined   d. Undefined

45. _____ is a metamorphic rock resulting from the metamorphism of limestone, composed mostly of calcite. It is extensively used for sculpture, as a building material, and in many other applications. The word '_____' is colloquially used to refer to many other stones that are capable of taking a high polish.
   a. Thing   b. Marble0
   c. Undefined   d. Undefined

46. _____ is a ferrimagnetic mineral one of several iron oxides and a member of the spinel group. The chemical IUPAC name is iron oxide and the common chemical name ferrous-ferric oxide.
   a. Magnetite0   b. Thing
   c. Undefined   d. Undefined

47. _____ is a very common mineral, colored black to steel or silver-gray, brown to reddish brown, or red. It is mined as the main ore of iron. Varieties include kidney ore, martite iron rose and specularite. While the forms of it vary, they all have a rust-red streak. it is harder than pure iron, but much more brittle.
   a. Hematite0   b. Thing
   c. Undefined   d. Undefined

48. The term _____ refers to several types of chemical compounds containing sulfur in its lowest oxidation number of -2.

Chapter 2. Atoms, Elements, and Minerals

a. Sulfide0
b. Thing
c. Undefined
d. Undefined

49. _____ is a description of the way light interacts with the surface of a crystal, rock, or mineral. For example, a diamond is said to have an adamantine _____ and pyrite is said to have a metallic _____.
   a. Thing
   b. Luster0
   c. Undefined
   d. Undefined

50. _____ are hydrous aluminium phyllosilicates, sometimes with variable amounts of iron, magnesium, alkali metals, alkaline earths and other cations. Clays have structures similar to the micas and therefore form flat hexagonal sheets. _____ are common weathering products and low temperature hydrothermal alteration products.
   a. Clay minerals0
   b. Thing
   c. Undefined
   d. Undefined

51. _____ is the characteristic of a solid material expressing its resistance to permanent deformation.
   a. Hardness0
   b. Thing
   c. Undefined
   d. Undefined

52. An _____ is a homogeneous mixture of two or more elements, at least one of which is a metal, and where the resulting material has metallic properties. The resulting metallic substance usually has different properties from those of its components.
   a. Alloy0
   b. Thing
   c. Undefined
   d. Undefined

53. _____, in mineralogy, is the tendency of crystalline materials to split along definite planes, creating smooth surfaces.
   a. Cleavage0
   b. Thing
   c. Undefined
   d. Undefined

54. _____ is a type of naturally-occurring glass formed as an extrusive igneous rock. It is produced when felsic lava erupted from a volcano cools rapidly through the glass transition temperature and freezes without sufficient time for crystal growth. _____ is commonly found within the margins of rhyolitic lava flows known as _____ flows, where cooling of the lava is rapid.
   a. Thing
   b. Obsidian0
   c. Undefined
   d. Undefined

55. _____, in everyday life, is most familiar as the agency that endows objects with weight. _____ is responsible for keeping the Earth and the other planets in their orbits around the Sun; for the formation of tides; and for various other phenomena that we observe. _____ is also the reason for the very existence of the Earth, the Sun, and most macroscopic objects in the universe; without it, matter would not have coalesced into these large masses, and life, as we know it, would not exist.
   a. Gravitation0
   b. Thing
   c. Undefined
   d. Undefined

56. In geology, glacial _____ are grooves or lines inscribed on the surface of a rock, produced by a geological process such as glacial flow.

Chapter 2. Atoms, Elements, and Minerals

a. Striations0
b. Thing
c. Undefined
d. Undefined

57. An _____ is a chemical compound containing an oxygen atom and other elements. Most of the earth's crust consists of them. They result when elements are oxidized by air.
a. Thing
b. Oxide0
c. Undefined
d. Undefined

58. _____ is one of the phenomena by which materials exert attractive or repulsive forces on other materials. Some well known materials that exhibit easily detectable magnetic properties are nickel, iron, some steels, and the mineral magnetite; however, all materials are influenced to greater or lesser degree by the presence of a magnetic field.
a. Thing
b. Magnetism0
c. Undefined
d. Undefined

59. _____ is the change in direction of a wave due to a change in its speed. This is most commonly seen when a wave passes from one medium to another.
a. Refraction0
b. Thing
c. Undefined
d. Undefined

60. A _____ is a process that results in the interconversion of chemical substances. The substance or substances initially involved in a _____ are called reactants. Chemical reactions are characterized by a chemical change, and they yield one or more products which are, in general, different from the reactants.
a. Thing
b. Chemical reaction0
c. Undefined
d. Undefined

Chapter 3. Igneous Rocks, Intrusive Activity, and the Origin of Igneous Rocks

1. A _____ is a naturally occurring substance formed through geological processes that has a characteristic chemical composition, a highly ordered atomic structure and specific physical properties. A rock, by comparison, is an aggregate of minerals and need not have a specific chemical composition. Minerals range in composition from pure elements and simple salts to very complex silicates with thousands of known forms.
   - a. Thing
   - b. Mineral0
   - c. Undefined
   - d. Undefined

2. _____ is a term used to describe a group of hydrous aluminium phyllosilicate minerals, that are typically less than 2 micrometres in diameter. _____ consists of a variety of phyllosilicate minerals rich in silicon and aluminium oxides and hydroxides which include variable amounts of structural water. Clays are generally formed by the chemical weathering of silicate-bearing rocks by carbonic acid but some are formed by hydrothermal activity.
   - a. Thing
   - b. Clay0
   - c. Undefined
   - d. Undefined

3. _____ are hydrous aluminium phyllosilicates, sometimes with variable amounts of iron, magnesium, alkali metals, alkaline earths and other cations. Clays have structures similar to the micas and therefore form flat hexagonal sheets. _____ are common weathering products and low temperature hydrothermal alteration products.
   - a. Thing
   - b. Clay minerals0
   - c. Undefined
   - d. Undefined

4. _____ is a field of study within geology concerned generally with the structures within the crust of the Earth, or other planets, and particularly with the forces and movements that have operated in a region to create these structures.
   - a. Tectonics0
   - b. Thing
   - c. Undefined
   - d. Undefined

5. _____, in everyday life, is most familiar as the agency that endows objects with weight. _____ is responsible for keeping the Earth and the other planets in their orbits around the Sun; for the formation of tides; and for various other phenomena that we observe. _____ is also the reason for the very existence of the Earth, the Sun, and most macroscopic objects in the universe; without it, matter would not have coalesced into these large masses, and life, as we know it, would not exist.
   - a. Gravitation0
   - b. Thing
   - c. Undefined
   - d. Undefined

6. _____ is any particulate matter that can be transported by fluid flow and which eventually is deposited as a layer of solid particles on the bed or bottom of a body of water or other liquid.
   - a. Thing
   - b. Sediment0
   - c. Undefined
   - d. Undefined

7. _____ is the condition of a system in which competing influences are balanced.
   - a. Thing
   - b. Equilibrium0
   - c. Undefined
   - d. Undefined

8. _____ is the science and study of the solid matter that constitute the Earth. Encompassing such things as rocks, soil, and gemstones, _____ studies the composition, structure, physical properties, history, and the processes that shape Earth's components.

Chapter 3. Igneous Rocks, Intrusive Activity, and the Origin of Igneous Rocks

    a. Thing
    b. Geology0
    c. Undefined
    d. Undefined

9. _____ can be defined as the solid state recrystallisation of pre-existing rocks due to changes in heat and/or pressure and/or introduction of fluids. There will be mineralogical, chemical and crystallographic changes. _____ produced with increasing pressure and temperature conditions is known as prograde _____. Conversely, decreasing temperatures and pressure characterize retrograde _____.
    a. Metamorphism0
    b. Thing
    c. Undefined
    d. Undefined

10. _____ is molten rock located beneath the surface of the Earth, and which often collects in a _____ chamber. _____ is a complex high-temperature fluid substance. Most are silicate solutions. It is capable of intrusion into adjacent rocks or of extrusion onto the surface as lava or ejected explosively as tephra to form pyroclastic rock. Environments of _____ formation include subduction zones, continental rift zones, mid-oceanic ridges, and hotspots, some of which are interpreted as mantle plumes.
    a. Magma0
    b. Thing
    c. Undefined
    d. Undefined

11. _____ rocks form when molten rock, magma, cools and solidifies, with or without crystallization, either below the surface as intrusive, plutonic rocks or on the surface as extrusive, volcanic, rocks.
    a. Thing
    b. Igneous0
    c. Undefined
    d. Undefined

12. _____ forms when rock cools and solidifies either below the surface as intrusive rocks or on the surface as extrusive rocks. This magma can be derived from partial melts of pre-existing rocks in either the Earth's mantle or crust. Typically, the melting is caused by one or more of the following processes -- an increase in temperature, a decrease in pressure, or a change in composition.
    a. Igneous rock0
    b. Thing
    c. Undefined
    d. Undefined

13. An _____ is a body of igneous rock that has crystallized from a molten magma below the surface of the Earth.
    a. Intrusion0
    b. Thing
    c. Undefined
    d. Undefined

14. _____ is displacement of solids by the agents of ocean currents, wind, water, or ice by downward or down-slope movement in response to gravity or by living organisms.
    a. Erosion0
    b. Thing
    c. Undefined
    d. Undefined

15. _____ is the process of breaking down rocks, soils and their minerals through direct contact with the atmosphere. _____ occurs without movement. Two main classifications of _____ processes exist. Mechanical or physical _____ involves the breakdown of rocks and soils through direct contact with atmospheric conditions. The second classification, chemical _____, involves the direct effect of atmospheric chemicals in the breakdown of rocks, soils and minerals.

Chapter 3. Igneous Rocks, Intrusive Activity, and the Origin of Igneous Rocks

    a. Weathering0
    b. Thing
    c. Undefined
    d. Undefined

16. _____ rock is one of the three main rock groups. Rock formed from these covers 75% of the Earth's land area, and includes common types such as chalk, limestone, dolomite, sandstone, and shale.
    a. Sedimentary0
    b. Thing
    c. Undefined
    d. Undefined

17. _____ is one of the three main rock groups. _____ covers 75% of the Earth's land area. Four basic processes are involved in the formation of a clastic _____: weathering caused mainly by friction of waves, transportation where the sediment is carried along by a current, deposition and compaction where the sediment is squashed together to form a rock of this kind.
    a. Sedimentary rock0
    b. Thing
    c. Undefined
    d. Undefined

18. _____ is the result of the transformation of a pre-existing rock type, the protolith, in a process called metamorphism, which means "change in form". The protolith is subjected to heat and extreme pressure causing profound physical and/or chemical change. The protolith may be sedimentary rock, igneous rock or another older rock.
    a. Thing
    b. Metamorphic rock0
    c. Undefined
    d. Undefined

19. The _____ is a fundamental concept in geology that describes the dynamic transitions through geologic time among the three main rock types: sedimentary, metamorphic, and igneous.
    a. Thing
    b. Rock cycle0
    c. Undefined
    d. Undefined

20. _____ is the process of heating a solid substance to a point where it turns into a liquid. An object that has melted is molten.
    a. Melting0
    b. Thing
    c. Undefined
    d. Undefined

21. Earth's _____ is a ~2,900 km thick rocky shell comprising approximately 70% of Earth's volume. It is predominantly solid and overlies the Earth's iron-rich core, which occupies about 30% of Earth's volume. Past episodes of melting and volcanism at the shallower levels of the _____ have produced a very thin crust of crystallized melt products near the surface, upon which we live.
    a. Thing
    b. Mantle0
    c. Undefined
    d. Undefined

22. _____ is a theory of geology that has been developed to explain the observed evidence for large scale motions of the Earth's lithosphere. The theory encompassed and superseded the older theory of continental drift.
    a. Plate tectonics0
    b. Thing
    c. Undefined
    d. Undefined

23. In plate tectonics, a _____ is an actively deforming region where two tectonic plates or fragments of lithosphere move towards one another. When two plates move toward one another, they form either a subduction zone or a continental collision.

Chapter 3. Igneous Rocks, Intrusive Activity, and the Origin of Igneous Rocks

a. Thing
b. Convergent boundary0
c. Undefined
d. Undefined

24. In geology, a _____ zone is an area on Earth where two tectonic plates meet and move towards one another, with one sliding underneath the other and moving down into the mantle, at rates typically measured in centimeters per year. An oceanic plate ordinarily slides underneath a continental plate; this often creates an orogenic zone with many volcanoes and earthquakes.
a. Thing
b. Subduction0
c. Undefined
d. Undefined

25. A _____ is an area on Earth where two tectonic plates meet and move towards one another, with one sliding underneath the other and moving down into the mantle, at rates typically measured in centimeters per year. In a sense, subduction zones are the opposite of divergent boundaries, areas where material rises up from the mantle and plates are moving apart.
a. Thing
b. Subduction zone0
c. Undefined
d. Undefined

26. An _____ is a layer of gases that may surround a material body of sufficient mass. The gases are attracted by the gravity of the body, and are retained for a longer duration if gravity is high and the _____'s temperature is low. Some planets consist mainly of various gases, and thus have very deep atmospheres.
a. Atmosphere0
b. Place
c. Undefined
d. Undefined

27. _____ is molten rock expelled by a volcano during an eruption. When first extruded from a volcanic vent, it is a liquid at temperatures from 700 °C to 1,200 °C.
a. Thing
b. Lava0
c. Undefined
d. Undefined

28. _____ is a common gray to black extrusive volcanic rock. It is usually fine-grained due to rapid cooling of lava on the Earth's surface. It may be porphyritic containing larger crystals in a fine matrix, or vesicular, or frothy scoria.
a. Thing
b. Basalt0
c. Undefined
d. Undefined

29. _____ is the oxide of silicon, chemical formula SiO_2, and is known for its hardness as early as the 16th century. It is a principle component in most types of glass and substances such as concrete.
a. Thing
b. Silica0
c. Undefined
d. Undefined

30. _____ is a common and widely occurring type of intrusive, felsic, igneous rock. Granites are usually medium to coarsely crystalline, occasionally with some individual crystals larger than the groundmass forming a rock known as porphyry. Granites can be pink to dark gray or even black, depending on their chemistry and mineralogy.
a. Thing
b. Granite0
c. Undefined
d. Undefined

Chapter 3. Igneous Rocks, Intrusive Activity, and the Origin of Igneous Rocks

31. _____ is the second most common mineral in the Earth's continental crust. It is made up of a lattice of silica tetrahedra. _____ belongs to the rhombohedral crystal system. In nature _____ crystals are often twinned, distorted, or so intergrown with adjacent crystals of _____ or other minerals as to only show part of this shape, or to lack obvious crystal faces altogether and appear massive.
    a. Thing
    b. Quartz0
    c. Undefined
    d. Undefined

32. _____ is an igneous rock of volcanic origin. They often have a vesicular texture, which is the result voids left by volatiles escaping from the molten lava. Pumice is a rock, which is an example of explosive volcanic eruption. It is so vesicular that it floats in water.
    a. Thing
    b. Volcanic rock0
    c. Undefined
    d. Undefined

33. _____ refers to the mode of igneous volcanic rock formation in which hot magma from inside the Earth flows out onto the surface as lava or explodes violently into the atmosphere to fall back as pyroclastics or tuff.
    a. Extrusive0
    b. Thing
    c. Undefined
    d. Undefined

34. _____ is an igneous, volcanic rock, of intermediate composition, with aphanitic to porphyritic texture.
    a. Thing
    b. Andesite0
    c. Undefined
    d. Undefined

35. _____ is an igneous, volcanic rock, of felsic composition. It may have any texture from aphanitic to porphyritic. The mineral assemblage is usually quartz, alkali feldspar and plagioclase. Biotite and pyroxene are common accessory minerals.
    a. Rhyolite0
    b. Thing
    c. Undefined
    d. Undefined

36. _____ is a grey to dark grey intermediate intrusive igneous rock composed principally of plagioclase feldspar, biotite, hornblende, and/or pyroxene. It may contain small amounts of quartz, microcline and olivine.
    a. Diorite0
    b. Thing
    c. Undefined
    d. Undefined

37. _____ is a dark, coarse-grained, intrusive igneous rock chemically equivalent to basalt. It is a plutonic rock, formed when molten magma is trapped beneath the Earth's surface and cools into a crystalline mass.
    a. Gabbro0
    b. Thing
    c. Undefined
    d. Undefined

38. The mineral _____ is a magnesium iron silicate. It is one of the most common minerals on Earth, and has also been identified on the Moon, Mars, and comet Wild 2.
    a. Olivine0
    b. Thing
    c. Undefined
    d. Undefined

39. _____ is a common phyllosilicate mineral within the mica group. Primarily a solid-solution series between the iron-endmember annite, and the magnesium-endmember phlogopite; more aluminous endmembers include siderophyllite.

Chapter 3. Igneous Rocks, Intrusive Activity, and the Origin of Igneous Rocks

    a. Biotite0
    c. Undefined
    b. Thing
    d. Undefined

40. _____, in mineralogy, is the tendency of crystalline materials to split along definite planes, creating smooth surfaces.
    a. Cleavage0
    c. Undefined
    b. Thing
    d. Undefined

41. _____ is an intrusive igneous rock similar to granite, but contains more plagioclase than potassium feldspar. It usually contains abundant biotite mica and hornblende, giving it a darker appearance than true granite.
    a. Granodiorite0
    c. Undefined
    b. Thing
    d. Undefined

42. In geology and astronomy, the term _____ is used to denote types of rock that consist predominantly of _____ minerals. Such rocks include a wide range of igneous, metamorphic and sedimentary types. Most of the Earth's mantle and crust are made up of _____ rocks. The same is true of the Moon and the other rocky planets.
    a. Thing
    c. Undefined
    b. Silicate0
    d. Undefined

43. In geology, _____ minerals and rocks are silicate minerals, magmas, and volcanic and intrusive igneous rocks that have relatively high concentrations of the heavier elements. The term is a combination of "magnesium" and ferrum.
    a. Mafic0
    c. Undefined
    b. Thing
    d. Undefined

44. An _____ is a chemical compound containing an oxygen atom and other elements. Most of the earth's crust consists of them. They result when elements are oxidized by air.
    a. Thing
    c. Undefined
    b. Oxide0
    d. Undefined

45. _____ is a term used in geology to refer to silicate minerals, magmas, and rocks which are enriched in the lighter elements such as silica, oxygen, aluminium, sodium, and potassium. _____ minerals are usually light in color and have specific gravities less than 3. Common _____ minerals include quartz, muscovite, orthoclase, and the sodium rich plagioclase feldspars.
    a. Felsic0
    c. Undefined
    b. Thing
    d. Undefined

46. _____ is a dense, coarse-grained igneous rock, consisting mostly of the minerals olivine and pyroxene. _____ is ultramafic and ultrabasic, as the rock contains less than 45% silica. This type of rock is derived from the Earth's mantle, either as solid blocks and fragments, or as crystals accumulated from magmas that formed in the mantle.
    a. Peridotite0
    c. Undefined
    b. Thing
    d. Undefined

47. In geology, a _____ is the outermost layer of a planet, part of its lithosphere. They are generally composed of a less dense material than its deeper layers. Earths' is composed mainly of basalt and granite. It is cooler and more rigid than the deeper layers of the mantle and core.

Chapter 3. Igneous Rocks, Intrusive Activity, and the Origin of Igneous Rocks

a. Crust0
b. Thing
c. Undefined
d. Undefined

48. A _____ is a volcanic landform created when lava hardens within a vent on an active volcano. When forming, a plug can cause an extreme build-up of pressure if volatile-charged magma is trapped beneath it, and this can sometimes lead to an explosive eruption.
a. Thing
b. Volcanic neck0
c. Undefined
d. Undefined

49. A _____ is an opening, or rupture, in the Earth's surface or crust, which allows hot, molten rock, ash and gases to escape from deep below the surface.
a. Thing
b. Volcano0
c. Undefined
d. Undefined

50. A _____ is an intrusion into a cross-cutting fissure, meaning a _____ cuts across other pre-existing layers or bodies of rock, this means that a _____ is always younger than the rocks that contain it. The thickness is usually much smaller than the other two dimensions. Thickness can vary from sub-centimeter scale to many meters in thickness and the lateral dimensions can extend over many kilometers.
a. Dike0
b. Thing
c. Undefined
d. Undefined

51. A _____ coastline occurs where bands of differing rock type run perpendicular to the coast.
a. Thing
b. Discordant0
c. Undefined
d. Undefined

52. In geology, a _____ is a tabular pluton that has intruded between older layers of sedimentary rock, beds of volcanic lava or tuff, or even along the direction of foliation in metamorphic rock. The term _____ is synonymous with concordant intrusive sheet. This means that the _____ does not cut across preexisting rocks. Contrast this with dikes.
a. Thing
b. Sill0
c. Undefined
d. Undefined

53. A _____ coastline occurs where the bands of differing rock types run parallel to the coast. The outer hard rock provides a protective barrier to erosion of the softer rocks further inland.
a. Concordant0
b. Thing
c. Undefined
d. Undefined

54. A _____ in geology is an intrusive igneous rock body that crystallized from a magma below the surface of the Earth. Plutons include batholiths, dikes, sills, laccoliths, lopoliths, and other igneous bodies. In practice, "_____" usually refers to a distinctive mass of igneous rock, typically kilometers in dimension, without a tabular shape like those of dikes and sills.
a. Thing
b. Pluton0
c. Undefined
d. Undefined

55. A _____ is a large emplacement of igneous intrusive rock that forms from cooled magma deep in the Earth's crust. They are almost always made mostly of felsic or intermediate rock-types, such as granite, quartz monzonite, or diorite.

Chapter 3. Igneous Rocks, Intrusive Activity, and the Origin of Igneous Rocks

a. Batholith0	b. Thing
c. Undefined	d. Undefined

56. A _____ is a landform that extends above the surrounding terrain in a limited area. A _____ is generally steeper than a hill, but there is no universally accepted standard definition for the height of a _____ or a hill although a _____ usually has an identifiable summit.

a. Mountain0	b. Place
c. Undefined	d. Undefined

57. The _____ is defined as the part of the land adjoining or near the ocean. A coastline is properly a line on a map indicating the disposition of a _____, but the word is often used to refer to the _____ itself. The adjective coastal describes something as being on, near to, or associated with a _____.

a. Place	b. Coast0
c. Undefined	d. Undefined

58. A _____ is a special-purpose map made to show geological features. The stratigraphic contour lines are drawn on the surface of a selected deep stratum, so that they can show the topographic trends of the strata under the ground. It is not always possible to properly show this when the strata are extremely fractured, mixed, in some discontinuities, or where they are otherwise disturbed.

a. Thing	b. Geologic map0
c. Undefined	d. Undefined

59. The _____ is the layer of granitic, sedimentary, and metamorphic rocks which form the continents and the areas of shallow seabed close to their shores, known as continental shelves. It is less dense than the material of the Earth's mantle and thus "floats" on top of it. _____ is also less dense than oceanic crust, though it is considerably thicker. About 40% of the Earth's surface is now underlain by _____.

a. Thing	b. Continental crust0
c. Undefined	d. Undefined

60. In geology, _____ refers to heat sources within the planet. The planet's internal heat was originally generated during its accretion, due to gravitational binding energy, and since then additional heat has continued to be generated by the radioactive decay of elements such as uranium, thorium, and potassium.

a. Geothermal0	b. Thing
c. Undefined	d. Undefined

61. The _____ is the rate of increase in temperature per unit depth in the Earth. It varies with location and is typically measured by determining the bottom open-hole temperature after the drilling of a borehole.

a. Geothermal gradient0	b. Thing
c. Undefined	d. Undefined

62. In thermal physics, _____ is the passage of thermal energy from a hot to a cold body. When a physical body, e.g. an object or fluid, is at a different temperature than its surroundings or another body, transfer of thermal energy, also known as _____, occurs in such a way that the body and the surroundings reach thermal equilibrium.

a. Heat transfer0	b. Thing
c. Undefined	d. Undefined

Chapter 3. Igneous Rocks, Intrusive Activity, and the Origin of Igneous Rocks

63. A _____ is an upwelling of abnormally hot rock within the Earth's mantle. As the heads of mantle plumes can partly melt when they reach shallow depths, they are thought to be the cause of volcanic centers known as hotspots and probably also to have caused flood basalts.
   a. Mantle plume0
   b. Event
   c. Undefined
   d. Undefined

64. _____ is the gas phase component of a another state of matter which does not completely fill its container. It is distinguished from the pure gas phase by the presence of the same substance in another state of matter. Hence when a liquid has completely evaporated, it is said that the system has been completely transformed to the gas phase.
   a. Vapor0
   b. Thing
   c. Undefined
   d. Undefined

65. A _____ is a solid in which the constituent atoms, molecules, or ions are packed in a regularly ordered, repeating pattern extending in all three spatial dimensions. Most metals encountered in everyday life are polycrystals. Crystals are often symmetrically intergrown to form _____ twins.
   a. Crystal0
   b. Thing
   c. Undefined
   d. Undefined

66. _____ is the part of Earth's lithosphere that surfaces in the ocean basins. _____ is primarily composed of mafic rocks, or sima. It is thinner than continental crust, or sial, generally less than 10 kilometers thick, however it is more dense, having a mean density of about 3.3 grams per cubic centimeter.
   a. Thing
   b. Oceanic crust0
   c. Undefined
   d. Undefined

67. _____ is the process of formation of solid crystals from a uniform solution. It is also a chemical solid-liquid separation technique, in which mass transfer of a solute from the liquid solution to a pure solid crystalline phase occurs.
   a. Thing
   b. Crystallization0
   c. Undefined
   d. Undefined

68. _____ is a very important series of tectosilicate minerals within the feldspar family. Rather than referring to a particular mineral with a specific chemical composition, it is a solid solution series.
   a. Plagioclase0
   b. Thing
   c. Undefined
   d. Undefined

69. _____ is the name of a group of rock-forming minerals which make up as much as sixty percent of the Earth's crust. Feldspars crystallize from magma in both intrusive and extrusive rocks, and they can also occur as compact minerals, as veins, and are also present in many types of metamorphic rock.
   a. Thing
   b. Feldspar0
   c. Undefined
   d. Undefined

70. A _____ is a unique arrangement of atoms in a crystal. It is composed of a unit cell, a set of atoms arranged in a particular way, which is periodically repeated in three dimensions on a lattice. The spacing between unit cells in various directions is called its lattice parameters. The symmetry properties of the crystal are embodied in its space group.
   a. Thing
   b. Crystal structure0
   c. Undefined
   d. Undefined

Chapter 3. Igneous Rocks, Intrusive Activity, and the Origin of Igneous Rocks

71. _____ is a phyllosilicate mineral of aluminium and potassium. It has a highly perfect basal cleavage yielding remarkably thin laminae , which are often highly elastic. Sheets of _____ 5 metres by 3 metres have been found in Nellore, India.
   a. Muscovite0
   b. Thing
   c. Undefined
   d. Undefined

72. A _____ is a large underground pool of molten rock lying under the surface of the earth's crust. The molten rock in such a chamber is under great pressure, and given enough time and pressure can gradually fracture the rock around it creating outlets for the magma.
   a. Magma chamber0
   b. Thing
   c. Undefined
   d. Undefined

73. An _____ is a volume of rock containing components or minerals in a mode of occurrence that renders it valuable for mining.
   a. Ore0
   b. Thing
   c. Undefined
   d. Undefined

74. A _____ is an intrusion caused by buoyancy and pressure differentials. A _____ is any relatively mobile mass that intrudes into preexisting strata. Diapirs commonly intrude vertically upward along fractures or zones of structural weakness through more dense overlying rocks because of density contrast between a less dense, lower rock mass and overlying denser rocks. The density contrast manifests as a force of buoyancy.
   a. Thing
   b. Diapir0
   c. Undefined
   d. Undefined

75. The _____ is the region of the Earth between 100-200 km below the surface that is the weak or "soft" zone in the upper mantle. It lies just below the lithosphere, which is involved in plate movements and isostatic adjustments. In spite of its heat, pressures keep it plastic, and it has a relatively low density. Seismic waves pass relatively slowly through the _____.
   a. Asthenosphere0
   b. Thing
   c. Undefined
   d. Undefined

76. The _____ is the solid outermost shell of a rocky planet. On the Earth, the _____ includes the crust and the uppermost mantle which is joined to the crust across the Mohorovièiæ discontinuity. _____ is underlain by asthenosphere, the weaker, hotter, and deeper part of the upper mantle.
   a. Lithosphere0
   b. Thing
   c. Undefined
   d. Undefined

77. A _____ is an area of highland, usually consisting of relatively flat rural area.
   a. Plateau0
   b. Place
   c. Undefined
   d. Undefined

78. A _____ is a type of excavation or depression in the ground. They are generally defined by being deeper than they are wide, and by being narrow compared to their length.
   a. Thing
   b. Trench0
   c. Undefined
   d. Undefined

79. A _____ is a geological feature that is also known as a Rip in the earth causing magma to flow out and forming an undersea volcano, it also has geological features, a continuous elevational crest for some distance. Ridges are usually termed hills or mountains as well, depending on size.
   a. Ridge0
   b. Thing
   c. Undefined
   d. Undefined

Chapter 4. Volcanism and Extrusive Rocks

1. _____ is molten rock located beneath the surface of the Earth, and which often collects in a _____ chamber. _____ is a complex high-temperature fluid substance. Most are silicate solutions. It is capable of intrusion into adjacent rocks or of extrusion onto the surface as lava or ejected explosively as tephra to form pyroclastic rock. Environments of _____ formation include subduction zones, continental rift zones, mid-oceanic ridges, and hotspots, some of which are interpreted as mantle plumes.
   a. Magma0 b. Thing
   c. Undefined d. Undefined

2. _____ is the oxide of silicon, chemical formula SiO_2, and is known for its hardness as early as the 16th century. It is a principle component in most types of glass and substances such as concrete.
   a. Thing b. Silica0
   c. Undefined d. Undefined

3. _____ is molten rock expelled by a volcano during an eruption. When first extruded from a volcanic vent, it is a liquid at temperatures from 700 °C to 1,200 °C.
   a. Lava0 b. Thing
   c. Undefined d. Undefined

4. _____ are clastic rocks composed solely or primarily of volcanic materials.
   a. Pyroclastics0 b. Thing
   c. Undefined d. Undefined

5. _____ is air-fall material produced by a volcanic eruption regardless of composition or fragment size. It is typically rhyolitic in composition as most explosive volcanoes are the product of the more viscous felsic or high silica magmas.
   a. Tephra0 b. Thing
   c. Undefined d. Undefined

6. _____ refers to the mode of igneous volcanic rock formation in which hot magma from inside the Earth flows out onto the surface as lava or explodes violently into the atmosphere to fall back as pyroclastics or tuff.
   a. Extrusive0 b. Thing
   c. Undefined d. Undefined

7. A _____ comprises a geomorphological unit, and is largely defined by its surface form and location in the landscape, as part of the terrain, and as such, is typically an element of topography. They are categorised by features such as elevation, slope, orientation, stratification, rock exposure, and soil type. They include berms, mounds, hills, cliffs, valleys, rivers and numerous other elements.
   a. Landform0 b. Thing
   c. Undefined d. Undefined

8. A _____ is an opening, or rupture, in the Earth's surface or crust, which allows hot, molten rock, ash and gases to escape from deep below the surface.
   a. Thing b. Volcano0
   c. Undefined d. Undefined

9. A _____ is a landform that extends above the surrounding terrain in a limited area. A _____ is generally steeper than a hill, but there is no universally accepted standard definition for the height of a _____ or a hill although a _____ usually has an identifiable summit.

Chapter 4. Volcanism and Extrusive Rocks

    a. Mountain0   b. Place
    c. Undefined   d. Undefined

10. A _____ is an area of highland, usually consisting of relatively flat rural area.
    a. Plateau0   b. Place
    c. Undefined   d. Undefined

11. A _____ is a flat, wide surface that is formed when lava comes out of the ground and spreads out very quickly.
    a. Thing   b. Lava plateau0
    c. Undefined   d. Undefined

12. _____ is the science and study of the solid matter that constitute the Earth. Encompassing such things as rocks, soil, and gemstones, _____ studies the composition, structure, physical properties, history, and the processes that shape Earth's components.
    a. Geology0   b. Thing
    c. Undefined   d. Undefined

13. In geology, a _____ is the outermost layer of a planet, part of its lithosphere. They are generally composed of a less dense material than its deeper layers.Earths' is composed mainly of basalt and granite. It is cooler and more rigid than the deeper layers of the mantle and core.
    a. Crust0   b. Thing
    c. Undefined   d. Undefined

14. Earth's _____ is a ~2,900 km thick rocky shell comprizing approximately 70% of Earth's volume. It is predominantly solid and overlies the Earth's iron-rich core, which occupies about 30% of Earth's volume. Past episodes of melting and volcanism at the shallower levels of the _____ have produced a very thin crust of crystallized melt products near the surface, upon which we live.
    a. Mantle0   b. Thing
    c. Undefined   d. Undefined

15. _____ consists of very fine rock and mineral particles less than 2 mm in diameter that are ejected from a volcanic vent. The very fine particles may be carried for many miles, settling out as a dust-like layer across the landscape
    a. Thing   b. Ash fall0
    c. Undefined   d. Undefined

16. Mean _____ is the average height of the sea, with reference to a suitable reference surface.
    a. Thing   b. Sea level0
    c. Undefined   d. Undefined

17. _____ is an igneous rock of volcanic origin. They often have a vesicular texture, which is the result voids left by volatiles escaping from the molten lava. Pumice is a rock, which is an example of explosive volcanic eruption. It is so vesicular that it floats in water.
    a. Volcanic rock0   b. Thing
    c. Undefined   d. Undefined

Chapter 4. Volcanism and Extrusive Rocks 31

18. An _____ is a layer of gases that may surround a material body of sufficient mass. The gases are attracted by the gravity of the body, and are retained for a longer duration if gravity is high and the _____'s temperature is low. Some planets consist mainly of various gases, and thus have very deep atmospheres.
   a. Place
   b. Atmosphere0
   c. Undefined
   d. Undefined

19. _____ is the increase in the average temperature of the Earth's near-surface air and oceans in recent decades and its projected continuation. An increase in global temperatures can in turn cause other changes, including sea level rise, and changes in the amount and pattern of precipitation resulting in floods and drought. There may also be changes in the frequency and intensity of extreme weather events.
   a. Thing
   b. Global warming0
   c. Undefined
   d. Undefined

20. A _____ is a large underground pool of molten rock lying under the surface of the earth's crust. The molten rock in such a chamber is under great pressure, and given enough time and pressure can gradually fracture the rock around it creating outlets for the magma.
   a. Thing
   b. Magma chamber0
   c. Undefined
   d. Undefined

21. A _____ is an approximately circular depression in the surface of a planet, moon or other solid body in the Solar System, formed by the hyper-velocity impact of a smaller body with the surface. Impact craters typically have raised rims, and they range from small, simple, bowl-shaped depressions to large, complex, multi-ringed, impact basins.
   a. Crater0
   b. Thing
   c. Undefined
   d. Undefined

22. A _____ is a special-purpose map made to show geological features. The stratigraphic contour lines are drawn on the surface of a selected deep stratum, so that they can show the topographic trends of the strata under the ground. It is not always possible to properly show this when the strata are extremely fractured, mixed, in some discontinuities, or where they are otherwise disturbed.
   a. Geologic map0
   b. Thing
   c. Undefined
   d. Undefined

23. A _____ is a common and devastating result of some volcanic eruptions. The flows are fast-moving fluidized bodies of hot gas, ash and rock. The flows normally hug the ground and travel downhill under gravity, their speed depending upon the gradient of the slope and the size of the flow.
   a. Thing
   b. Pyroclastic flow0
   c. Undefined
   d. Undefined

24. _____ is a measure of the resistance of a fluid to deform under shear stress. It is commonly perceived as "thickness", or resistance to flow. _____ describes a fluid's internal resistance to flow and may be thought of as a measure of fluid friction.
   a. Viscosity0
   b. Thing
   c. Undefined
   d. Undefined

25. In geology, _____ minerals and rocks are silicate minerals, magmas, and volcanic and intrusive igneous rocks that have relatively high concentrations of the heavier elements. The term is a combination of "magnesium" and ferrum.

Chapter 4. Volcanism and Extrusive Rocks

a. Mafic0
b. Thing
c. Undefined
d. Undefined

26. _____ is a term used in geology to refer to silicate minerals, magmas, and rocks which are enriched in the lighter elements such as silica, oxygen, aluminium, sodium, and potassium. _____ minerals are usually light in color and have specific gravities less than 3. Common _____ minerals include quartz, muscovite, orthoclase, and the sodium rich plagioclase feldspars.
    a. Felsic0
    b. Thing
    c. Undefined
    d. Undefined

27. _____ is an igneous, volcanic rock, of felsic composition. It may have any texture from aphanitic to porphyritic. The mineral assemblage is usually quartz, alkali feldspar and plagioclase. Biotite and pyroxene are common accessory minerals.
    a. Thing
    b. Rhyolite0
    c. Undefined
    d. Undefined

28. _____ is a common gray to black extrusive volcanic rock. It is usually fine-grained due to rapid cooling of lava on the Earth's surface. It may be porphyritic containing larger crystals in a fine matrix, or vesicular, or frothy scoria.
    a. Thing
    b. Basalt0
    c. Undefined
    d. Undefined

29. _____ is an igneous, volcanic rock, of intermediate composition, with aphanitic to porphyritic texture.
    a. Thing
    b. Andesite0
    c. Undefined
    d. Undefined

30. _____ rocks form when molten rock, magma, cools and solidifies, with or without crystallization, either below the surface as intrusive, plutonic rocks or on the surface as extrusive, volcanic, rocks.
    a. Thing
    b. Igneous0
    c. Undefined
    d. Undefined

31. _____ forms when rock cools and solidifies either below the surface as intrusive rocks or on the surface as extrusive rocks. This magma can be derived from partial melts of pre-existing rocks in either the Earth's mantle or crust. Typically, the melting is caused by one or more of the following processes -- an increase in temperature, a decrease in pressure, or a change in composition.
    a. Igneous rock0
    b. Thing
    c. Undefined
    d. Undefined

32. A _____ is a naturally occurring substance formed through geological processes that has a characteristic chemical composition, a highly ordered atomic structure and specific physical properties. A rock, by comparison, is an aggregate of minerals and need not have a specific chemical composition. Minerals range in composition from pure elements and simple salts to very complex silicates with thousands of known forms.
    a. Thing
    b. Mineral0
    c. Undefined
    d. Undefined

33. _____ is the process of formation of solid crystals from a uniform solution. It is also a chemical solid-liquid separation technique, in which mass transfer of a solute from the liquid solution to a pure solid crystalline phase occurs.

Chapter 4. Volcanism and Extrusive Rocks

    a. Thing
    b. Crystallization0
    c. Undefined
    d. Undefined

34. In geology and astronomy, the term _____ is used to denote types of rock that consist predominantly of _____ minerals. Such rocks include a wide range of igneous, metamorphic and sedimentary types. Most of the Earth's mantle and crust are made up of _____ rocks. The same is true of the Moon and the other rocky planets.
    a. Silicate0
    b. Thing
    c. Undefined
    d. Undefined

35. _____ is the gas phase component of a another state of matter which does not completely fill its container. It is distinguished from the pure gas phase by the presence of the same substance in another state of matter. Hence when a liquid has completely evaporated, it is said that the system has been completely transformed to the gas phase.
    a. Vapor0
    b. Thing
    c. Undefined
    d. Undefined

36. The term _____ refers to several types of chemical compounds containing sulfur in its lowest oxidation number of −2.
    a. Thing
    b. Sulfide0
    c. Undefined
    d. Undefined

37. _____, in everyday life, is most familiar as the agency that endows objects with weight. _____ is responsible for keeping the Earth and the other planets in their orbits around the Sun; for the formation of tides; and for various other phenomena that we observe. _____ is also the reason for the very existence of the Earth, the Sun, and most macroscopic objects in the universe; without it, matter would not have coalesced into these large masses, and life, as we know it, would not exist.
    a. Thing
    b. Gravitation0
    c. Undefined
    d. Undefined

38. _____ is a highly vesicular pyroclastic extrusive igneous rock of intermediate to siliceous magmas including rhyolite, trachyte and phonolite. _____ is usually light in color ranging from white, yellowish, gray, gray brown, and a dull red. Most of the time, it is white. As an extrusive rock it was made from a volcanic eruption.
    a. Thing
    b. Pumice0
    c. Undefined
    d. Undefined

39. _____ is the second most common mineral in the Earth's continental crust. It is made up of a lattice of silica tetrahedra. _____ belongs to the rhombohedral crystal system. In nature _____ crystals are often twinned, distorted, or so intergrown with adjacent crystals of _____ or other minerals as to only show part of this shape, or to lack obvious crystal faces altogether and appear massive.
    a. Thing
    b. Quartz0
    c. Undefined
    d. Undefined

40. _____ is a common and widely occurring type of intrusive, felsic, igneous rock. Granites are usually medium to coarsely crystalline, occasionally with some individual crystals larger than the groundmass forming a rock known as porphyry. Granites can be pink to dark gray or even black, depending on their chemistry and mineralogy.

Chapter 4. Volcanism and Extrusive Rocks

    a. Granite0   b. Thing
    c. Undefined   d. Undefined

41. _____ is a high-silica igneous, volcanic rock. It is intermediate in compositions between andesite and rhyolite, and, like andesite, it consists mostly of plagioclase feldspar with biotite, hornblende, and pyroxene.
    a. Dacite0   b. Thing
    c. Undefined   d. Undefined

42. The mineral _____ is a magnesium iron silicate. It is one of the most common minerals on Earth, and has also been identified on the Moon, Mars, and comet Wild 2.
    a. Thing   b. Olivine0
    c. Undefined   d. Undefined

43. _____ is a very important series of tectosilicate minerals within the feldspar family. Rather than referring to a particular mineral with a specific chemical composition, it is a solid solution series.
    a. Plagioclase0   b. Thing
    c. Undefined   d. Undefined

44. _____ is the name of a group of rock-forming minerals which make up as much as sixty percent of the Earth's crust. Feldspars crystallize from magma in both intrusive and extrusive rocks, and they can also occur as compact minerals, as veins, and are also present in many types of metamorphic rock.
    a. Thing   b. Feldspar0
    c. Undefined   d. Undefined

45. _____ is a type of naturally-occurring glass formed as an extrusive igneous rock. It is produced when felsic lava erupted from a volcano cools rapidly through the glass transition temperature and freezes without sufficient time for crystal growth. _____ is commonly found within the margins of rhyolitic lava flows known as _____ flows, where cooling of the lava is rapid.
    a. Obsidian0   b. Thing
    c. Undefined   d. Undefined

46. An _____ is a body of igneous rock that has crystallized from a molten magma below the surface of the Earth.
    a. Thing   b. Intrusion0
    c. Undefined   d. Undefined

47. _____ rock is the fine-grained mass of material in which larger grains or crystals are embedded. The _____ of an igneous rock consists of fine-grained, often microscopic, crystals in which larger crystals are embedded. This porphyritic texture is indicative of multi-stage cooling of magma.
    a. Thing   b. Groundmass0
    c. Undefined   d. Undefined

48. _____ is a volcanic rock texture characterized by, or containing, many vesicles. The texture is often found in extrusive aphanitic, or glassy, igneous rock. The vesicles are small cavities formed by the expansion of bubbles of gas or steam during the solidification of the rock.

Chapter 4. Volcanism and Extrusive Rocks   35

    a. Vesicular texture0   b. Thing
    c. Undefined   d. Undefined

49. In cell biology, a _____ is a relatively small and enclosed compartment, separated from the cytosol by at least one lipid bilayer.
    a. Thing   b. Vesicle0
    c. Undefined   d. Undefined

50. _____ is the vesicular ejecta of basaltic and andesitic magmas. Generally a dark brownish black or red, _____ is generally thought of as the mafic version of pumice, forming when magma rich in dissolved gases is vented. _____ is composed of volcanic glass fragments, and has few mineral crystals.
    a. Scoria0   b. Thing
    c. Undefined   d. Undefined

51. A _____ is a fragment of cooled pyroclastic material, lava or magma.
    a. Thing   b. Cinder0
    c. Undefined   d. Undefined

52. _____ is a type of rock consisting of consolidated volcanic ash ejected from vents during a volcanic eruption.
    a. Tuff0   b. Thing
    c. Undefined   d. Undefined

53. _____ are pyroclastic rocks formed by explosive eruption of lava and any rocks which are entrained within the eruptive column. This may include rocks plucked off the wall of the magma conduit, or physically picked up by the ensuing pyroclastic surge.
    a. Thing   b. Volcanic breccia0
    c. Undefined   d. Undefined

54. _____ is a rock composed of angular fragments of rocks or minerals in a matrix, that is a cementing material, that may be similar or different in composition to the fragments.
    a. Breccia0   b. Thing
    c. Undefined   d. Undefined

55. In geology, a _____ is a deformational feature consisting of symmetrically-dipping anticlines; their general outline on a geologic map is circular or oval.
    a. Thing   b. Dome0
    c. Undefined   d. Undefined

56. A _____ flow typically advances as a series of small lobes and toes that continually break out from a cooled crust. Also forms lava tubes where the minimal heat loss maintains low viscosity.
    a. Pāhoehoe0   b. Thing
    c. Undefined   d. Undefined

57. A _____ is formed of molten lava ejected from a vent somewhat like taffy. Expanding gases in the lava fountains tear the liquid rock into irregular gobs that fall back to earth, forming a heap around the vent.

Chapter 4. Volcanism and Extrusive Rocks

    a. Spatter cone0
    c. Undefined
    b. Thing
    d. Undefined

58. The _____ is used by geologists and other scientists to describe the timing and relationships between events that have occurred during the history of Earth.
    a. Geological time scale0
    c. Undefined
    b. Thing
    d. Undefined

59. A _____, is a tall, conical volcano composed of many layers of hardened lava, tephra, and volcanic ash. These volcanoes are characterized by a steep profile and periodic, explosive eruptions. The lava that flows from them is viscous, and cools and hardens before spreading very far.
    a. Stratovolcano0
    c. Undefined
    b. Thing
    d. Undefined

60. _____ is displacement of solids by the agents of ocean currents, wind, water, or ice by downward or down-slope movement in response to gravity or by living organisms.
    a. Erosion0
    c. Undefined
    b. Thing
    d. Undefined

61. A _____ is a roughy circular mound-shaped protrusion resulting from the slow eruption of felsic lava from a volcano. The viscosity, or stickiness, of the lava does not allow for the lava to flow very far from its vent before solidifying. Domes may reach heights of several hundred meters, and can grow slowly and steadily for months or years. The sides of these structures are composed of unstable rock debris.
    a. Lava dome0
    c. Undefined
    b. Thing
    d. Undefined

62. A _____ is a large, slow moving river of ice, formed from compacted layers of snow, that slowly deforms and flows in response to gravity. _____ ice is the largest reservoir of fresh water on Earth, and second only to oceans as the largest reservoir of total water. Glaciers cover vast areas of polar regions but are restricted to the highest mountains in the tropics.
    a. Glacier0
    c. Undefined
    b. Thing
    d. Undefined

63. _____ is a reaction force applied by a stretched string, rope or a similar object on the objects which stretch it. The direction of the force of it is parallel to the string, towards the string.
    a. Thing
    c. Undefined
    b. Tension0
    d. Undefined

64. A _____ is a large volcano with shallowly-sloping sides. A _____ is formed by lava flows of low viscosity — lava that flows easily. Consequently, a volcanic mountain having a broad profile is built up over time by flow after flow of relatively fluid basaltic lava issuing from vents or fissures on the surface of the volcano.
    a. Thing
    c. Undefined
    b. Shield volcano0
    d. Undefined

Chapter 4. Volcanism and Extrusive Rocks

65. A _____ is a geological feature that is also known as a Rip in the earth causing magma to flow out and forming an undersea volcano, it also has geological features, a continuous elevational crest for some distance. Ridges are usually termed hills or mountains as well, depending on size.
    a. Ridge0
    b. Thing
    c. Undefined
    d. Undefined

66. In plate tectonics, a _____ a linear feature that exists between two tectonic plates that are moving away from each other. These areas can form in the middle of continents but eventually form ocean basins.
    a. Divergent plate boundary0
    b. Thing
    c. Undefined
    d. Undefined

67. A _____ is an intrusion into a cross-cutting fissure, meaning a _____ cuts across other pre-existing layers or bodies of rock, this means that a _____ is always younger than the rocks that contain it. The thickness is usually much smaller than the other two dimensions. Thickness can vary from sub-centimeter scale to many meters in thickness and the lateral dimensions can extend over many kilometers.
    a. Dike0
    b. Thing
    c. Undefined
    d. Undefined

Chapter 5. Weathering and Soil

1. _____ is the process of breaking down rocks, soils and their minerals through direct contact with the atmosphere. _____ occurs without movement. Two main classifications of _____ processes exist. Mechanical or physical _____ involves the breakdown of rocks and soils through direct contact with atmospheric conditions. The second classification, chemical _____, involves the direct effect of atmospheric chemicals in the breakdown of rocks, soils and minerals.
   a. Weathering0
   b. Thing
   c. Undefined
   d. Undefined

2. _____ is displacement of solids by the agents of ocean currents, wind, water, or ice by downward or down-slope movement in response to gravity or by living organisms.
   a. Thing
   b. Erosion0
   c. Undefined
   d. Undefined

3. A _____ is a body of water with a current, confined within a bed and banks. Streams are important as conduits in the water cycle, instruments in aquifer recharge, and corridors for fish and wildlife migration.
   a. Thing
   b. Stream0
   c. Undefined
   d. Undefined

4. _____ involves the change in the composition of rock, often leading to a 'break down' in its form.
   a. Chemical weathering0
   b. Thing
   c. Undefined
   d. Undefined

5. _____ is the gas phase component of a another state of matter which does not completely fill its container. It is distinguished from the pure gas phase by the presence of the same substance in another state of matter. Hence when a liquid has completely evaporated, it is said that the system has been completely transformed to the gas phase.
   a. Vapor0
   b. Thing
   c. Undefined
   d. Undefined

6. _____ is a common and widely occurring type of intrusive, felsic, igneous rock. Granites are usually medium to coarsely crystalline, occasionally with some individual crystals larger than the groundmass forming a rock known as porphyry. Granites can be pink to dark gray or even black, depending on their chemistry and mineralogy.
   a. Granite0
   b. Thing
   c. Undefined
   d. Undefined

7. _____ is a solid deposition of water vapor from saturated air. If solid surfaces in contact with the air are chilled below the deposition point, then spicules of ice grow out from the solid surface. _____ is often observed around cracks in wooden sidewalks due to the moist air escaping from the ground below. Other objects on which _____ develops are those with low specific heat and high thermal emissivity, such as blackened metals.
   a. Thing
   b. Frost0
   c. Undefined
   d. Undefined

8. _____ is the second most common mineral in the Earth's continental crust. It is made up of a lattice of silica tetrahedra. _____ belongs to the rhombohedral crystal system. In nature _____ crystals are often twinned, distorted, or so intergrown with adjacent crystals of _____ or other minerals as to only show part of this shape, or to lack obvious crystal faces altogether and appear massive.

Chapter 5. Weathering and Soil

   a. Quartz0
   b. Thing
   c. Undefined
   d. Undefined

9. A _____ is a naturally occurring substance formed through geological processes that has a characteristic chemical composition, a highly ordered atomic structure and specific physical properties. A rock, by comparison, is an aggregate of minerals and need not have a specific chemical composition. Minerals range in composition from pure elements and simple salts to very complex silicates with thousands of known forms.
   a. Thing
   b. Mineral0
   c. Undefined
   d. Undefined

10. _____ is a term used to describe a group of hydrous aluminium phyllosilicate minerals, that are typically less than 2 micrometres in diameter. _____ consists of a variety of phyllosilicate minerals rich in silicon and aluminium oxides and hydroxides which include variable amounts of structural water. Clays are generally formed by the chemical weathering of silicate-bearing rocks by carbonic acid but some are formed by hydrothermal activity.
   a. Clay0
   b. Thing
   c. Undefined
   d. Undefined

11. A _____ is a solid in which the constituent atoms, molecules, or ions are packed in a regularly ordered, repeating pattern extending in all three spatial dimensions. Most metals encountered in everyday life are polycrystals. Crystals are often symmetrically intergrown to form _____ twins.
   a. Crystal0
   b. Thing
   c. Undefined
   d. Undefined

12. A _____ is a unique arrangement of atoms in a crystal. It is composed of a unit cell, a set of atoms arranged in a particular way, which is periodically repeated in three dimensions on a lattice. The spacing between unit cells in various directions is called its lattice parameters. The symmetry properties of the crystal are embodied in its space group.
   a. Thing
   b. Crystal structure0
   c. Undefined
   d. Undefined

13. _____ is a sedimentary rock composed largely of the mineral calcite. _____ often contains variable amounts of silica in the form of chert or flint, as well as varying amounts of clay, silt and sand as disseminations, nodules, or layers within the rock. The primary source of the calcite in _____ is most commonly marine organisms. These organisms secrete shells that settle out of the water column and are deposited on ocean floors as pelagic ooze or alternatively is conglomerated in a coral reef.
   a. Thing
   b. Limestone0
   c. Undefined
   d. Undefined

14. _____ is a metamorphic rock resulting from the metamorphism of limestone, composed mostly of calcite. It is extensively used for sculpture, as a building material, and in many other applications. The word '_____' is colloquially used to refer to many other stones that are capable of taking a high polish.
   a. Marble0
   b. Thing
   c. Undefined
   d. Undefined

15. _____ is a fine-grained, homogeneous, metamorphic rock derived from an original shale-type sedimentary rock composed of clay or volcanic ash through low grade regional metamorphism. The result is a foliated rock in which the foliation may not correspond to the original sedimentary layering.

a. Thing
b. Slate0
c. Undefined
d. Undefined

16. In geology and astronomy, the term _____ is used to denote types of rock that consist predominantly of _____ minerals. Such rocks include a wide range of igneous, metamorphic and sedimentary types. Most of the Earth's mantle and crust are made up of _____ rocks. The same is true of the Moon and the other rocky planets.
   a. Silicate0
   b. Thing
   c. Undefined
   d. Undefined

17. _____ is a type of chemical weathering that creates rounded boulders and helps to create domed monoliths. This should not be confused with stream abrasion, a physical process which also creates rounded rocks on a much smaller scale.
   a. Spheroidal weathering0
   b. Thing
   c. Undefined
   d. Undefined

18. A _____ is a large emplacement of igneous intrusive rock that forms from cooled magma deep in the Earth's crust. They are almost always made mostly of felsic or intermediate rock-types, such as granite, quartz monzonite, or diorite.
   a. Thing
   b. Batholith0
   c. Undefined
   d. Undefined

19. _____, in everyday life, is most familiar as the agency that endows objects with weight. _____ is responsible for keeping the Earth and the other planets in their orbits around the Sun; for the formation of tides; and for various other phenomena that we observe. _____ is also the reason for the very existence of the Earth, the Sun, and most macroscopic objects in the universe; without it, matter would not have coalesced into these large masses, and life, as we know it, would not exist.
   a. Thing
   b. Gravitation0
   c. Undefined
   d. Undefined

20. _____ in geology is a weathering process, mainly caused in arid areas by differential heating and cooling of rock surfaces. There needs to be a high diurnal temperature range.
   a. Exfoliation0
   b. Thing
   c. Undefined
   d. Undefined

21. A _____ is a landform that extends above the surrounding terrain in a limited area. A _____ is generally steeper than a hill, but there is no universally accepted standard definition for the height of a _____ or a hill although a _____ usually has an identifiable summit.
   a. Place
   b. Mountain0
   c. Undefined
   d. Undefined

22. In geology, a _____ is a deformational feature consisting of symmetrically-dipping anticlines; their general outline on a geologic map is circular or oval.
   a. Thing
   b. Dome0
   c. Undefined
   d. Undefined

Chapter 5. Weathering and Soil

23. In geography, a _____ is a landscape form or region that receives very little precipitation. They are defined as areas that receive an average annual precipitation of less than 250 mm. A _____ where vegetation cover is exceedingly sparse correspond to the 'hyperarid' regions of the earth, where rainfall is exceedingly rare and infrequent.
    a. Desert0
    b. Place
    c. Undefined
    d. Undefined

24. _____ is molten rock located beneath the surface of the Earth, and which often collects in a _____ chamber. _____ is a complex high-temperature fluid substance. Most are silicate solutions. It is capable of intrusion into adjacent rocks or of extrusion onto the surface as lava or ejected explosively as tephra to form pyroclastic rock. Environments of _____ formation include subduction zones, continental rift zones, mid-oceanic ridges, and hotspots, some of which are interpreted as mantle plumes.
    a. Magma0
    b. Thing
    c. Undefined
    d. Undefined

25. An _____ is a layer of gases that may surround a material body of sufficient mass. The gases are attracted by the gravity of the body, and are retained for a longer duration if gravity is high and the _____'s temperature is low. Some planets consist mainly of various gases, and thus have very deep atmospheres.
    a. Atmosphere0
    b. Place
    c. Undefined
    d. Undefined

26. _____ is the condition of a system in which competing influences are balanced.
    a. Equilibrium0
    b. Thing
    c. Undefined
    d. Undefined

27. An _____ is a chemical compound containing an oxygen atom and other elements. Most of the earth's crust consists of them. They result when elements are oxidized by air.
    a. Oxide0
    b. Thing
    c. Undefined
    d. Undefined

28. _____ is a common phyllosilicate mineral within the mica group. Primarily a solid-solution series between the iron-endmember annite, and the magnesium-endmember phlogopite; more aluminous endmembers include siderophyllite.
    a. Biotite0
    b. Thing
    c. Undefined
    d. Undefined

29. The mineral _____ is a magnesium iron silicate. It is one of the most common minerals on Earth, and has also been identified on the Moon, Mars, and comet Wild 2.
    a. Thing
    b. Olivine0
    c. Undefined
    d. Undefined

30. _____ is the oxide of silicon, chemical formula SiO_2, and is known for its hardness as early as the 16th century. It is a principle component in most types of glass and substances such as concrete.
    a. Thing
    b. Silica0
    c. Undefined
    d. Undefined

31. _____ is an ore consisting in a mixture of hydrated iron oxide-hydroxide of varying composition. It often contains a varying amount of oxide compared to hydroxide.

Chapter 5. Weathering and Soil

a. Limonite0
b. Thing
c. Undefined
d. Undefined

32. An _____ solid is a solid in which there is no long-range order of the positions of the atoms. These materials are often prepared by rapidly cooling molten material, such as glass. The cooling reduces the mobility of the material's molecules before they can pack into a more thermodynamically favorable crystalline state.
   a. Amorphous0
   b. Thing
   c. Undefined
   d. Undefined

33. _____ rock is one of the three main rock groups. Rock formed from these covers 75% of the Earth's land area, and includes common types such as chalk, limestone, dolomite, sandstone, and shale.
   a. Sedimentary0
   b. Thing
   c. Undefined
   d. Undefined

34. _____ is one of the three main rock groups. _____ covers 75% of the Earth's land area. Four basic processes are involved in the formation of a clastic _____: weathering caused mainly by friction of waves, transportation where the sediment is carried along by a current, deposition and compaction where the sediment is squashed together to form a rock of this kind.
   a. Thing
   b. Sedimentary rock0
   c. Undefined
   d. Undefined

35. _____ is a very common mineral, colored black to steel or silver-gray, brown to reddish brown, or red. It is mined as the main ore of iron. Varieties include kidney ore, martite iron rose and specularite. While the forms of it vary, they all have a rust-red streak. it is harder than pure iron, but much more brittle.
   a. Hematite0
   b. Thing
   c. Undefined
   d. Undefined

36. An _____ is an atom or group of atoms which have lost or gained one or more electrons, making them negatively or positively charged.
   a. Ion0
   b. Thing
   c. Undefined
   d. Undefined

37. _____ is the result of the transformation of a pre-existing rock type, the protolith, in a process called metamorphism, which means "change in form". The protolith is subjected to heat and extreme pressure causing profound physical and/or chemical change. The protolith may be sedimentary rock, igneous rock or another older rock.
   a. Thing
   b. Metamorphic rock0
   c. Undefined
   d. Undefined

38. _____ can be defined as the solid state recrystallisation of pre-existing rocks due to changes in heat and/or pressure and/or introduction of fluids. There will be mineralogical, chemical and crystallographic changes. _____ produced with increasing pressure and temperature conditions is known as prograde _____. Conversely, decreasing temperatures and pressure characterize retrograde _____.
   a. Thing
   b. Metamorphism0
   c. Undefined
   d. Undefined

Chapter 5. Weathering and Soil

39. _____ are hydrous aluminium phyllosilicates, sometimes with variable amounts of iron, magnesium, alkali metals, alkaline earths and other cations. Clays have structures similar to the micas and therefore form flat hexagonal sheets. _____ are common weathering products and low temperature hydrothermal alteration products.
   a. Clay minerals0
   b. Thing
   c. Undefined
   d. Undefined

40. _____ is a form of chemical bonding that is characterized by the sharing of pairs of electrons between atoms.
   a. Covalent bonding0
   b. Thing
   c. Undefined
   d. Undefined

41. Earth's _____ is a ~2,900 km thick rocky shell comprizing approximately 70% of Earth's volume. It is predominantly solid and overlies the Earth's iron-rich core, which occupies about 30% of Earth's volume. Past episodes of melting and volcanism at the shallower levels of the _____ have produced a very thin crust of crystallized melt products near the surface, upon which we live.
   a. Thing
   b. Mantle0
   c. Undefined
   d. Undefined

42. _____ is a fine-grained sedimentary rock whose original constituents were clays or muds. It is characterized by thin laminae breaking with an irregular curving fracture, often splintery and usually parallel to the often-indistinguishable bedding plane.
   a. Shale0
   b. Thing
   c. Undefined
   d. Undefined

43. _____ is a sedimentary rock composed mainly of sand-size mineral or rock grains. Most _____ is composed of quartz and/or feldspar because these are the most common minerals in the Earth's crust. Like sand, _____ may be any color, but the most common colors are tan, brown, yellow, red, gray and white.
   a. Sandstone0
   b. Thing
   c. Undefined
   d. Undefined

44. _____ is the average and variations of weather over long periods of time. _____ zones can be defined using parameters such as temperature and rainfall.
   a. Thing
   b. Climate0
   c. Undefined
   d. Undefined

45. In organic chemistry, a _____ is a salt of carbonic acid.
   a. Thing
   b. Carbonate0
   c. Undefined
   d. Undefined

46. _____ is the native consolidated rock underlying the Earth's surface. Above the _____ is usually an area of broken and weathered unconsolidated rock in the basal subsoil.
   a. Thing
   b. Bedrock0
   c. Undefined
   d. Undefined

47. _____ is a layer of loose, heterogeneous material covering solid rock. _____ is present on Earth, the Moon, some asteroids, and other planets.

a. Regolith0   b. Thing
c. Undefined   d. Undefined

48. _____ is any particulate matter that can be transported by fluid flow and which eventually is deposited as a layer of solid particles on the bed or bottom of a body of water or other liquid.
   a. Sediment0   b. Thing
   c. Undefined   d. Undefined

49. _____ is soil composed of sand, silt, and clay in relatively even concentration. Loams are gritty, plastic when moist, and retain water easily. They generally contain more nutrients than sandy soils.
   a. Loam0   b. Thing
   c. Undefined   d. Undefined

50. _____ is the layer of soil under the topsoil on the surface of the ground. The _____ may include substances such as clay and has only been partially broken down by air, sunlight, water, etc., to produce true soil.
   a. Subsoil0   b. Thing
   c. Undefined   d. Undefined

51. In chemistry, a _____ is defined as a sufficiently stable electrically neutral group of at least two atoms in a definite arrangement held together by strong chemical bonds.
   a. Thing   b. Molecule0
   c. Undefined   d. Undefined

52. _____ is the process of extracting a substance from a solid by dissolving it in a liquid.
   a. Leaching0   b. Thing
   c. Undefined   d. Undefined

53. _____ consist of mineral layers which may contain concentrations of clay or minerals such as iron or aluminium, or organic material. In addition, they are defined by having a distinctly different structure or consistence to the A horizon above and the horizons below.
   a. B horizon0   b. Thing
   c. Undefined   d. Undefined

54. On a glacier, the _____ is the area above the firn line, where snowfall accumulates and exceeds the losses from ablation.
   a. Accumulation zone0   b. Thing
   c. Undefined   d. Undefined

55. _____ is simply named so because they come 'after' A and B within the soil profile. These layers are little affected by soil forming processes, and their lack of pedological development is one of their defining attributes
   a. Thing   b. C horizon0
   c. Undefined   d. Undefined

56. _____, in soil science, means the underlying geological material in which soil horizons form. Soils typically get a great deal of structure and minerals from their _____.

Chapter 5. Weathering and Soil

a. Parent material0
b. Thing
c. Undefined
d. Undefined

57. _____ occurs when snow falls on a glacier, is compressed, and becomes part of a glacier that winds its way toward a body of water.
 a. Thing
 b. Blue ice0
 c. Undefined
 d. Undefined

58. Among the classifications of soil types, _____, is a fine, silty, windblown type of unconsolidated deposit. It is derived from glacial deposits, where glacial activity has ground rocks very fine. After drying, these deposits are highly susceptible to wind erosion, and downwind deposits may become very deep. _____ deposits are geologically unstable by nature, and will erode even without being disturbed by humans.
 a. Thing
 b. Loess0
 c. Undefined
 d. Undefined

59. _____ is a common gray to black extrusive volcanic rock. It is usually fine-grained due to rapid cooling of lava on the Earth's surface. It may be porphyritic containing larger crystals in a fine matrix, or vesicular, or frothy scoria.
 a. Basalt0
 b. Thing
 c. Undefined
 d. Undefined

60. _____ consists of very fine rock and mineral particles less than 2 mm in diameter that are ejected from a volcanic vent. The very fine particles may be carried for many miles, settling out as a dust-like layer across the landscape
 a. Ash fall0
 b. Thing
 c. Undefined
 d. Undefined

61. _____ is molten rock expelled by a volcano during an eruption. When first extruded from a volcanic vent, it is a liquid at temperatures from 700 °C to 1,200 °C.
 a. Lava0
 b. Thing
 c. Undefined
 d. Undefined

62. _____ is the process by which molecules in a liquid state become a gas.
 a. Evaporation0
 b. Thing
 c. Undefined
 d. Undefined

63. _____ is the ability of a substance to draw another substance into it. The standard reference is to a tube in plants but can be seen readily with porous paper. It occurs when the adhesive intermolecular forces between the liquid and a substance are stronger than the cohesive intermolecular forces inside the liquid. The effect causes a concave meniscus to form where the substance is touching a vertical surface. The same effect is what causes porous materials to soak up liquids.
 a. Capillary action0
 b. Thing
 c. Undefined
 d. Undefined

64. _____ is any product of the condensation of atmospheric water vapor that is deposited on the earth's surface. It occurs when the atmosphere becomes saturated with water vapour and the water condenses and falls out of solution. Air becomes saturated via two processes, cooling and adding moisture.

Chapter 5. Weathering and Soil

a. Thing
b. Precipitation0
c. Undefined
d. Undefined

65. _____ is a hardened deposit of calcium carbonate. This calcium carbonate cements together other materials, including gravel, sand, clay, and silt. It is found in aridisol and mollisol soil orders. _____ occurs worldwide, generally in arid or semi-arid regions.
a. Thing
b. Caliche0
c. Undefined
d. Undefined

66. An _____ is a volume of rock containing components or minerals in a mode of occurrence that renders it valuable for mining.
a. Ore0
b. Thing
c. Undefined
d. Undefined

67. _____ is an aluminium ore. It consists largely of the Al minerals gibbsite, boehmite and diaspore, together with the iron oxides goethite and hematite, the clay mineral kaolinite and small amounts of anatase.
a. Thing
b. Bauxite0
c. Undefined
d. Undefined

68. _____ rocks form when molten rock, magma, cools and solidifies, with or without crystallization, either below the surface as intrusive, plutonic rocks or on the surface as extrusive, volcanic, rocks.
a. Thing
b. Igneous0
c. Undefined
d. Undefined

69. _____ forms when rock cools and solidifies either below the surface as intrusive rocks or on the surface as extrusive rocks. This magma can be derived from partial melts of pre-existing rocks in either the Earth's mantle or crust. Typically, the melting is caused by one or more of the following processes -- an increase in temperature, a decrease in pressure, or a change in composition.
a. Thing
b. Igneous rock0
c. Undefined
d. Undefined

70. _____ is a surface formation in hot and wet tropical areas which is enriched in iron and aluminium and develops by intensive and long lasting weathering of the underlying parent rock. Nearly all kinds of rocks can be deeply decomposed by the action of high rainfall and elevated temperatures. This gives rise to a residual concentration of more insoluble elements.
a. Laterite0
b. Thing
c. Undefined
d. Undefined

71. _____ can refer to two meanings. The first meaning, is simply that of a former soil preserved by burial underneath either sediments or volcanic deposits, which in case of older deposits, have lithified into rock. In general, it is the typical and accepted practice to use the term "_____" to designate such "fossil" soils found buried within either sedimentary or volcanic deposits exposed in all continents.
a. Paleosol0
b. Thing
c. Undefined
d. Undefined

72. _____ is the study of Earth's surface features or those of other planets, moons, and asteroids

a. Thing
b. Topography0
c. Undefined
d. Undefined

Chapter 6. Sediments and Sedimentary Rocks

1. _____ is any particulate matter that can be transported by fluid flow and which eventually is deposited as a layer of solid particles on the bed or bottom of a body of water or other liquid.
   - a. Thing
   - b. Sediment0
   - c. Undefined
   - d. Undefined

2. _____ rock is one of the three main rock groups. Rock formed from these covers 75% of the Earth's land area, and includes common types such as chalk, limestone, dolomite, sandstone, and shale.
   - a. Thing
   - b. Sedimentary0
   - c. Undefined
   - d. Undefined

3. _____ is one of the three main rock groups. _____ covers 75% of the Earth's land area. Four basic processes are involved in the formation of a clastic _____: weathering caused mainly by friction of waves, transportation where the sediment is carried along by a current, deposition and compaction where the sediment is squashed together to form a rock of this kind.
   - a. Sedimentary rock0
   - b. Thing
   - c. Undefined
   - d. Undefined

4. _____ is any product of the condensation of atmospheric water vapor that is deposited on the earth's surface. It occurs when the atmosphere becomes saturated with water vapour and the water condenses and falls out of solution. Air becomes saturated via two processes, cooling and adding moisture.
   - a. Thing
   - b. Precipitation0
   - c. Undefined
   - d. Undefined

5. A _____ is a rock, sandbar, or other feature lying beneath the surface of the water yet shallow enough to be a hazard to ships. They result from abiotic processes—deposition of sand, wave erosion planning down rock outcrops, and other natural processes.
   - a. Reef0
   - b. Thing
   - c. Undefined
   - d. Undefined

6. _____ is the process of breaking down rocks, soils and their minerals through direct contact with the atmosphere. _____ occurs without movement. Two main classifications of _____ processes exist. Mechanical or physical _____ involves the breakdown of rocks and soils through direct contact with atmospheric conditions. The second classification, chemical _____, involves the direct effect of atmospheric chemicals in the breakdown of rocks, soils and minerals.
   - a. Thing
   - b. Weathering0
   - c. Undefined
   - d. Undefined

7. _____ is displacement of solids by the agents of ocean currents, wind, water, or ice by downward or down-slope movement in response to gravity or by living organisms.
   - a. Erosion0
   - b. Thing
   - c. Undefined
   - d. Undefined

8. _____ is rock that is of a certain particle size range. In geology, _____ is any loose rock that is at least two millimeters in its largest dimension and no more than 75 millimeters.
   - a. Gravel0
   - b. Thing
   - c. Undefined
   - d. Undefined

Chapter 6. Sediments and Sedimentary Rocks 49

9. A _____ is a naturally occurring substance formed through geological processes that has a characteristic chemical composition, a highly ordered atomic structure and specific physical properties. A rock, by comparison, is an aggregate of minerals and need not have a specific chemical composition. Minerals range in composition from pure elements and simple salts to very complex silicates with thousands of known forms.
- a. Mineral0
- b. Thing
- c. Undefined
- d. Undefined

10. _____ is a term used to describe a group of hydrous aluminium phyllosilicate minerals, that are typically less than 2 micrometres in diameter. _____ consists of a variety of phyllosilicate minerals rich in silicon and aluminium oxides and hydroxides which include variable amounts of structural water. Clays are generally formed by the chemical weathering of silicate-bearing rocks by carbonic acid but some are formed by hydrothermal activity.
- a. Clay0
- b. Thing
- c. Undefined
- d. Undefined

11. In geology and astronomy, the term _____ is used to denote types of rock that consist predominantly of _____ minerals. Such rocks include a wide range of igneous, metamorphic and sedimentary types. Most of the Earth's mantle and crust are made up of _____ rocks. The same is true of the Moon and the other rocky planets.
- a. Silicate0
- b. Thing
- c. Undefined
- d. Undefined

12. _____ are hydrous aluminium phyllosilicates, sometimes with variable amounts of iron, magnesium, alkali metals, alkaline earths and other cations. Clays have structures similar to the micas and therefore form flat hexagonal sheets. _____ are common weathering products and low temperature hydrothermal alteration products.
- a. Thing
- b. Clay minerals0
- c. Undefined
- d. Undefined

13. _____ involves the change in the composition of rock, often leading to a 'break down' in its form.
- a. Thing
- b. Chemical weathering0
- c. Undefined
- d. Undefined

14. _____ is the second most common mineral in the Earth's continental crust. It is made up of a lattice of silica tetrahedra. _____ belongs to the rhombohedral crystal system. In nature _____ crystals are often twinned, distorted, or so intergrown with adjacent crystals of _____ or other minerals as to only show part of this shape, or to lack obvious crystal faces altogether and appear massive.
- a. Quartz0
- b. Thing
- c. Undefined
- d. Undefined

15. _____ consists of clay-sized particles of rock, generated by glacial erosion or by artificial grinding to a similar size. Because the material is very small, it is suspended in river water making the water appear cloudy. If the river flows into a glacial lake, the lake may appear turquoise in color as a result.
- a. Thing
- b. Rock flour0
- c. Undefined
- d. Undefined

16. _____ is the geological process whereby material is added to a landform. This is the process by which wind and water create a sediment deposit, through the laying down of granular material that has been eroded and transported from another geographical location.

Chapter 6. Sediments and Sedimentary Rocks

    a. Deposition0   b. Thing
    c. Undefined   d. Undefined

17. A _____ is a body of water with a current, confined within a bed and banks. Streams are important as conduits in the water cycle, instruments in aquifer recharge, and corridors for fish and wildlife migration.
    a. Stream0   b. Thing
    c. Undefined   d. Undefined

18. _____ is a type of chemical weathering that creates rounded boulders and helps to create domed monoliths. This should not be confused with stream abrasion, a physical process which also creates rounded rocks on a much smaller scale.
    a. Spheroidal weathering0   b. Thing
    c. Undefined   d. Undefined

19. _____, in everyday life, is most familiar as the agency that endows objects with weight. _____ is responsible for keeping the Earth and the other planets in their orbits around the Sun; for the formation of tides; and for various other phenomena that we observe. _____ is also the reason for the very existence of the Earth, the Sun, and most macroscopic objects in the universe; without it, matter would not have coalesced into these large masses, and life, as we know it, would not exist.
    a. Gravitation0   b. Thing
    c. Undefined   d. Undefined

20. _____ is a measure of the resistance of a fluid to deform under shear stress. It is commonly perceived as "thickness", or resistance to flow. _____ describes a fluid's internal resistance to flow and may be thought of as a measure of fluid friction.
    a. Viscosity0   b. Thing
    c. Undefined   d. Undefined

21. _____ occurs when snow falls on a glacier, is compressed, and becomes part of a glacier that winds its way toward a body of water.
    a. Thing   b. Blue ice0
    c. Undefined   d. Undefined

22. _____ is the oxide of silicon, chemical formula SiO_2, and is known for its hardness as early as the 16th century. It is a principle component in most types of glass and substances such as concrete.
    a. Silica0   b. Thing
    c. Undefined   d. Undefined

23. In geography, a _____ is a landscape form or region that receives very little precipitation. They are defined as areas that receive an average annual precipitation of less than 250 mm. A _____ where vegetation cover is exceedingly sparse correspond to the 'hyperarid' regions of the earth, where rainfall is exceedingly rare and infrequent.
    a. Desert0   b. Place
    c. Undefined   d. Undefined

Chapter 6. Sediments and Sedimentary Rocks

24. _____ refer to marine animals from the class Anthozoa and exist as small sea anemone-like polyps, typically in colonies of many identical individuals. The group includes the important reef builders that are found in tropical oceans, which secrete calcium carbonate to form a hard skeleton.
    a. Coral0
    b. Thing
    c. Undefined
    d. Undefined

25. A _____ is an aragonite structure produced by living organisms, found in shallow, tropical marine waters with little to no nutrients in the water.
    a. Coral reef0
    b. Thing
    c. Undefined
    d. Undefined

26. A _____ is a hill of sand built by eolian processes. Dunes are subject to different forms and sizes based on their interaction with the wind. Most kinds of _____ are longer on the windward side where the sand is pushed up the _____, and a shorter in the lee of the wind. The trough between dunes is called a slack. A "_____ field" is an area covered by extensive sand dunes. Large _____ fields are known as ergs.
    a. Dune0
    b. Thing
    c. Undefined
    d. Undefined

27. Mean _____ is the average height of the sea, with reference to a suitable reference surface.
    a. Sea level0
    b. Thing
    c. Undefined
    d. Undefined

28. _____ is the process in which sediments compact under pressure, expel connate fluids, and gradually become solid rock.
    a. Lithification0
    b. Thing
    c. Undefined
    d. Undefined

29. _____ is the process of a material being more closely packed together.
    a. Compaction0
    b. Thing
    c. Undefined
    d. Undefined

30. _____ is the process of deposition of dissolved mineral components in the interstices of sediments. It is an important factor in the consolidation of coarse-grained clastic sedimentary rocks such as sandstones, conglomerates, or breccias during diagenesis or lithification. Cementing materials may include silica, carbonates, iron oxides, or clay minerals.
    a. Cementation0
    b. Thing
    c. Undefined
    d. Undefined

31. _____ is the process of formation of solid crystals from a uniform solution. It is also a chemical solid-liquid separation technique, in which mass transfer of a solute from the liquid solution to a pure solid crystalline phase occurs.
    a. Crystallization0
    b. Thing
    c. Undefined
    d. Undefined

32. _____ is a term used in geology to denote the pressure imposed on a stratigraphic layer by the weight of overlying layers of material.

Chapter 6. Sediments and Sedimentary Rocks

a. Lithostatic pressure0
b. Event
c. Undefined
d. Undefined

33. _____ is a sedimentary rock composed mainly of sand-size mineral or rock grains. Most _____ is composed of quartz and/or feldspar because these are the most common minerals in the Earth's crust. Like sand, _____ may be any color, but the most common colors are tan, brown, yellow, red, gray and white.
   a. Thing
   b. Sandstone0
   c. Undefined
   d. Undefined

34. In organic chemistry, a _____ is a salt of carbonic acid.
   a. Carbonate0
   b. Thing
   c. Undefined
   d. Undefined

35. _____ rocks are rocks formed from fragments of pre-existing rock.
   a. Clastic0
   b. Thing
   c. Undefined
   d. Undefined

36. _____ rocks form when molten rock, magma, cools and solidifies, with or without crystallization, either below the surface as intrusive, plutonic rocks or on the surface as extrusive, volcanic, rocks.
   a. Thing
   b. Igneous0
   c. Undefined
   d. Undefined

37. _____ forms when rock cools and solidifies either below the surface as intrusive rocks or on the surface as extrusive rocks. This magma can be derived from partial melts of pre-existing rocks in either the Earth's mantle or crust. Typically, the melting is caused by one or more of the following processes -- an increase in temperature, a decrease in pressure, or a change in composition.
   a. Igneous rock0
   b. Thing
   c. Undefined
   d. Undefined

38. _____ is molten rock located beneath the surface of the Earth, and which often collects in a _____ chamber. _____ is a complex high-temperature fluid substance. Most are silicate solutions. It is capable of intrusion into adjacent rocks or of extrusion onto the surface as lava or ejected explosively as tephra to form pyroclastic rock. Environments of _____ formation include subduction zones, continental rift zones, mid-oceanic ridges, and hotspots, some of which are interpreted as mantle plumes.
   a. Magma0
   b. Thing
   c. Undefined
   d. Undefined

39. In materials science, _____ is the distribution of crystallographic orientations of a sample.
   a. Crystalline texture0
   b. Thing
   c. Undefined
   d. Undefined

40. _____ is an essentially physical process that has meanings in chemistry, metallurgy and geology. In geology, solid-state _____ is a metamorphic process that occurs under situations of intense temperature and pressure where grains, atoms or molecules of a rock or mineral are packed closer together, creating a new crystal structure.

Chapter 6. Sediments and Sedimentary Rocks

a. Recrystallization0
b. Thing
c. Undefined
d. Undefined

41. _____ is a common and widely occurring type of intrusive, felsic, igneous rock. Granites are usually medium to coarsely crystalline, occasionally with some individual crystals larger than the groundmass forming a rock known as porphyry. Granites can be pink to dark gray or even black, depending on their chemistry and mineralogy.
a. Thing
b. Granite0
c. Undefined
d. Undefined

42. _____ is a fine-grained sedimentary rock whose original constituents were clays or muds. It is characterized by thin laminae breaking with an irregular curving fracture, often splintery and usually parallel to the often-indistinguishable bedding plane.
a. Thing
b. Shale0
c. Undefined
d. Undefined

43. A _____ is a rock consisting of individual stones that have become cemented together. Conglomerates are sedimentary rocks consisting of rounded fragements and are thus differentiated from breccias, which consist of angular clasts. Both conglomerates and breccias are characterized by clasts larger than sand.
a. Conglomerate0
b. Thing
c. Undefined
d. Undefined

44. _____ is the mineral form of sodium chloride. _____ forms isometric crystals. It commonly occurs with other evaporite deposit minerals such as several of the sulfates, halides and borates. _____ occurs in vast lakes of sedimentary evaporite minerals that result from the drying up of enclosed beds, playas, and seas.
a. Thing
b. Halite0
c. Undefined
d. Undefined

45. _____ is a fossil fuel formed in swamp ecosystems where plant remains were saved by water and mud from oxidization and biodegradation. It is a sedimentary rock, but the harder forms, such as anthracite _____, can be regarded as metamorphic rocks because of later exposure to elevated temperature and pressure. It is composed primarily of carbon along with assorted other elements, including sulfur.
a. Thing
b. Coal0
c. Undefined
d. Undefined

46. In geology the term _____ refers to the system of forces that tend to decrease the volume of or shorten rocks. Compressive strength refers to the maximum compressive stress that can be applied to a material before failure occurs.
a. Thing
b. Compression0
c. Undefined
d. Undefined

47. _____ is a sedimentary rock composed largely of the mineral calcite. _____ often contains variable amounts of silica in the form of chert or flint, as well as varying amounts of clay, silt and sand as disseminations, nodules, or layers within the rock. The primary source of the calcite in _____ is most commonly marine organisms. These organisms secrete shells that settle out of the water column and are deposited on ocean floors as pelagic ooze or alternatively is conglomerated in a coral reef.

Chapter 6. Sediments and Sedimentary Rocks

    a. Thing   b. Limestone0
    c. Undefined   d. Undefined

48. _____ is a rock composed of angular fragments of rocks or minerals in a matrix, that is a cementing material, that may be similar or different in composition to the fragments.
    a. Thing   b. Breccia0
    c. Undefined   d. Undefined

49. _____ is a detrital sedimentary rock, specifically a type of sandstone containing at least 25% feldspar. Arkosic sand is sand that is similarly rich in feldspar, and thus the potential precursor of _____. The other mineral components may vary, but quartz is commonly dominant, and minor mica is often present. Apart from the mineral content, rock fragments may also be a significant component.
    a. Arkose0   b. Thing
    c. Undefined   d. Undefined

50. _____ is the average and variations of weather over long periods of time. _____ zones can be defined using parameters such as temperature and rainfall.
    a. Climate0   b. Thing
    c. Undefined   d. Undefined

51. _____ is the result of the transformation of a pre-existing rock type, the protolith, in a process called metamorphism, which means "change in form". The protolith is subjected to heat and extreme pressure causing profound physical and/or chemical change. The protolith may be sedimentary rock, igneous rock or another older rock.
    a. Thing   b. Metamorphic rock0
    c. Undefined   d. Undefined

52. Metamorphic rock is the result of the transformation of a pre-existing rock type, the protolith, in a process called metamorphism. The protolith is subjected to heat and extreme pressure causing profound physical and/or chemical change. _____ make up a large part of the Earth's crust. They are formed deep beneath the Earth's surface by great stresses from rocks above and high pressures and temperatures.
    a. Metamorphic rocks0   b. Thing
    c. Undefined   d. Undefined

53. _____ can be defined as the solid state recrystallisation of pre-existing rocks due to changes in heat and/or pressure and/or introduction of fluids. There will be mineralogical, chemical and crystallographic changes. _____ produced with increasing pressure and temperature conditions is known as prograde _____. Conversely, decreasing temperatures and pressure characterize retrograde _____.
    a. Metamorphism0   b. Thing
    c. Undefined   d. Undefined

54. _____ is a sedimentary rock which has a composition intermediate in grain size between the coarser sandstones and the finer mudstones and shales.
    a. Siltstone0   b. Thing
    c. Undefined   d. Undefined

55. _____ is a geological term used to describe a sedimentary rock that is composed primarily of clay-sized particles.
- a. Thing
- b. Claystone0
- c. Undefined
- d. Undefined

56. _____ is a fine-grained sedimentary rock whose original constituents were clays or muds. Grain size is up to 0.0625 mm with individual grains too small to be distinguished without a microscope.
- a. Mudstone0
- b. Thing
- c. Undefined
- d. Undefined

57. _____ is a fine-grained silica-rich cryptocrystalline sedimentary rock that may contain small fossils. It varies greatly in color from white to black, but most often manifests as gray, brown, grayish brown and light green to rusty red; its color is an expression of trace elements present in the rock, and both red and green are most often related to traces of iron.
- a. Chert0
- b. Thing
- c. Undefined
- d. Undefined

58. Fossils are the mineralized or otherwise preserved remains or traces of animals, plants, and other organisms. The totality of fossils, both discovered and undiscovered, and their placement in fossiliferous rock formations and sedimentary layers is known as the _____ record.
- a. Fossil0
- b. Thing
- c. Undefined
- d. Undefined

59. _____ is an incompletely consolidated sedimentary rock of biochemical origin, mainly composed of mineral calcite, often including some phosphate, in the form of seashells or coral. It is created in association with marine reefs. While not usually referred to as such, it is actually a subset of limestone.
- a. Coquina0
- b. Thing
- c. Undefined
- d. Undefined

60. _____ is a soft, white, porous sedimentary rock, a form of limestone composed of the mineral calcite. It forms under relatively deep marine conditions from the gradual accumulation of minute calcite plates shed from micro-organisms called coccolithophores. It is common to find flint nodules embedded in it.
- a. Chalk0
- b. Thing
- c. Undefined
- d. Undefined

61. _____ is the name for an unusual geological form of calcite rock. _____ is a rough, thick, rock-like calcium carbonate deposit that forms by precipitation from bodies of water with a high dissolved calcium content.
- a. Tufa0
- b. Thing
- c. Undefined
- d. Undefined

62. _____ is a sedimentary rock. _____ is a natural chemical precipitate of carbonate minerals; typically aragonite, but often recrystallized to or primarily calcite; which is deposited from the water of mineral springs or streams saturated with calcium carbonate.
- a. Travertine0
- b. Thing
- c. Undefined
- d. Undefined

Chapter 6. Sediments and Sedimentary Rocks

63. A _____ is a natural underground void large enough for a human to enter. Some people suggest that the term '_____' should only apply to cavities that have some part which does not receive daylight; however, in popular usage, the term includes smaller spaces like a sea _____, rock shelters, and grottos.
   a. Cave0
   b. Place
   c. Undefined
   d. Undefined

64. _____ is a sedimentary carbonate rock that contains a high percentage of the mineral dolomite. It is usually referred to as dolomite rock. In old U.S.G.S. publications it was referred to as magnesian limestone.
   a. Dolostone0
   b. Thing
   c. Undefined
   d. Undefined

65. _____ is the process by which molecules in a liquid state become a gas.
   a. Evaporation0
   b. Thing
   c. Undefined
   d. Undefined

66. _____ is a very soft mineral composed of calcium sulfate dihydrate, with the chemical formula $CaSO_4 \cdot 2H_2O$. _____ occurs in nature as flattened and often twinned crystals and transparent cleavable masses. It may also occur silky and fibrous. Finally it may also be granular or quite compact.
   a. Gypsum0
   b. Thing
   c. Undefined
   d. Undefined

67. _____ refers to water-soluble, mineral sediments that result from the evaporation of bodies of surficial water.
   a. Thing
   b. Evaporite0
   c. Undefined
   d. Undefined

68. _____ is an accumulation of partially decayed vegetation matter. It forms in wetlands.
   a. Peat0
   b. Thing
   c. Undefined
   d. Undefined

69. _____ is a gaseous fossil fuel consisting primarily of methane but including significant quantities of ethane, butane, propane, carbon dioxide, nitrogen, helium and hydrogen sulfide.
   a. Thing
   b. Natural gas0
   c. Undefined
   d. Undefined

70. _____ is a naturally occurring liquid found in formations in the Earth consisting of a complex mixture of hydrocarbons of various lengths.
   a. Thing
   b. Petroleum0
   c. Undefined
   d. Undefined

71. The principle or _____ states that sediments are deposited under the influence of gravity as nearly horizontal beds. Observations in a wide variety of sedimentary environments support this principle. If we find folded or faulted strata, we know that the layers were deformed by tectonic forces after the sediments were deposited. This principle can be combined with the principle of superposition.
   a. Original horizontality0
   b. Thing
   c. Undefined
   d. Undefined

Chapter 6. Sediments and Sedimentary Rocks

72. The basic idea of this is that an object, event or entity can be spanned across multiple realities or universes. When combined, these multiple, unique, pan-dimensional segments of the object, consciousness or event, make up parts or constituents of its _____.
    a. Superposition0
    b. Thing
    c. Undefined
    d. Undefined

73. The _____ is an axiom that forms one of the bases of the sciences of geology, archaeology, and other fields dealing with stratigraphy. In its plainest form, that is: layers are arranged in a time sequence, with the oldest on the bottom and the youngest on the top, unless later processes disturb this arrangement.
    a. Law of Superposition0
    b. Thing
    c. Undefined
    d. Undefined

74. _____ are where one sedimetary deposit ends and another one begins. The rock is prone to breakage at these points because of the weakness between the layers.
    a. Bedding planes0
    b. Thing
    c. Undefined
    d. Undefined

75. In geology, a _____ is one characterized by coarse sediments at its base, which grade upward into progressively finer ones. They are perhaps best represented in turbidite strata, where they indicate a sudden strong current that deposits heavy, coarse sediments first, with finer ones following as the current weakens.
    a. Graded bed0
    b. Thing
    c. Undefined
    d. Undefined

76. _____ is a cloudiness or haziness of water caused by individual particles that are generally invisible to the naked eye, thus being much like smoke in air. _____ is generally caused by phytoplankton. Measurement of _____ is a key test of water quality.
    a. Turbidity0
    b. Thing
    c. Undefined
    d. Undefined

77. A _____ is a current of rapidly moving, sediment-laden water moving down a slope through air, water, or another fluid. The current moves because it has a higher density and turbidity than the fluid through which it flows.
    a. Thing
    b. Turbidity current0
    c. Undefined
    d. Undefined

78. Ocean _____ are any more or less continuous, directed movement of ocean water that flows in one of the Earth's oceans. They are rivers of hot or cold water within the ocean. They are generated from the forces acting upon the water like the earth's rotation, the wind, the temperature and salinity differences and the gravitation of the moon.
    a. Thing
    b. Currents0
    c. Undefined
    d. Undefined

79. _____ refers to the cyclic rizing and falling of Earth's ocean surface caused by the tidal forces of the Moon and the sun acting on the oceans. They cause changes in the depth of the marine and estuarine water bodies and produce oscillating currents known as tidal streams, making prediction of tides important for coastal navigation.
    a. Thing
    b. Tide0
    c. Undefined
    d. Undefined

Chapter 6. Sediments and Sedimentary Rocks

80. In geology, _____ are sedimentary structures that indicate agitation by or wind.
    a. Ripple marks0
    b. Thing
    c. Undefined
    d. Undefined

81. Fossil fuels are hydrocarbons, primarily coal and petroleum, formed from the fossilized remains of dead plants and animals. In common parlance, the term _____ also includes hydrocarbon-containing natural resources that are not derived from animal or plant sources. Fossil fuels have made large-scale industrial development possible and have largely supplanted water-driven mills, as well as the combustion of wood or peat for heat.
    a. Fossil fuel0
    b. Thing
    c. Undefined
    d. Undefined

82. _____ are hydrocarbons, primarily coal and petroleum, formed from the fossilized remains of dead plants and animals by exposure to heat and pressure in the Earth's crust over hundreds of millions of years. The burning of _____ by humans is the largest source of emissions of carbon dioxide, which is one of the greenhouse gases that enhances radiative forcing and contributes to global warming.
    a. Thing
    b. Fossil fuels0
    c. Undefined
    d. Undefined

83. _____ is the science and study of the solid matter that constitute the Earth. Encompassing such things as rocks, soil, and gemstones, _____ studies the composition, structure, physical properties, history, and the processes that shape Earth's components.
    a. Geology0
    b. Thing
    c. Undefined
    d. Undefined

84. _____ is a common gray to black extrusive volcanic rock. It is usually fine-grained due to rapid cooling of lava on the Earth's surface. It may be porphyritic containing larger crystals in a fine matrix, or vesicular, or frothy scoria.
    a. Thing
    b. Basalt0
    c. Undefined
    d. Undefined

85. _____ is a common and widely distributed type of rock formed by high-grade regional metamorphic processes from preexisting formations that were originally either igneous or sedimentary rocks. Gneissic rocks are usually medium to coarse foliated and largely recrystallized but do not carry large quantities of micas, chlorite or other platy minerals.
    a. Thing
    b. Gneiss0
    c. Undefined
    d. Undefined

86. _____ is a common phyllosilicate mineral within the mica group. Primarily a solid-solution series between the iron-endmember annite, and the magnesium-endmember phlogopite; more aluminous endmembers include siderophyllite.
    a. Biotite0
    b. Thing
    c. Undefined
    d. Undefined

87. _____ is the third or vertical dimension of land surface. When _____ is described underwater, the term bathymetry is used.
    a. Thing
    b. Terrain0
    c. Undefined
    d. Undefined

Chapter 6. Sediments and Sedimentary Rocks

88. _____ is mechanical scraping of a rock surface by friction between rocks and moving particles during their transport in wind, glacier, waves, gravity or running water.
   a. Abrasion0
   b. Thing
   c. Undefined
   d. Undefined

89. An _____ plain is a relatively flat and gently sloping landform found at the base of a range of hills or mountains, formed by the deposition of _____ soil over a long period of time by one or more rivers coming from the mountains.
   a. Alluvial0
   b. Thing
   c. Undefined
   d. Undefined

90. _____ is a very common mineral, colored black to steel or silver-gray, brown to reddish brown, or red. It is mined as the main ore of iron. Varieties include kidney ore, martite iron rose and specularite. While the forms of it vary, they all have a rust-red streak. it is harder than pure iron, but much more brittle.
   a. Thing
   b. Hematite0
   c. Undefined
   d. Undefined

91. A _____ is a landform where the mouth of a river flows into an ocean, sea, desert, estuary or lake. It builds up sediment outwards into the flat area which the river's flow encounters transported by the water and set down as the currents slow.
   a. Delta0
   b. Thing
   c. Undefined
   d. Undefined

92. An _____ is any piece of land that is completely surrounded by water, above high tide. There are two main types of islands: continental islands and oceanic islands. There are also artificial islands. A grouping of geographically and/or geologically related islands is called an archipelago.
   a. Thing
   b. Island0
   c. Undefined
   d. Undefined

93. _____ is a field of study within geology concerned generally with the structures within the crust of the Earth, or other planets, and particularly with the forces and movements that have operated in a region to create these structures.
   a. Thing
   b. Tectonics0
   c. Undefined
   d. Undefined

94. _____ is a theory of geology that has been developed to explain the observed evidence for large scale motions of the Earth's lithosphere. The theory encompassed and superseded the older theory of continental drift.
   a. Thing
   b. Plate tectonics0
   c. Undefined
   d. Undefined

95. A _____ is a landform that extends above the surrounding terrain in a limited area. A _____ is generally steeper than a hill, but there is no universally accepted standard definition for the height of a _____ or a hill although a _____ usually has an identifiable summit.
   a. Place
   b. Mountain0
   c. Undefined
   d. Undefined

96. _____ geological formations have their origins in turbidity current deposits, deposits from a form of underwater avalanche that are responsible for distributing vast amounts of clastic sediment into the deep ocean.

a. Turbidite0 b. Thing
c. Undefined d. Undefined

97. Faults are planar rock fractures, which show evidence of relative movement. Large faults within the Earth's crust are the result of shear motion and active _____ zones are the causal locations of most earthquakes. Earthquakes are caused by energy release during rapid slippage along faults. The largest examples are at tectonic plate boundaries but many faults occur far from active plate boundaries. Since faults do not usually consist of a single, clean fracture, the term _____ zone is used when referring to the zone of complex deformation that is associated with the _____ plane.
  a. Fault0 b. Thing
  c. Undefined d. Undefined

98. A _____ is a geological fault that is a special case of strike-slip faulting which terminates abruptly, at both ends, at a major transverse geological feature. Also known as a conservative plate boundary.
  a. Thing b. Transform fault0
  c. Undefined d. Undefined

99. In plate tectonics, a _____ a linear feature that exists between two tectonic plates that are moving away from each other. These areas can form in the middle of continents but eventually form ocean basins.
  a. Thing b. Divergent plate boundary0
  c. Undefined d. Undefined

100. In geology, a _____ is a place where the Earth's crust and lithosphere are being pulled apart.
  a. Thing b. Rift0
  c. Undefined d. Undefined

101. A _____ in geology is a valley created by the formation of a rift.
  a. Rift valley0 b. Thing
  c. Undefined d. Undefined

102. In geology, a _____ is a depression with predominant extent in one direction. The terms U-shaped and V-shaped are descriptive terms of geography to characterize the form of valleys. Most valleys belong to one of these two main types or a mixture of them, at least with respect of the cross section of the slopes or hillsides.
  a. Valley0 b. Thing
  c. Undefined d. Undefined

103. A _____ is a feature of some volcanoes in which a linear series of fissures in the volcanic edifice allows lava to be erupted from the volcano's flank instead of from its summit.
  a. Rift zone0 b. Thing
  c. Undefined d. Undefined

Chapter 7. Metamorphism, Metamorphic Rocks, and Hydrothermal Rocks   61

1. The _____ is a fundamental concept in geology that describes the dynamic transitions through geologic time among the three main rock types: sedimentary, metamorphic, and igneous.
- a. Rock cycle0
- b. Thing
- c. Undefined
- d. Undefined

2. _____ is molten rock located beneath the surface of the Earth, and which often collects in a _____ chamber. _____ is a complex high-temperature fluid substance. Most are silicate solutions. It is capable of intrusion into adjacent rocks or of extrusion onto the surface as lava or ejected explosively as tephra to form pyroclastic rock. Environments of _____ formation include subduction zones, continental rift zones, mid-oceanic ridges, and hotspots, some of which are interpreted as mantle plumes.
- a. Thing
- b. Magma0
- c. Undefined
- d. Undefined

3. _____ can be defined as the solid state recrystallisation of pre-existing rocks due to changes in heat and/or pressure and/or introduction of fluids. There will be mineralogical, chemical and crystallographic changes. _____ produced with increasing pressure and temperature conditions is known as prograde _____. Conversely, decreasing temperatures and pressure characterize retrograde _____.
- a. Metamorphism0
- b. Thing
- c. Undefined
- d. Undefined

4. A _____ is a naturally occurring substance formed through geological processes that has a characteristic chemical composition, a highly ordered atomic structure and specific physical properties. A rock, by comparison, is an aggregate of minerals and need not have a specific chemical composition. Minerals range in composition from pure elements and simple salts to very complex silicates with thousands of known forms.
- a. Thing
- b. Mineral0
- c. Undefined
- d. Undefined

5. _____ is the result of the transformation of a pre-existing rock type, the protolith, in a process called metamorphism, which means "change in form". The protolith is subjected to heat and extreme pressure causing profound physical and/or chemical change. The protolith may be sedimentary rock, igneous rock or another older rock.
- a. Metamorphic rock0
- b. Thing
- c. Undefined
- d. Undefined

6. In geology, a _____ is the outermost layer of a planet, part of its lithosphere. They are generally composed of a less dense material than its deeper layers.Earths' is composed mainly of basalt and granite. It is cooler and more rigid than the deeper layers of the mantle and core.
- a. Thing
- b. Crust0
- c. Undefined
- d. Undefined

7. Metamorphic rock is the result of the transformation of a pre-existing rock type, the protolith, in a process called metamorphism. The protolith is subjected to heat and extreme pressure causing profound physical and/or chemical change. _____ make up a large part of the Earth's crust. They are formed deep beneath the Earth's surface by great stresses from rocks above and high pressures and temperatures.
- a. Thing
- b. Metamorphic rocks0
- c. Undefined
- d. Undefined

Chapter 7. Metamorphism, Metamorphic Rocks, and Hydrothermal Rocks

8. _____ is displacement of solids by the agents of ocean currents, wind, water, or ice by downward or down-slope movement in response to gravity or by living organisms.
   a. Erosion0
   b. Thing
   c. Undefined
   d. Undefined

9. A _____ is a landform that extends above the surrounding terrain in a limited area. A _____ is generally steeper than a hill, but there is no universally accepted standard definition for the height of a _____ or a hill although a _____ usually has an identifiable summit.
   a. Mountain0
   b. Place
   c. Undefined
   d. Undefined

10. _____ is the rise of land masses that were depressed by the huge weight of ice sheets during the last ice age, through a process known as isostatic depression. It affects northern Europe, especially Scotland and Scandinavia, Siberia, Canada, and the Great Lakes of Canada and the United States.
    a. Thing
    b. Post glacial rebound0
    c. Undefined
    d. Undefined

11. _____ is the rise of land masses that were depressed by the huge weight of ice sheets during the last ice age, through a process known as isostatic depression.
    a. Thing
    b. Post-glacial rebound0
    c. Undefined
    d. Undefined

12. The _____ is the layer of granitic, sedimentary, and metamorphic rocks which form the continents and the areas of shallow seabed close to their shores, known as continental shelves. It is less dense than the material of the Earth's mantle and thus "floats" on top of it. _____ is also less dense than oceanic crust, though it is considerably thicker. About 40% of the Earth's surface is now underlain by _____.
    a. Continental crust0
    b. Thing
    c. Undefined
    d. Undefined

13. The _____ is an informal name for the eons of the geologic timescale that came before the current Phanerozoic eon. It spans from the formation of Earth around 4500 Ma to the evolution of abundant macroscopic hard-shelled animals, which marked the beginning of the Cambrian, the first period of the first era of the Phanerozoic eon, some 542 Ma.
    a. Precambrian0
    b. Thing
    c. Undefined
    d. Undefined

14. _____ rocks form when molten rock, magma, cools and solidifies, with or without crystallization, either below the surface as intrusive, plutonic rocks or on the surface as extrusive, volcanic, rocks.
    a. Thing
    b. Igneous0
    c. Undefined
    d. Undefined

15. _____ forms when rock cools and solidifies either below the surface as intrusive rocks or on the surface as extrusive rocks. This magma can be derived from partial melts of pre-existing rocks in either the Earth's mantle or crust. Typically, the melting is caused by one or more of the following processes -- an increase in temperature, a decrease in pressure, or a change in composition.

Chapter 7. Metamorphism, Metamorphic Rocks, and Hydrothermal Rocks

a. Thing
b. Igneous rock0
c. Undefined
d. Undefined

16. _____ rock is one of the three main rock groups. Rock formed from these covers 75% of the Earth's land area, and includes common types such as chalk, limestone, dolomite, sandstone, and shale.
a. Sedimentary0
b. Thing
c. Undefined
d. Undefined

17. _____ is one of the three main rock groups. _____ covers 75% of the Earth's land area. Four basic processes are involved in the formation of a clastic _____: weathering caused mainly by friction of waves, transportation where the sediment is carried along by a current, deposition and compaction where the sediment is squashed together to form a rock of this kind.
a. Thing
b. Sedimentary rock0
c. Undefined
d. Undefined

18. _____ is a sedimentary rock composed largely of the mineral calcite. _____ often contains variable amounts of silica in the form of chert or flint, as well as varying amounts of clay, silt and sand as disseminations, nodules, or layers within the rock. The primary source of the calcite in _____ is most commonly marine organisms. These organisms secrete shells that settle out of the water column and are deposited on ocean floors as pelagic ooze or alternatively is conglomerated in a coral reef.
a. Thing
b. Limestone0
c. Undefined
d. Undefined

19. _____ is a metamorphic rock resulting from the metamorphism of limestone, composed mostly of calcite. It is extensively used for sculpture, as a building material, and in many other applications. The word '_____' is colloquially used to refer to many other stones that are capable of taking a high polish.
a. Thing
b. Marble0
c. Undefined
d. Undefined

20. _____ is the condition of a system in which competing influences are balanced.
a. Thing
b. Equilibrium0
c. Undefined
d. Undefined

21. _____ is a term used to describe a group of hydrous aluminium phyllosilicate minerals, that are typically less than 2 micrometres in diameter. _____ consists of a variety of phyllosilicate minerals rich in silicon and aluminium oxides and hydroxides which include variable amounts of structural water. Clays are generally formed by the chemical weathering of silicate-bearing rocks by carbonic acid but some are formed by hydrothermal activity.
a. Thing
b. Clay0
c. Undefined
d. Undefined

22. _____ are hydrous aluminium phyllosilicates, sometimes with variable amounts of iron, magnesium, alkali metals, alkaline earths and other cations. Clays have structures similar to the micas and therefore form flat hexagonal sheets. _____ are common weathering products and low temperature hydrothermal alteration products.
a. Clay minerals0
b. Thing
c. Undefined
d. Undefined

Chapter 7. Metamorphism, Metamorphic Rocks, and Hydrothermal Rocks

23. _____ is a fine-grained sedimentary rock whose original constituents were clays or muds. It is characterized by thin laminae breaking with an irregular curving fracture, often splintery and usually parallel to the often-indistinguishable bedding plane.
   a. Shale0
   b. Thing
   c. Undefined
   d. Undefined

24. _____ is a sedimentary rock composed mainly of sand-size mineral or rock grains. Most _____ is composed of quartz and/or feldspar because these are the most common minerals in the Earth's crust. Like sand, _____ may be any color, but the most common colors are tan, brown, yellow, red, gray and white.
   a. Thing
   b. Sandstone0
   c. Undefined
   d. Undefined

25. _____ is the second most common mineral in the Earth's continental crust. It is made up of a lattice of silica tetrahedra. _____ belongs to the rhombohedral crystal system. In nature _____ crystals are often twinned, distorted, or so intergrown with adjacent crystals of _____ or other minerals as to only show part of this shape, or to lack obvious crystal faces altogether and appear massive.
   a. Thing
   b. Quartz0
   c. Undefined
   d. Undefined

26. _____ is a common and widely occurring type of intrusive, felsic, igneous rock. Granites are usually medium to coarsely crystalline, occasionally with some individual crystals larger than the groundmass forming a rock known as porphyry. Granites can be pink to dark gray or even black, depending on their chemistry and mineralogy.
   a. Thing
   b. Granite0
   c. Undefined
   d. Undefined

27. _____ is the process of formation of solid crystals from a uniform solution. It is also a chemical solid-liquid separation technique, in which mass transfer of a solute from the liquid solution to a pure solid crystalline phase occurs.
   a. Crystallization0
   b. Thing
   c. Undefined
   d. Undefined

28. _____ is a field of study within geology concerned generally with the structures within the crust of the Earth, or other planets, and particularly with the forces and movements that have operated in a region to create these structures.
   a. Thing
   b. Tectonics0
   c. Undefined
   d. Undefined

29. _____ is the chemical alteration of a rock by hydrothermal and other fluids. _____ can occur via the action of hydrothermal fluids from an igneous or metamorphic source. In the metamorphic environment, _____ is created by mass transfer from a volume of metamorphic rock at higher stress and temperature into a zone with lower stress and temperature, with metamorphic hydrothermal solutions acting as a solvent.
   a. Metasomatism0
   b. Thing
   c. Undefined
   d. Undefined

30. _____ is a common gray to black extrusive volcanic rock. It is usually fine-grained due to rapid cooling of lava on the Earth's surface. It may be porphyritic containing larger crystals in a fine matrix, or vesicular, or frothy scoria.

a. Thing
b. Basalt0
c. Undefined
d. Undefined

31. _____ is the oxide of silicon, chemical formula SiO_2, and is known for its hardness as early as the 16th century. It is a principle component in most types of glass and substances such as concrete.
 a. Silica0
 b. Thing
 c. Undefined
 d. Undefined

32. In geology, _____ refers to heat sources within the planet. The planet's internal heat was originally generated during its accretion, due to gravitational binding energy, and since then additional heat has continued to be generated by the radioactive decay of elements such as uranium, thorium, and potassium.
 a. Geothermal0
 b. Thing
 c. Undefined
 d. Undefined

33. _____ is the use of geothermal heat to generate electricity.
 a. Thing
 b. Geothermal power0
 c. Undefined
 d. Undefined

34. The _____ is the rate of increase in temperature per unit depth in the Earth. It varies with location and is typically measured by determining the bottom open-hole temperature after the drilling of a borehole.
 a. Geothermal gradient0
 b. Thing
 c. Undefined
 d. Undefined

35. _____, in everyday life, is most familiar as the agency that endows objects with weight. _____ is responsible for keeping the Earth and the other planets in their orbits around the Sun; for the formation of tides; and for various other phenomena that we observe. _____ is also the reason for the very existence of the Earth, the Sun, and most macroscopic objects in the universe; without it, matter would not have coalesced into these large masses, and life, as we know it, would not exist.
 a. Thing
 b. Gravitation0
 c. Undefined
 d. Undefined

36. A _____ is a solid in which the constituent atoms, molecules, or ions are packed in a regularly ordered, repeating pattern extending in all three spatial dimensions. Most metals encountered in everyday life are polycrystals. Crystals are often symmetrically intergrown to form _____ twins.
 a. Crystal0
 b. Thing
 c. Undefined
 d. Undefined

37. A _____ is a unique arrangement of atoms in a crystal. It is composed of a unit cell, a set of atoms arranged in a particular way, which is periodically repeated in three dimensions on a lattice. The spacing between unit cells in various directions is called its lattice parameters. The symmetry properties of the crystal are embodied in its space group.
 a. Crystal structure0
 b. Thing
 c. Undefined
 d. Undefined

38. _____ is the process of heating a solid substance to a point where it turns into a liquid. An object that has melted is molten.

Chapter 7. Metamorphism, Metamorphic Rocks, and Hydrothermal Rocks

a. Thing
b. Melting0
c. Undefined
d. Undefined

39. In geology and astronomy, the term _____ is used to denote types of rock that consist predominantly of _____ minerals. Such rocks include a wide range of igneous, metamorphic and sedimentary types. Most of the Earth's mantle and crust are made up of _____ rocks. The same is true of the Moon and the other rocky planets.
a. Silicate0
b. Thing
c. Undefined
d. Undefined

40. _____ is an igneous, volcanic rock, of felsic composition. It may have any texture from aphanitic to porphyritic. The mineral assemblage is usually quartz, alkali feldspar and plagioclase. Biotite and pyroxene are common accessory minerals.
a. Thing
b. Rhyolite0
c. Undefined
d. Undefined

41. Overburden, or _____ pressure, is a term used in geology to denote the pressure imposed on a stratigraphic layer by the weight of overlying layers of material.
a. Thing
b. Lithostatic0
c. Undefined
d. Undefined

42. _____ is a term used in geology to denote the pressure imposed on a stratigraphic layer by the weight of overlying layers of material.
a. Lithostatic pressure0
b. Event
c. Undefined
d. Undefined

43. _____ is the stress applied to materials resulting in their compaction, decrease of volume.
a. Thing
b. Compression stress0
c. Undefined
d. Undefined

44. A _____ is a rock consisting of individual stones that have become cemented together. Conglomerates are sedimentary rocks consisting of rounded fragements and are thus differentiated from breccias, which consist of angular clasts. Both conglomerates and breccias are characterized by clasts larger than sand.
a. Conglomerate0
b. Thing
c. Undefined
d. Undefined

45. _____ is a complex inosilicate series of minerals. _____ is not a recognized mineral, in its own right but the name is used as a general or field term, to refer to a dark amphibole. It is an isomorphous mixture of three molecules; a calcium-iron-magnesium silicate, an aluminium-iron-magnesium silicate and an iron-magnesium silicate.
a. Thing
b. Hornblende0
c. Undefined
d. Undefined

46. _____, in mineralogy, is the tendency of crystalline materials to split along definite planes, creating smooth surfaces.
a. Cleavage0
b. Thing
c. Undefined
d. Undefined

Chapter 7. Metamorphism, Metamorphic Rocks, and Hydrothermal Rocks 67

47. _____ is the gas phase component of a another state of matter which does not completely fill its container. It is distinguished from the pure gas phase by the presence of the same substance in another state of matter. Hence when a liquid has completely evaporated, it is said that the system has been completely transformed to the gas phase.
- a. Thing
- b. Vapor0
- c. Undefined
- d. Undefined

48. A _____ in geology is an intrusive igneous rock body that crystallized from a magma below the surface of the Earth. Plutons include batholiths, dikes, sills, laccoliths, lopoliths, and other igneous bodies. In practice, "_____" usually refers to a distinctive mass of igneous rock, typically kilometers in dimension, without a tabular shape like those of dikes and sills.
- a. Thing
- b. Pluton0
- c. Undefined
- d. Undefined

49. A _____ is a process that results in the interconversion of chemical substances. The substance or substances initially involved in a _____ are called reactants. Chemical reactions are characterized by a chemical change, and they yield one or more products which are, in general, different from the reactants.
- a. Chemical reaction0
- b. Thing
- c. Undefined
- d. Undefined

50. An _____ is a type of atom that is defined by its atomic number; that is, by the number of protons in its nucleus.
- a. Element0
- b. Thing
- c. Undefined
- d. Undefined

51. _____ has penetrative planar fabric present within it. It is common to rocks affected by regional metamorphic compression typical of orogenic belts.
- a. Foliated metamorphic rock0
- b. Thing
- c. Undefined
- d. Undefined

52. _____ is a hard, metamorphic rock which was originally sandstone. Sandstone is converted into _____ through heating and pressure usually related to tectonic compression within orogenic belts.
- a. Thing
- b. Quartzite0
- c. Undefined
- d. Undefined

53. The _____ refers to a group of medium-grade metamorphic rocks, chiefly notable for the preponderance of lamellar minerals such as micas, chlorite, talc, hornblende, graphite, and others. Quartz often occurs in drawn-out grains to such an extent that a particular form called quartz _____ is produced.
- a. Thing
- b. Schist0
- c. Undefined
- d. Undefined

54. A _____ column is a column of rizing air in the lower altitudes of the Earth's atmosphere. Thermals are created by the uneven heating of the Earth's surface from solar radiation, and are an example of convection. The Sun warms the ground, which in turn warms the air directly above it.
- a. Thing
- b. Thermal0
- c. Undefined
- d. Undefined

Chapter 7. Metamorphism, Metamorphic Rocks, and Hydrothermal Rocks

55. _____ is the group designation for a series of contact metamorphic rocks that have been baked and indurated by the heat of intrusive igneous masses and have been rendered massive, hard, splintery, and in some cases exceedingly tough and durable. Most _____ are fine-grained.
   a. Thing
   b. Hornfels0
   c. Undefined
   d. Undefined

56. _____ is the process of breaking down rocks, soils and their minerals through direct contact with the atmosphere. _____ occurs without movement. Two main classifications of _____ processes exist. Mechanical or physical _____ involves the breakdown of rocks and soils through direct contact with atmospheric conditions. The second classification, chemical _____, involves the direct effect of atmospheric chemicals in the breakdown of rocks, soils and minerals.
   a. Thing
   b. Weathering0
   c. Undefined
   d. Undefined

57. _____ involves the change in the composition of rock, often leading to a 'break down' in its form.
   a. Chemical weathering0
   b. Thing
   c. Undefined
   d. Undefined

58. _____ is the characteristic of a solid material expressing its resistance to permanent deformation.
   a. Thing
   b. Hardness0
   c. Undefined
   d. Undefined

59. _____ is an essentially physical process that has meanings in chemistry, metallurgy and geology. In geology, solid-state _____ is a metamorphic process that occurs under situations of intense temperature and pressure where grains, atoms or molecules of a rock or mineral are packed closer together, creating a new crystal structure.
   a. Thing
   b. Recrystallization0
   c. Undefined
   d. Undefined

60. _____ is a general field petrologic term applied to metamorphic and/or altered mafic volcanic rock. The green is due to abundant green chlorite, actinolite and epidote minerals that dominate the rock.
   a. Greenschist0
   b. Thing
   c. Undefined
   d. Undefined

61. _____ is the name given to a rock consisting mainly of hornblende amphibole, the use of the term being restricted, however, to metamorphic rocks. The modern terminology for a holocrystalline plutonic igneous rocks rock composed primarily of hornblende amphibole is a hornblendite, which are usually crystal cumulates.
   a. Thing
   b. Amphibolite0
   c. Undefined
   d. Undefined

62. _____ is a very important series of tectosilicate minerals within the feldspar family. Rather than referring to a particular mineral with a specific chemical composition, it is a solid solution series.
   a. Thing
   b. Plagioclase0
   c. Undefined
   d. Undefined

Chapter 7. Metamorphism, Metamorphic Rocks, and Hydrothermal Rocks

63. _____ is the name of a group of rock-forming minerals which make up as much as sixty percent of the Earth's crust. Feldspars crystallize from magma in both intrusive and extrusive rocks, and they can also occur as compact minerals, as veins, and are also present in many types of metamorphic rock.
   a. Thing
   b. Feldspar0
   c. Undefined
   d. Undefined

64. _____ is a fine-grained, homogeneous, metamorphic rock derived from an original shale-type sedimentary rock composed of clay or volcanic ash through low grade regional metamorphism. The result is a foliated rock in which the foliation may not correspond to the original sedimentary layering.
   a. Slate0
   b. Thing
   c. Undefined
   d. Undefined

65. _____ is a type of foliated metamorphic rock primarily composed of quartz, sericite mica, and chlorite; the rock represents a gradation in the degree of metamorphism between slate and mica schist. Minute crystals of graphite, sericite, or chlorite impart a silky, sometimes golden sheen to the surfaces of cleavage.
   a. Phyllite0
   b. Thing
   c. Undefined
   d. Undefined

66. _____ is a common and widely distributed type of rock formed by high-grade regional metamorphic processes from preexisting formations that were originally either igneous or sedimentary rocks. Gneissic rocks are usually medium to coarse foliated and largely recrystallized but do not carry large quantities of micas, chlorite or other platy minerals.
   a. Gneiss0
   b. Thing
   c. Undefined
   d. Undefined

67. _____ is a grey to dark grey intermediate intrusive igneous rock composed principally of plagioclase feldspar, biotite, hornblende, and/or pyroxene. It may contain small amounts of quartz, microcline and olivine.
   a. Diorite0
   b. Thing
   c. Undefined
   d. Undefined

68. _____ is a rock at the frontier between igneous and metamorphic rocks. They can also be known as diatexite.
   a. Migmatite0
   b. Thing
   c. Undefined
   d. Undefined

69. _____ in meteorology are large scale patterns in the atmospheric pressure field that are nearly stationary, effectively "blocking" or redirecting migratory cyclones. These _____ can remain in place for several days or even weeks, causing the areas affected by them to have the same kind of weather for an extended period of time.
   a. Blocks0
   b. Thing
   c. Undefined
   d. Undefined

70. Earth's _____ is a ~2,900 km thick rocky shell comprizing approximately 70% of Earth's volume. It is predominantly solid and overlies the Earth's iron-rich core, which occupies about 30% of Earth's volume. Past episodes of melting and volcanism at the shallower levels of the _____ have produced a very thin crust of crystallized melt products near the surface, upon which we live.
   a. Mantle0
   b. Thing
   c. Undefined
   d. Undefined

Chapter 7. Metamorphism, Metamorphic Rocks, and Hydrothermal Rocks

71. _____ is a theory of geology that has been developed to explain the observed evidence for large scale motions of the Earth's lithosphere. The theory encompassed and superseded the older theory of continental drift.
   a. Plate tectonics0
   b. Thing
   c. Undefined
   d. Undefined

72. In plate tectonics, a _____ is an actively deforming region where two tectonic plates or fragments of lithosphere move towards one another. When two plates move toward one another, they form either a subduction zone or a continental collision.
   a. Thing
   b. Convergent boundary0
   c. Undefined
   d. Undefined

73. The _____ is the solid outermost shell of a rocky planet. On the Earth, the _____ includes the crust and the uppermost mantle which is joined to the crust across the Mohorovièiæ discontinuity. _____ is underlain by asthenosphere, the weaker, hotter, and deeper part of the upper mantle.
   a. Thing
   b. Lithosphere0
   c. Undefined
   d. Undefined

74. In geology, a _____ zone is an area on Earth where two tectonic plates meet and move towards one another, with one sliding underneath the other and moving down into the mantle, at rates typically measured in centimeters per year. An oceanic plate ordinarily slides underneath a continental plate; this often creates an orogenic zone with many volcanoes and earthquakes.
   a. Subduction0
   b. Thing
   c. Undefined
   d. Undefined

75. A _____ is an area on Earth where two tectonic plates meet and move towards one another, with one sliding underneath the other and moving down into the mantle, at rates typically measured in centimeters per year. In a sense, subduction zones are the opposite of divergent boundaries, areas where material rises up from the mantle and plates are moving apart.
   a. Thing
   b. Subduction zone0
   c. Undefined
   d. Undefined

76. _____ is the part of Earth's lithosphere that surfaces in the ocean basins. _____ is primarily composed of mafic rocks, or sima. It is thinner than continental crust, or sial, generally less than 10 kilometers thick, however it is more dense, having a mean density of about 3.3 grams per cubic centimeter.
   a. Thing
   b. Oceanic crust0
   c. Undefined
   d. Undefined

77. The _____ is the region of the Earth between 100-200 km below the surface that is the weak or "soft" zone in the upper mantle. It lies just below the lithosphere, which is involved in plate movements and isostatic adjustments. In spite of its heat, pressures keep it plastic, and it has a relatively low density. Seismic waves pass relatively slowly through the _____.
   a. Asthenosphere0
   b. Thing
   c. Undefined
   d. Undefined

78. A _____ should ideally be a distinctive rock that forms under certain conditions of sedimentation, reflecting a particular process or environment.

Chapter 7. Metamorphism, Metamorphic Rocks, and Hydrothermal Rocks

a. Facies0
b. Thing
c. Undefined
d. Undefined

79. _____ is any product of the condensation of atmospheric water vapor that is deposited on the earth's surface. It occurs when the atmosphere becomes saturated with water vapour and the water condenses and falls out of solution. Air becomes saturated via two processes, cooling and adding moisture.
   a. Thing
   b. Precipitation0
   c. Undefined
   d. Undefined

80. _____ is a rock that forms by the metamorphism of basalt and rocks with similar composition at high pressures and low temperatures, approximately corresponding to a depth of 15 to 30 kilometers and 200 to ~500 degrees Celsius. The blue color of the rock comes from the presence of the mineral glaucophane.
   a. Thing
   b. Blueschist0
   c. Undefined
   d. Undefined

81. _____ is a dark, coarse-grained, intrusive igneous rock chemically equivalent to basalt. It is a plutonic rock, formed when molten magma is trapped beneath the Earth's surface and cools into a crystalline mass.
   a. Thing
   b. Gabbro0
   c. Undefined
   d. Undefined

82. In plate tectonics, a _____ a linear feature that exists between two tectonic plates that are moving away from each other. These areas can form in the middle of continents but eventually form ocean basins.
   a. Divergent plate boundary0
   b. Thing
   c. Undefined
   d. Undefined

83. The mineral _____ is a magnesium iron silicate. It is one of the most common minerals on Earth, and has also been identified on the Moon, Mars, and comet Wild 2.
   a. Olivine0
   b. Thing
   c. Undefined
   d. Undefined

84. A _____ is a spring that is produced by the emergence of geothermally-heated groundwater from the earth's crust. They are all over the earth, on every continent and even under the oceans and seas.
   a. Hot spring0
   b. Thing
   c. Undefined
   d. Undefined

85. An _____ is a volume of rock containing components or minerals in a mode of occurrence that renders it valuable for mining.
   a. Thing
   b. Ore0
   c. Undefined
   d. Undefined

86. In geology, a _____ is a place where the Earth's crust and lithosphere are being pulled apart.
   a. Thing
   b. Rift0
   c. Undefined
   d. Undefined

87. The term _____ refers to several types of chemical compounds containing sulfur in its lowest oxidation number of −2.

Chapter 7. Metamorphism, Metamorphic Rocks, and Hydrothermal Rocks

a. Sulfide0
b. Thing
c. Undefined
d. Undefined

88. An _____ is an atom or group of atoms which have lost or gained one or more electrons, making them negatively or positively charged.
  a. Ion0
  b. Thing
  c. Undefined
  d. Undefined

89. _____ is a ferrimagnetic mineral one of several iron oxides and a member of the spinel group. The chemical IUPAC name is iron oxide and the common chemical name ferrous-ferric oxide.
  a. Magnetite0
  b. Thing
  c. Undefined
  d. Undefined

90. An _____ is a chemical compound containing an oxygen atom and other elements. Most of the earth's crust consists of them. They result when elements are oxidized by air.
  a. Thing
  b. Oxide0
  c. Undefined
  d. Undefined

91. _____ is any particulate matter that can be transported by fluid flow and which eventually is deposited as a layer of solid particles on the bed or bottom of a body of water or other liquid.
  a. Sediment0
  b. Thing
  c. Undefined
  d. Undefined

Chapter 8. Time and Geology

1. The _____ is used by geologists and other scientists to describe the timing and relationships between events that have occurred during the history of Earth.
   a. Thing
   b. Geological time scale0
   c. Undefined
   d. Undefined

2. Mean _____ is the average height of the sea, with reference to a suitable reference surface.
   a. Sea level0
   b. Thing
   c. Undefined
   d. Undefined

3. _____ is any particulate matter that can be transported by fluid flow and which eventually is deposited as a layer of solid particles on the bed or bottom of a body of water or other liquid.
   a. Thing
   b. Sediment0
   c. Undefined
   d. Undefined

4. _____ is the science and study of the solid matter that constitute the Earth. Encompassing such things as rocks, soil, and gemstones, _____ studies the composition, structure, physical properties, history, and the processes that shape Earth's components.
   a. Thing
   b. Geology0
   c. Undefined
   d. Undefined

5. _____ is displacement of solids by the agents of ocean currents, wind, water, or ice by downward or down-slope movement in response to gravity or by living organisms.
   a. Erosion0
   b. Thing
   c. Undefined
   d. Undefined

6. _____ rock is one of the three main rock groups. Rock formed from these covers 75% of the Earth's land area, and includes common types such as chalk, limestone, dolomite, sandstone, and shale.
   a. Thing
   b. Sedimentary0
   c. Undefined
   d. Undefined

7. _____ is one of the three main rock groups. _____ covers 75% of the Earth's land area. Four basic processes are involved in the formation of a clastic _____: weathering caused mainly by friction of waves, transportation where the sediment is carried along by a current, deposition and compaction where the sediment is squashed together to form a rock of this kind.
   a. Sedimentary rock0
   b. Thing
   c. Undefined
   d. Undefined

8. _____ refers to the principle that the same processes that shape the universe occurred in the past as they do now, and that the same laws of physics apply in all parts of the knowable universe.
   a. Thing
   b. Uniformitarianism0
   c. Undefined
   d. Undefined

9. _____ is the process in which an unstable atomic nucleus loses energy by emitting radiation in the form of particles or electromagnetic waves.
   a. Radioactive decay0
   b. Thing
   c. Undefined
   d. Undefined

10. _____ is the result of the transformation of a pre-existing rock type, the protolith, in a process called metamorphism, which means "change in form". The protolith is subjected to heat and extreme pressure causing profound physical and/or chemical change. The protolith may be sedimentary rock, igneous rock or another older rock.
   a. Metamorphic rock0
   b. Thing
   c. Undefined
   d. Undefined

11. _____ can be defined as the solid state recrystallisation of pre-existing rocks due to changes in heat and/or pressure and/or introduction of fluids. There will be mineralogical, chemical and crystallographic changes. _____ produced with increasing pressure and temperature conditions is known as prograde _____. Conversely, decreasing temperatures and pressure characterize retrograde _____.
   a. Thing
   b. Metamorphism0
   c. Undefined
   d. Undefined

12. _____ in meteorology are large scale patterns in the atmospheric pressure field that are nearly stationary, effectively "blocking" or redirecting migratory cyclones. These _____ can remain in place for several days or even weeks, causing the areas affected by them to have the same kind of weather for an extended period of time.
   a. Blocks0
   b. Thing
   c. Undefined
   d. Undefined

13. _____ is a common and widely occurring type of intrusive, felsic, igneous rock. Granites are usually medium to coarsely crystalline, occasionally with some individual crystals larger than the groundmass forming a rock known as porphyry. Granites can be pink to dark gray or even black, depending on their chemistry and mineralogy.
   a. Granite0
   b. Thing
   c. Undefined
   d. Undefined

14. A _____ is an intrusion into a cross-cutting fissure, meaning a _____ cuts across other pre-existing layers or bodies of rock, this means that a _____ is always younger than the rocks that contain it. The thickness is usually much smaller than the other two dimensions. Thickness can vary from sub-centimeter scale to many meters in thickness and the lateral dimensions can extend over many kilometers.
   a. Thing
   b. Dike0
   c. Undefined
   d. Undefined

15. The principle or _____ states that sediments are deposited under the influence of gravity as nearly horizontal beds. Observations in a wide variety of sedimentary environments support this principle. If we find folded or faulted strata, we know that the layers were deformed by tectonic forces after the sediments were deposited. This principle can be combined with the principle of superposition.
   a. Original horizontality0
   b. Thing
   c. Undefined
   d. Undefined

16. The basic idea of this is that an object, event or entity can be spanned across multiple realities or universes. When combined, these multiple, unique, pan-dimensional segments of the object, consciousness or event, make up parts or constituents of its _____.
   a. Superposition0
   b. Thing
   c. Undefined
   d. Undefined

Chapter 8. Time and Geology

17. _____ is a sedimentary rock composed largely of the mineral calcite. _____ often contains variable amounts of silica in the form of chert or flint, as well as varying amounts of clay, silt and sand as disseminations, nodules, or layers within the rock. The primary source of the calcite in _____ is most commonly marine organisms. These organisms secrete shells that settle out of the water column and are deposited on ocean floors as pelagic ooze or alternatively is conglomerated in a coral reef.
   - a. Limestone0
   - b. Thing
   - c. Undefined
   - d. Undefined

18. _____ is the native consolidated rock underlying the Earth's surface. Above the _____ is usually an area of broken and weathered unconsolidated rock in the basal subsoil.
   - a. Bedrock0
   - b. Thing
   - c. Undefined
   - d. Undefined

19. _____ is the geological process whereby material is added to a landform. This is the process by which wind and water create a sediment deposit, through the laying down of granular material that has been eroded and transported from another geographical location.
   - a. Thing
   - b. Deposition0
   - c. Undefined
   - d. Undefined

20. The _____ is an axiom that forms one of the bases of the sciences of geology, archaeology, and other fields dealing with stratigraphy. In its plainest form, that is: layers are arranged in a time sequence, with the oldest on the bottom and the youngest on the top, unless later processes disturb this arrangement.
   - a. Law of Superposition0
   - b. Thing
   - c. Undefined
   - d. Undefined

21. _____ is molten rock expelled by a volcano during an eruption. When first extruded from a volcanic vent, it is a liquid at temperatures from 700 °C to 1,200 °C.
   - a. Thing
   - b. Lava0
   - c. Undefined
   - d. Undefined

22. In geology, a _____ is a depression with predominant extent in one direction. The terms U-shaped and V-shaped are descriptive terms of geography to characterize the form of valleys. Most valleys belong to one of these two main types or a mixture of them, at least with respect of the cross section of the slopes or hillsides.
   - a. Thing
   - b. Valley0
   - c. Undefined
   - d. Undefined

23. An _____ is a body of igneous rock that has crystallized from a molten magma below the surface of the Earth.
   - a. Intrusion0
   - b. Thing
   - c. Undefined
   - d. Undefined

24. A _____ is a body of water with a current, confined within a bed and banks. Streams are important as conduits in the water cycle, instruments in aquifer recharge, and corridors for fish and wildlife migration.
   - a. Thing
   - b. Stream0
   - c. Undefined
   - d. Undefined

Chapter 8. Time and Geology

25. _____ is a field of study within geology concerned generally with the structures within the crust of the Earth, or other planets, and particularly with the forces and movements that have operated in a region to create these structures.
    a. Tectonics0
    b. Thing
    c. Undefined
    d. Undefined

26. An _____ is a buried erosion surface separating two rock masses or strata of different ages, indicating that sediment deposition was not continuous. In general, the older layer was exposed to erosion for an interval of time before deposition of the younger, but the term is used to describe any break in the sedimentary geologic record.
    a. Unconformity0
    b. Thing
    c. Undefined
    d. Undefined

27. A _____ is an unconformity between parallel layers of sedimentary rocks which represents a period of erosion or non-deposition.
    a. Disconformity0
    b. Thing
    c. Undefined
    d. Undefined

28. Fossils are the mineralized or otherwise preserved remains or traces of animals, plants, and other organisms. The totality of fossils, both discovered and undiscovered, and their placement in fossiliferous rock formations and sedimentary layers is known as the _____ record.
    a. Thing
    b. Fossil0
    c. Undefined
    d. Undefined

29. _____ is an unconformity where horizontally parallel strata of sedimentary rock are deposited on tilted and eroded layers that may be either vertical or at an angle to the overlying horizontal layers
    a. Angular unconformity0
    b. Thing
    c. Undefined
    d. Undefined

30. _____ is the process in which sediments compact under pressure, expel connate fluids, and gradually become solid rock.
    a. Lithification0
    b. Thing
    c. Undefined
    d. Undefined

31. In geology, engineering, and surveying, _____ is the motion of a surface as it shifts downward relative to a datum such as sea-level. The opposite of _____ is uplift, which results in an increase in elevation. In meteorology, _____ refers to the downward movement of air.
    a. Thing
    b. Subsidence0
    c. Undefined
    d. Undefined

32. _____ is an igneous rock of volcanic origin. They often have a vesicular texture, which is the result voids left by volatiles escaping from the molten lava. Pumice is a rock, which is an example of explosive volcanic eruption. It is so vesicular that it floats in water.
    a. Volcanic rock0
    b. Thing
    c. Undefined
    d. Undefined

Chapter 8. Time and Geology

33. In geology, a _____ is the outermost layer of a planet, part of its lithosphere. They are generally composed of a less dense material than its deeper layers. Earths' is composed mainly of basalt and granite. It is cooler and more rigid than the deeper layers of the mantle and core.
    a. Crust0
    b. Thing
    c. Undefined
    d. Undefined

34. _____ is the process of formation of solid crystals from a uniform solution. It is also a chemical solid-liquid separation technique, in which mass transfer of a solute from the liquid solution to a pure solid crystalline phase occurs.
    a. Thing
    b. Crystallization0
    c. Undefined
    d. Undefined

35. A _____ in geology is an intrusive igneous rock body that crystallized from a magma below the surface of the Earth. Plutons include batholiths, dikes, sills, laccoliths, lopoliths, and other igneous bodies. In practice, "_____" usually refers to a distinctive mass of igneous rock, typically kilometers in dimension, without a tabular shape like those of dikes and sills.
    a. Pluton0
    b. Thing
    c. Undefined
    d. Undefined

36. _____ is a sedimentary rock composed mainly of sand-size mineral or rock grains. Most _____ is composed of quartz and/or feldspar because these are the most common minerals in the Earth's crust. Like sand, _____ may be any color, but the most common colors are tan, brown, yellow, red, gray and white.
    a. Thing
    b. Sandstone0
    c. Undefined
    d. Undefined

37. _____ is a fine-grained sedimentary rock whose original constituents were clays or muds. It is characterized by thin laminae breaking with an irregular curving fracture, often splintery and usually parallel to the often-indistinguishable bedding plane.
    a. Thing
    b. Shale0
    c. Undefined
    d. Undefined

38. _____ is a common gray to black extrusive volcanic rock. It is usually fine-grained due to rapid cooling of lava on the Earth's surface. It may be porphyritic containing larger crystals in a fine matrix, or vesicular, or frothy scoria.
    a. Basalt0
    b. Thing
    c. Undefined
    d. Undefined

39. _____ refers to the movement of the Earth's continents relative to each other. _____ is a concept that said the shapes of continents on either side of the Atlantic Ocean seem to fit together and the similarity of southern continent fossil faunae could mean that all the continents had once been joined into a supercontinent. It was suggested that the continents had been pulled apart by the centrifugal pseudoforce of the Earth's rotation.
    a. Continental drift0
    b. Thing
    c. Undefined
    d. Undefined

40. A _____ is a large, slow moving river of ice, formed from compacted layers of snow, that slowly deforms and flows in response to gravity. _____ ice is the largest reservoir of fresh water on Earth, and second only to oceans as the largest reservoir of total water. Glaciers cover vast areas of polar regions but are restricted to the highest mountains in the tropics.

Chapter 8. Time and Geology

   a. Glacier0
   c. Undefined
   b. Thing
   d. Undefined

41. _____ is a fossil fuel formed in swamp ecosystems where plant remains were saved by water and mud from oxidization and biodegradation. It is a sedimentary rock, but the harder forms, such as anthracite _____, can be regarded as metamorphic rocks because of later exposure to elevated temperature and pressure. It is composed primarily of carbon along with assorted other elements, including sulfur.
   a. Coal0
   c. Undefined
   b. Thing
   d. Undefined

42. _____ is the use of the principles of geology to reconstruct and understand the history of the Earth. It focuses on geologic processes that change the Earth's surface and subsurface; and the use of stratigraphy, structural geology and paleontology to tell the sequence of these events. It also focuses on the evolution of plants and animals during different time periods in the geological timescale.
   a. Thing
   c. Undefined
   b. Historical geology0
   d. Undefined

43. The _____ is an informal name for the eons of the geologic timescale that came before the current Phanerozoic eon. It spans from the formation of Earth around 4500 Ma to the evolution of abundant macroscopic hard-shelled animals, which marked the beginning of the Cambrian, the first period of the first era of the Phanerozoic eon, some 542 Ma.
   a. Precambrian0
   c. Undefined
   b. Thing
   d. Undefined

44. The _____ is the earliest of three geologic eras of the Phanerozoic eon. The _____ is subdivided into six geologic periods; from oldest to youngest they are: the Cambrian, Ordovician, Silurian, Devonian, Carboniferous, and Permian.
   a. Paleozoic0
   c. Undefined
   b. Thing
   d. Undefined

45. An _____ is a long period of time with different technical and colloquial meanings, and usages in language. It begins with some beginning event known as an epoch, epochal date, epochal event or epochal moment.
   a. Era0
   c. Undefined
   b. Thing
   d. Undefined

46. The _____ is one of three geologic eras of the Phanerozoic eon. The _____ was a time of tectonic, climatic and evolutionary activity, shifting from a state of connectedness into their present configuration. The climate was exceptionally warm throughout the period, also playing an important role in the evolution and diversification of new animal species. By the end of the era, the basis of modern life was in place.
   a. Thing
   c. Undefined
   b. Mesozoic0
   d. Undefined

47. The _____ is part of the Neogene and Quaternary periods. Human civilization dates entirely within the _____. The _____ was preceded by the Younger Dryas cold period, the final part of the Pleistocene epoch. The _____ starts late in the retreat of the Pleistocene glaciers. It can be considered an interglacial in the current ice age.

Chapter 8. Time and Geology

    a. Thing
    b. Holocene0
    c. Undefined
    d. Undefined

48. _____ can refer to: a period of time; a distinctive historical period or era, a unit of the geologic time scale, less than a period and greater than an age, or a phase in the development of the universe with distinctive properties.
    a. Epoch0
    b. Thing
    c. Undefined
    d. Undefined

49. The _____ Era meaning "new life", is the most recent of the three classic geological eras. It covers the 65.5 million years since the Cretaceous-Tertiary extinction event at the end of the Cretaceous that marked the demise of the last non-avian dinosaurs and the end of the Mesozoic Era. The _____ era is ongoing.
    a. Cenozoic0
    b. Thing
    c. Undefined
    d. Undefined

50. The _____ is the most recent of the three classic geological eras. It covers the 65.5 million years since the Cretaceous-Tertiary extinction event at the end of the Cretaceous that marked the demise of the last non-avian dinosaurs and the end of the Mesozoic Era.
    a. Cenozoic era0
    b. Thing
    c. Undefined
    d. Undefined

51. The _____ on the geologic timescale had been intended to cover the world's recent period of repeated glaciations. The _____ follows the Pliocene and is followed by the Holocene. The _____ is the third epoch of the Neogene period or 6th epoch of the Cenozoic era. The end of the _____ corresponds with the end of the Paleolithic age used in archaeology. The _____ is divided into the Early _____, Middle _____ and Late _____, and numerous faunal stages.
    a. Thing
    b. Pleistocene0
    c. Undefined
    d. Undefined

52. The _____ is a geologic period of the Paleozoic era. During the _____ the first fish evolved legs and started to walk on land as tetrapods and the first insects and spiders also started to colonize terrestrial habitats. The first seed-bearing plants spread across dry land, forming huge forests. In the oceans, Primitive sharks became more numerous. The first ammonite mollusks appeared, and trilobites as well as great coral reefs were still common.
    a. Thing
    b. Devonian0
    c. Undefined
    d. Undefined

53. A _____ is a naturally occurring substance formed through geological processes that has a characteristic chemical composition, a highly ordered atomic structure and specific physical properties. A rock, by comparison, is an aggregate of minerals and need not have a specific chemical composition. Minerals range in composition from pure elements and simple salts to very complex silicates with thousands of known forms.
    a. Mineral0
    b. Thing
    c. Undefined
    d. Undefined

54. A _____ is a solid in which the constituent atoms, molecules, or ions are packed in a regularly ordered, repeating pattern extending in all three spatial dimensions. Most metals encountered in everyday life are polycrystals. Crystals are often symmetrically intergrown to form _____ twins.

Chapter 8. Time and Geology

a. Crystal0   b. Thing
c. Undefined   d. Undefined

55. _____ is molten rock located beneath the surface of the Earth, and which often collects in a _____ chamber. _____ is a complex high-temperature fluid substance. Most are silicate solutions. It is capable of intrusion into adjacent rocks or of extrusion onto the surface as lava or ejected explosively as tephra to form pyroclastic rock. Environments of _____ formation include subduction zones, continental rift zones, mid-oceanic ridges, and hotspots, some of which are interpreted as mantle plumes.
   a. Magma0   b. Thing
   c. Undefined   d. Undefined

56. An _____ is a type of atom that is defined by its atomic number; that is, by the number of protons in its nucleus.
   a. Thing   b. Element0
   c. Undefined   d. Undefined

57. _____ is a technique used to date materials based on a knowledge of the decay rates of naturally occurring isotopes, and the current abundances. It is the principal source of information about the age of the Earth and a significant source of information about rates of evolutionary change.
   a. Thing   b. Radiometric dating0
   c. Undefined   d. Undefined

58. In optics, _____ is the field that studies the measurement of electromagnetic radiation, including visible light. Note that light is also measured using the techniques of photometry, which deal with brightness as perceived by the human eye, rather than absolute power.
   a. Radiometry0   b. Thing
   c. Undefined   d. Undefined

59. _____ are any of the several different forms of an element each having different atomic mass. _____ of an element have nuclei with the same number of protons but different numbers of neutrons.
   a. Isotopes0   b. Thing
   c. Undefined   d. Undefined

60. In chemistry and physics, the _____ is the number of protons found in the nucleus of an atom. It is traditionally represented by the symbol Z.
   a. Thing   b. Atomic number0
   c. Undefined   d. Undefined

61. The _____ is the mass of an atom at rest, most often expressed in unified _____ units.[
   a. Atomic mass0   b. Thing
   c. Undefined   d. Undefined

62. In nuclear physics, a decay product, also known as a _____, daughter isotope or daughter nuclide, is a nuclide resulting from the radioactive decay of a parent isotope or precursor nuclide. The _____ may be stable or it may decay to form a _____ of its own. The daughter of a _____ is sometimes called a granddaughter product.

Chapter 8. Time and Geology

a. Thing
b. Daughter product0
c. Undefined
d. Undefined

63. The _____ is a fundamental subatomic particle that carries a negative electric charge.
a. Electron0
b. Thing
c. Undefined
d. Undefined

64. In physics, the _____ is a subatomic particle with no net electric charge.
a. Thing
b. Neutron0
c. Undefined
d. Undefined

65. In physics, the _____ is a subatomic particle with an electric charge of one positive fundamental unit a diameter of about 1.5×10^{-15} m, and a mass of 938.27231(28) MeV/c2 (1.6726×10^{-27} kg), 1.007 276 466 88(13) u or about 1836 times the mass of an electron.
a. Proton0
b. Thing
c. Undefined
d. Undefined

66. An _____ is a layer of gases that may surround a material body of sufficient mass. The gases are attracted by the gravity of the body, and are retained for a longer duration if gravity is high and the _____ 's temperature is low. Some planets consist mainly of various gases, and thus have very deep atmospheres.
a. Atmosphere0
b. Place
c. Undefined
d. Undefined

67. _____ rocks form when molten rock, magma, cools and solidifies, with or without crystallization, either below the surface as intrusive, plutonic rocks or on the surface as extrusive, volcanic, rocks.
a. Thing
b. Igneous0
c. Undefined
d. Undefined

68. _____ forms when rock cools and solidifies either below the surface as intrusive rocks or on the surface as extrusive rocks. This magma can be derived from partial melts of pre-existing rocks in either the Earth's mantle or crust. Typically, the melting is caused by one or more of the following processes -- an increase in temperature, a decrease in pressure, or a change in composition.
a. Igneous rock0
b. Thing
c. Undefined
d. Undefined

69. Metamorphic rock is the result of the transformation of a pre-existing rock type, the protolith, in a process called metamorphism. The protolith is subjected to heat and extreme pressure causing profound physical and/or chemical change. _____ make up a large part of the Earth's crust. They are formed deep beneath the Earth's surface by great stresses from rocks above and high pressures and temperatures.
a. Metamorphic rocks0
b. Thing
c. Undefined
d. Undefined

70. _____ is the process of breaking down rocks, soils and their minerals through direct contact with the atmosphere. _____ occurs without movement. Two main classifications of _____ processes exist. Mechanical or physical _____ involves the breakdown of rocks and soils through direct contact with atmospheric conditions. The second classification, chemical _____, involves the direct effect of atmospheric chemicals in the breakdown of rocks, soils and minerals.
- a. Weathering0
- b. Thing
- c. Undefined
- d. Undefined

71. _____ consists of very fine rock and mineral particles less than 2 mm in diameter that are ejected from a volcanic vent. The very fine particles may be carried for many miles, settling out as a dust-like layer across the landscape
- a. Thing
- b. Ash fall0
- c. Undefined
- d. Undefined

72. The _____ is the current eon in the geologic timescale, and the one during which abundant animal life has existed. It covers roughly 545 million years and goes back to the time when diverse hard-shelled animals first appeared.
- a. Thing
- b. Phanerozoic0
- c. Undefined
- d. Undefined

73. The _____ is the current eon in the geologic timescale, and the one during which abundant animal life has existed. It covers roughly 545 million years and goes back to the time when diverse hard-shelled animals first appeared.
- a. Phanerozoic Eon0
- b. Thing
- c. Undefined
- d. Undefined

74. An _____ is a period of long-term reduction in the temperature of Earth's climate, resulting in an expansion of the continental ice sheets, polar ice sheets and mountain glaciers .
- a. Ice Age0
- b. Thing
- c. Undefined
- d. Undefined

Chapter 9. Mass Wasting

1. _____ is a field of study within geology concerned generally with the structures within the crust of the Earth, or other planets, and particularly with the forces and movements that have operated in a region to create these structures.
   a. Thing
   b. Tectonics0
   c. Undefined
   d. Undefined

2. _____ is the process of breaking down rocks, soils and their minerals through direct contact with the atmosphere. _____ occurs without movement. Two main classifications of _____ processes exist. Mechanical or physical _____ involves the breakdown of rocks and soils through direct contact with atmospheric conditions. The second classification, chemical _____, involves the direct effect of atmospheric chemicals in the breakdown of rocks, soils and minerals.
   a. Weathering0
   b. Thing
   c. Undefined
   d. Undefined

3. _____ is displacement of solids by the agents of ocean currents, wind, water, or ice by downward or down-slope movement in response to gravity or by living organisms.
   a. Erosion0
   b. Thing
   c. Undefined
   d. Undefined

4. A _____ is a landform that extends above the surrounding terrain in a limited area. A _____ is generally steeper than a hill, but there is no universally accepted standard definition for the height of a _____ or a hill although a _____ usually has an identifiable summit.
   a. Mountain0
   b. Place
   c. Undefined
   d. Undefined

5. _____ is the condition of a system in which competing influences are balanced.
   a. Thing
   b. Equilibrium0
   c. Undefined
   d. Undefined

6. _____, in everyday life, is most familiar as the agency that endows objects with weight. _____ is responsible for keeping the Earth and the other planets in their orbits around the Sun; for the formation of tides; and for various other phenomena that we observe. _____ is also the reason for the very existence of the Earth, the Sun, and most macroscopic objects in the universe; without it, matter would not have coalesced into these large masses, and life, as we know it, would not exist.
   a. Thing
   b. Gravitation0
   c. Undefined
   d. Undefined

7. _____ is the geomorphic process by which soil, regolith, and rock move downslope under the force of gravity. Types of _____ include creep, slides, flows, topples, and falls, each with their own characteristic features, and take place over timescales from seconds to years. _____ occurs on both terrestrial and submarine slopes, and has been observed on Earth, Mars, and Venus.
   a. Thing
   b. Mass wasting0
   c. Undefined
   d. Undefined

8. _____ is the native consolidated rock underlying the Earth's surface. Above the _____ is usually an area of broken and weathered unconsolidated rock in the basal subsoil.

Chapter 9. Mass Wasting

a. Thing
b. Bedrock0
c. Undefined
d. Undefined

9. _____, is the slow downward progression of rock and soil down a low grade slope; it can also refer to slow deformation of such materials as a result of prolonged pressure and stress.
a. Creep0
b. Thing
c. Undefined
d. Undefined

10. _____ is the science and study of the solid matter that constitute the Earth. Encompassing such things as rocks, soil, and gemstones, _____ studies the composition, structure, physical properties, history, and the processes that shape Earth's components.
a. Thing
b. Geology0
c. Undefined
d. Undefined

11. A _____ is a geological phenomenon which includes a wide range of ground movement, such as rock falls, deep failure of slopes and shallow debris flows. Although gravity's action on an over-steepened slope is the primary reason for a _____, there are other contributing factors affecting the original slope stability.
a. Landslide0
b. Thing
c. Undefined
d. Undefined

12. _____ is a form of mass wasting event that occurs when loosely consolidated materials or rock layers move a short distance down a slope. When the movement occurs in soil, there is often a distinctive rotational movement to the mass, that cuts vertically through bedding planes.
a. Slump0
b. Thing
c. Undefined
d. Undefined

13. _____ are very large slides of snow or rock down a mountainside, caused when a buildup of snow is released down a slope, and is one of the major dangers faced in the mountains.
a. Avalanches0
b. Thing
c. Undefined
d. Undefined

14. _____ is the third or vertical dimension of land surface. When _____ is described underwater, the term bathymetry is used.
a. Thing
b. Terrain0
c. Undefined
d. Undefined

15. In geology, a _____ is a depression with predominant extent in one direction. The terms U-shaped and V-shaped are descriptive terms of geography to characterize the form of valleys. Most valleys belong to one of these two main types or a mixture of them, at least with respect of the cross section of the slopes or hillsides.
a. Valley0
b. Thing
c. Undefined
d. Undefined

16. An _____ is the result from the sudden release of stored energy in the Earth's crust that creates seismic waves. At the Earth's surface, earthquakes may manifest themselves by a shaking or displacement of the ground. An _____ is caused by tectonic plates getting stuck and putting a strain on the ground. The strain becomes so great that rocks give way by breaking and sliding along fault planes.

Chapter 9. Mass Wasting

    a. Thing
    c. Undefined
    b. Earthquake0
    d. Undefined

17. _____ are where one sedimetary deposit ends and another one begins. The rock is prone to breakage at these points because of the weakness between the layers.
   a. Thing
   b. Bedding planes0
   c. Undefined
   d. Undefined

18. _____ in meteorology are large scale patterns in the atmospheric pressure field that are nearly stationary, effectively "blocking" or redirecting migratory cyclones. These _____ can remain in place for several days or even weeks, causing the areas affected by them to have the same kind of weather for an extended period of time.
   a. Thing
   b. Blocks0
   c. Undefined
   d. Undefined

19. _____ is an effect within the surface layer of a liquid that causes that layer to behave as an elastic sheet. This effect allows insects to walk on water. It allows small metal objects such as needles, razor blades, or foil fragments to float on the surface of water, and causes capillary action.
   a. Thing
   b. Surface tension0
   c. Undefined
   d. Undefined

20. _____ is a reaction force applied by a stretched string, rope or a similar object on the objects which stretch it. The direction of the force of it is parallel to the string, towards the string.
   a. Thing
   b. Tension0
   c. Undefined
   d. Undefined

21. _____ refers to the cyclic rizing and falling of Earth's ocean surface caused by the tidal forces of the Moon and the sun acting on the oceans. They cause changes in the depth of the marine and estuarine water bodies and produce oscillating currents known as tidal streams, making prediction of tides important for coastal navigation.
   a. Thing
   b. Tide0
   c. Undefined
   d. Undefined

22. A _____ is the most rapid up to 80 km/h and fluid type of downhill mass wasting.
   a. Mudflow0
   b. Thing
   c. Undefined
   d. Undefined

23. A _____ is a body of water with a current, confined within a bed and banks. Streams are important as conduits in the water cycle, instruments in aquifer recharge, and corridors for fish and wildlife migration.
   a. Stream0
   b. Thing
   c. Undefined
   d. Undefined

24. _____ often refers to mudslides, mudflows, jökulhlaups, or debris avalanches. They consist primarily of geological material mixed with water. They may be generated when hillside colluvium or landslide material becomes rapidly saturated with water and flows into a channel.
   a. Thing
   b. Debris flow0
   c. Undefined
   d. Undefined

Chapter 9. Mass Wasting

25. _____ are downslope, viscous flows of saturated, fine-grained materials, that move at any speed from slow to fast. Typically, they can move at speeds from .17 to 20 km/h. Though these are a lot like mudflows, overall they are slower moving and are covered with solid material carried along by flow from within.
- a. Earthflows0
- b. Thing
- c. Undefined
- d. Undefined

26. An _____ is a transition zone between different physiogeographic provinces that involves an elevation differential, often involving high cliffs. Most commonly, an _____, is a transition from one series of sedimentary rocks to another series of a different age and composition. In such cases, the _____ usually represents the line of erosional loss of the newer rock over the older.
- a. Thing
- b. Escarpment0
- c. Undefined
- d. Undefined

27. A _____ is a significant vertical, or near vertical, rock exposure. Cliffs are categorized as erosion landforms due to the processes of erosion and weathering that produce them. Cliffs are common on coasts, in mountainous areas, escarpments and along rivers. Cliffs are usually formed by rock that is resistant to erosion and weathering.
- a. Cliff0
- b. Thing
- c. Undefined
- d. Undefined

28. A _____ is the fringe of land at the edge of a large body of water, such as an ocean, sea, or lake. A strict definition is the strip of land along a water body that is alternately exposed and covered by waves and tides.
- a. Shoreline0
- b. Thing
- c. Undefined
- d. Undefined

29. In geology, _____, is a type of mass wasting where waterlogged sediment slowly moves downslope over impermeable material. It can occur in any climate where the ground is saturated by water, though it is most often found in periglacial environments where the ground is permanently frozen.
- a. Thing
- b. Solifluction0
- c. Undefined
- d. Undefined

30. In geology, _____ is soil at or below the freezing point of water for two or more years. Ice is not always present, as may be in the case of nonporous bedrock, but it frequently occurs and it may be in amounts exceeding the potential hydraulic saturation of the ground material. Most _____ is located in high latitudes, but alpine _____ exists at high altitudes.
- a. Thing
- b. Permafrost0
- c. Undefined
- d. Undefined

31. _____ is any particulate matter that can be transported by fluid flow and which eventually is deposited as a layer of solid particles on the bed or bottom of a body of water or other liquid.
- a. Sediment0
- b. Thing
- c. Undefined
- d. Undefined

32. _____ is a measure of the resistance of a fluid to deform under shear stress. It is commonly perceived as "thickness", or resistance to flow. _____ describes a fluid's internal resistance to flow and may be thought of as a measure of fluid friction.

Chapter 9. Mass Wasting

a. Thing
b. Viscosity0
c. Undefined
d. Undefined

33. In geography, a _____ is a landscape form or region that receives very little precipitation. They are defined as areas that receive an average annual precipitation of less than 250 mm. A _____ where vegetation cover is exceedingly sparse correspond to the 'hyperarid' regions of the earth, where rainfall is exceedingly rare and infrequent.
a. Place
b. Desert0
c. Undefined
d. Undefined

34. _____ are clastic rocks composed solely or primarily of volcanic materials.
a. Pyroclastics0
b. Thing
c. Undefined
d. Undefined

35. _____ is molten rock expelled by a volcano during an eruption. When first extruded from a volcanic vent, it is a liquid at temperatures from 700 °C to 1,200 °C.
a. Lava0
b. Thing
c. Undefined
d. Undefined

36. _____ is the result of the transformation of a pre-existing rock type, the protolith, in a process called metamorphism, which means "change in form". The protolith is subjected to heat and extreme pressure causing profound physical and/or chemical change. The protolith may be sedimentary rock, igneous rock or another older rock.
a. Metamorphic rock0
b. Thing
c. Undefined
d. Undefined

37. Metamorphic rock is the result of the transformation of a pre-existing rock type, the protolith, in a process called metamorphism. The protolith is subjected to heat and extreme pressure causing profound physical and/or chemical change. _____ make up a large part of the Earth's crust. They are formed deep beneath the Earth's surface by great stresses from rocks above and high pressures and temperatures.
a. Metamorphic rocks0
b. Thing
c. Undefined
d. Undefined

38. _____ can be defined as the solid state recrystallisation of pre-existing rocks due to changes in heat and/or pressure and/or introduction of fluids. There will be mineralogical, chemical and crystallographic changes. _____ produced with increasing pressure and temperature conditions is known as prograde _____. Conversely, decreasing temperatures and pressure characterize retrograde _____.
a. Metamorphism0
b. Thing
c. Undefined
d. Undefined

39. _____ is a solid deposition of water vapor from saturated air. If solid surfaces in contact with the air are chilled below the deposition point, then spicules of ice grow out from the solid surface. _____ is often observed around cracks in wooden sidewalks due to the moist air escaping from the ground below. Other objects on which _____ develops are those with low specific heat and high thermal emissivity, such as blackened metals.
a. Frost0
b. Thing
c. Undefined
d. Undefined

Chapter 9. Mass Wasting

40. _____ is a term given to broken rock that appears at the bottom of crags, mountain cliffs or valley shoulders, forming a _____ slope. The maximum inclination of such deposits corresponds to the angle of repose of the mean debris size.
   a. Thing
   b. Scree0
   c. Undefined
   d. Undefined

41. A _____ is a large, slow moving river of ice, formed from compacted layers of snow, that slowly deforms and flows in response to gravity. _____ ice is the largest reservoir of fresh water on Earth, and second only to oceans as the largest reservoir of total water. Glaciers cover vast areas of polar regions but are restricted to the highest mountains in the tropics.
   a. Glacier0
   b. Thing
   c. Undefined
   d. Undefined

42. _____ is a sedimentary rock composed largely of the mineral calcite. _____ often contains variable amounts of silica in the form of chert or flint, as well as varying amounts of clay, silt and sand as disseminations, nodules, or layers within the rock. The primary source of the calcite in _____ is most commonly marine organisms. These organisms secrete shells that settle out of the water column and are deposited on ocean floors as pelagic ooze or alternatively is conglomerated in a coral reef.
   a. Limestone0
   b. Thing
   c. Undefined
   d. Undefined

43. Most often, a _____ refers to an artificial lake, used to store water for various uses. Reservoirs are created first by building a sturdy dam, usually out of cement, earth, rock, or a mixture. Once the dam is completed, a stream is allowed to flow behind it and eventually fill it to capacity.
   a. Reservoir0
   b. Thing
   c. Undefined
   d. Undefined

44. _____ is a sedimentary rock composed mainly of sand-size mineral or rock grains. Most _____ is composed of quartz and/or feldspar because these are the most common minerals in the Earth's crust. Like sand, _____ may be any color, but the most common colors are tan, brown, yellow, red, gray and white.
   a. Sandstone0
   b. Thing
   c. Undefined
   d. Undefined

45. _____ is a fine-grained sedimentary rock whose original constituents were clays or muds. It is characterized by thin laminae breaking with an irregular curving fracture, often splintery and usually parallel to the often-indistinguishable bedding plane.
   a. Thing
   b. Shale0
   c. Undefined
   d. Undefined

46. _____ rock is one of the three main rock groups. Rock formed from these covers 75% of the Earth's land area, and includes common types such as chalk, limestone, dolomite, sandstone, and shale.
   a. Sedimentary0
   b. Thing
   c. Undefined
   d. Undefined

47. _____ is one of the three main rock groups. _____ covers 75% of the Earth's land area. Four basic processes are involved in the formation of a clastic _____: weathering caused mainly by friction of waves, transportation where the sediment is carried along by a current, deposition and compaction where the sediment is squashed together to form a rock of this kind.
   a. Thing
   b. Sedimentary rock0
   c. Undefined
   d. Undefined

Chapter 10. Streams and Floods

1. _____ is the gas phase component of a another state of matter which does not completely fill its container. It is distinguished from the pure gas phase by the presence of the same substance in another state of matter. Hence when a liquid has completely evaporated, it is said that the system has been completely transformed to the gas phase.
   - a. Vapor0
   - b. Thing
   - c. Undefined
   - d. Undefined

2. An _____ is a layer of gases that may surround a material body of sufficient mass. The gases are attracted by the gravity of the body, and are retained for a longer duration if gravity is high and the _____'s temperature is low. Some planets consist mainly of various gases, and thus have very deep atmospheres.
   - a. Atmosphere0
   - b. Place
   - c. Undefined
   - d. Undefined

3. The Earth's water is always in movement, and the _____, describes the continuous movement of water on, above, and below the surface of the Earth. Since the _____ is truly a "cycle," there is no beginning or end. Water can change states among liquid, vapor, and ice at various places in the _____, with these processes happening in the blink of an eye and over millions of years. Although the balance of water on Earth remains fairly constant over time, individual water molecules can come and go in a hurry.
   - a. Hydrologic cycle0
   - b. Thing
   - c. Undefined
   - d. Undefined

4. _____ is the process by which molecules in a liquid state become a gas.
   - a. Evaporation0
   - b. Thing
   - c. Undefined
   - d. Undefined

5. _____ is the evaporation of water from aerial parts and of plants, especially leaves but also stems, flowers and fruits. _____ is a side effect of the plant needing to open its stomata in order to obtain carbon dioxide gas from the air for photosynthesis. _____ also cools plants and enables mass flow of mineral nutrients from roots to shoots.
   - a. Transpiration0
   - b. Thing
   - c. Undefined
   - d. Undefined

6. A _____ is a body of water with a current, confined within a bed and banks. Streams are important as conduits in the water cycle, instruments in aquifer recharge, and corridors for fish and wildlife migration.
   - a. Thing
   - b. Stream0
   - c. Undefined
   - d. Undefined

7. _____, in everyday life, is most familiar as the agency that endows objects with weight. _____ is responsible for keeping the Earth and the other planets in their orbits around the Sun; for the formation of tides; and for various other phenomena that we observe. _____ is also the reason for the very existence of the Earth, the Sun, and most macroscopic objects in the universe; without it, matter would not have coalesced into these large masses, and life, as we know it, would not exist.
   - a. Gravitation0
   - b. Thing
   - c. Undefined
   - d. Undefined

8. In geology, a _____ is a depression with predominant extent in one direction. The terms U-shaped and V-shaped are descriptive terms of geography to characterize the form of valleys. Most valleys belong to one of these two main types or a mixture of them, at least with respect of the cross section of the slopes or hillsides.

Chapter 10. Streams and Floods

a. Valley0
b. Thing
c. Undefined
d. Undefined

9. A _____ is flat or nearly flat land adjacent to a stream or river that experiences occasional or periodic flooding. It includes the floodway, which consists of the stream channel and adjacent areas that carry flood flows, and the flood fringe, which are areas covered by the flood, but which do not experience a strong current.
   a. Thing
   b. Floodplain0
   c. Undefined
   d. Undefined

10. _____ is any particulate matter that can be transported by fluid flow and which eventually is deposited as a layer of solid particles on the bed or bottom of a body of water or other liquid.
    a. Sediment0
    b. Thing
    c. Undefined
    d. Undefined

11. _____ is the result of heavy rain on bare soil where water flows as a sheet down any gradient, carrying soil particles.
    a. Sheet erosion0
    b. Thing
    c. Undefined
    d. Undefined

12. _____ is displacement of solids by the agents of ocean currents, wind, water, or ice by downward or down-slope movement in response to gravity or by living organisms.
    a. Erosion0
    b. Thing
    c. Undefined
    d. Undefined

13. _____ is the geomorphic process by which soil, regolith, and rock move downslope under the force of gravity. Types of _____ include creep, slides, flows, topples, and falls, each with their own characteristic features, and take place over timescales from seconds to years. _____ occurs on both terrestrial and submarine slopes, and has been observed on Earth, Mars, and Venus.
    a. Thing
    b. Mass wasting0
    c. Undefined
    d. Undefined

14. A _____ is a narrow and shallow incision into soil resulting from erosion by overland flow that has been focused into a thin thread by soil surface roughness.
    a. Rill0
    b. Thing
    c. Undefined
    d. Undefined

15. _____ is the natural or artificial removal of surface and sub-surface water from a given area. Many agricultural soils need _____ to improve production or to manage water supplies.
    a. Drainage0
    b. Thing
    c. Undefined
    d. Undefined

16. A _____ is a region of land where water from rain or snow melt drains downhill into a body of water, such as a river, lake, dam, estuary, wetland, sea or ocean. The _____ includes both the streams and rivers that convey the water as well as the land surfaces from which water drains into those channels. The _____ acts like a funnel - collecting all the water within the area covered by the basin and channeling it into a waterway.

Chapter 10. Streams and Floods

    a. Drainage basin0   b. Thing
    c. Undefined   d. Undefined

17. A _____ is a stream or river which flows into a mainstem river, and which does not flow directly into a sea. In orography, they are ordered from those nearest to the source of the river to those nearest to the mouth of the river.
    a. Tributary0   b. Thing
    c. Undefined   d. Undefined

18. _____ is the name given to the North American portion of the mountainous ridge which separates the watersheds that drain into the Pacific Ocean from the river systems which drain into the Atlantic Ocean, and the river systems which drain into the Arctic Ocean. A secondary, non-mountainous divide further separates other river systems that drain into the Arctic Ocean from those which drain into the Atlantic Ocean.
    a. Continental Divide0   b. Thing
    c. Undefined   d. Undefined

19. _____ is a layer of loose, heterogeneous material covering solid rock. _____ is present on Earth, the Moon, some asteroids, and other planets.
    a. Thing   b. Regolith0
    c. Undefined   d. Undefined

20. _____ is a sedimentary rock composed mainly of sand-size mineral or rock grains. Most _____ is composed of quartz and/or feldspar because these are the most common minerals in the Earth's crust. Like sand, _____ may be any color, but the most common colors are tan, brown, yellow, red, gray and white.
    a. Sandstone0   b. Thing
    c. Undefined   d. Undefined

21. _____ is a fine-grained sedimentary rock whose original constituents were clays or muds. It is characterized by thin laminae breaking with an irregular curving fracture, often splintery and usually parallel to the often-indistinguishable bedding plane.
    a. Shale0   b. Thing
    c. Undefined   d. Undefined

22. _____ is the study of Earth's surface features or those of other planets, moons, and asteroids
    a. Topography0   b. Thing
    c. Undefined   d. Undefined

23. _____ is the geological process whereby material is added to a landform. This is the process by which wind and water create a sediment deposit, through the laying down of granular material that has been eroded and transported from another geographical location.
    a. Deposition0   b. Thing
    c. Undefined   d. Undefined

24. _____ is the ratio of drop in a stream per unit distance, usually expressed as feet per mile or meters per kilometer. A high gradient indicates a steep slope and rapid flow of water; whereas a low gradient indicates a more nearly level stream bed and sluggishly moving water, that may be able to carry only small amounts of very fine sediment.

Chapter 10. Streams and Floods

a. Stream gradient0
b. Thing
c. Undefined
d. Undefined

25. In physics, _____ is defined as the rate of change of displacement or the rate of displacement. Simply put, it is distance per units of time.
    a. Velocity0
    b. Thing
    c. Undefined
    d. Undefined

26. _____ is the term for the fine particles that are light enough to be carried in a stream without touching the stream bed. These particles are generally of the sand, silt and clay size, although they can be larger, especially in cases of high discharge, such as during floods. This is in contrast to bed load which is carried along the bottom of the stream.
    a. Suspended load0
    b. Thing
    c. Undefined
    d. Undefined

27. A _____ is a landform that extends above the surrounding terrain in a limited area. A _____ is generally steeper than a hill, but there is no universally accepted standard definition for the height of a _____ or a hill although a _____ usually has an identifiable summit.
    a. Place
    b. Mountain0
    c. Undefined
    d. Undefined

28. A _____ is a section of a river of relatively steep gradient causing an increase in water flow and turbulence. A _____ is a hydrological feature between a run and a cascade. It is characterized by the river becoming shallower and having some rocks exposed above the flow surface.
    a. Rapid0
    b. Thing
    c. Undefined
    d. Undefined

29. _____ in meteorology are large scale patterns in the atmospheric pressure field that are nearly stationary, effectively "blocking" or redirecting migratory cyclones. These _____ can remain in place for several days or even weeks, causing the areas affected by them to have the same kind of weather for an extended period of time.
    a. Blocks0
    b. Thing
    c. Undefined
    d. Undefined

30. _____ is the average and variations of weather over long periods of time. _____ zones can be defined using parameters such as temperature and rainfall.
    a. Thing
    b. Climate0
    c. Undefined
    d. Undefined

31. _____ is a form of mechanical weathering caused by the force of moving water currents rushing into a crack in the rockface. The water compresses the air in the crack, pushing it right to the back. As the wave retreats, the highly pressurised air is suddenly released with explosive force, capable of chipping away the rockface over time.
    a. Hydraulic action0
    b. Thing
    c. Undefined
    d. Undefined

32. _____ is mechanical scraping of a rock surface by friction between rocks and moving particles during their transport in wind, glacier, waves, gravity or running water.

Chapter 10. Streams and Floods

   a. Thing   b. Abrasion0
   c. Undefined   d. Undefined

33. A _____ is usually a geological formation resulting from water, often in the form of a stream, flowing over an erosion-resistant rock formation that forms a sudden break in elevation or nickpoint.
   a. Place   b. Waterfall0
   c. Undefined   d. Undefined

34. _____ is the process of breaking down rocks, soils and their minerals through direct contact with the atmosphere. _____ occurs without movement. Two main classifications of _____ processes exist. Mechanical or physical _____ involves the breakdown of rocks and soils through direct contact with atmospheric conditions. The second classification, chemical _____, involves the direct effect of atmospheric chemicals in the breakdown of rocks, soils and minerals.
   a. Weathering0   b. Thing
   c. Undefined   d. Undefined

35. _____ is a sedimentary rock composed largely of the mineral calcite. _____ often contains variable amounts of silica in the form of chert or flint, as well as varying amounts of clay, silt and sand as disseminations, nodules, or layers within the rock. The primary source of the calcite in _____ is most commonly marine organisms. These organisms secrete shells that settle out of the water column and are deposited on ocean floors as pelagic ooze or alternatively is conglomerated in a coral reef.
   a. Limestone0   b. Thing
   c. Undefined   d. Undefined

36. _____ rock is one of the three main rock groups. Rock formed from these covers 75% of the Earth's land area, and includes common types such as chalk, limestone, dolomite, sandstone, and shale.
   a. Sedimentary0   b. Thing
   c. Undefined   d. Undefined

37. _____ is one of the three main rock groups. _____ covers 75% of the Earth's land area. Four basic processes are involved in the formation of a clastic _____: weathering caused mainly by friction of waves, transportation where the sediment is carried along by a current, deposition and compaction where the sediment is squashed together to form a rock of this kind.
   a. Sedimentary rock0   b. Thing
   c. Undefined   d. Undefined

38. _____ is rock that is of a certain particle size range. In geology, _____ is any loose rock that is at least two millimeters in its largest dimension and no more than 75 millimeters.
   a. Gravel0   b. Thing
   c. Undefined   d. Undefined

39. _____ is a term to describe the larger particles, relative to the suspended load, that are carried along the bottom of a stream.
   a. Thing   b. Bed load0
   c. Undefined   d. Undefined

Chapter 10. Streams and Floods

40. The ways in which sediments are transported by streams, or the stream load is comprised of three types: Bed Loads, _____, Suspended Loads.
   a. Dissolved loads0
   b. Thing
   c. Undefined
   d. Undefined

41. _____ is a specific type of particle transport by fluids. It occurs when loose material is removed from a bed and carried by the fluid, before being transported back to the surface.
   a. Saltation0
   b. Thing
   c. Undefined
   d. Undefined

42. _____ involves the change in the composition of rock, often leading to a 'break down' in its form.
   a. Thing
   b. Chemical weathering0
   c. Undefined
   d. Undefined

43. In inorganic chemistry, a _____ is a salt of sulfuric acid
   a. Thing
   b. Sulfate0
   c. Undefined
   d. Undefined

44. _____ refers to water-soluble, mineral sediments that result from the evaporation of bodies of surficial water.
   a. Thing
   b. Evaporite0
   c. Undefined
   d. Undefined

45. A _____ is a landform where the mouth of a river flows into an ocean, sea, desert, estuary or lake. It builds up sediment outwards into the flat area which the river's flow encounters transported by the water and set down as the currents slow.
   a. Thing
   b. Delta0
   c. Undefined
   d. Undefined

46. An _____ plain is a relatively flat and gently sloping landform found at the base of a range of hills or mountains, formed by the deposition of _____ soil over a long period of time by one or more rivers coming from the mountains.
   a. Thing
   b. Alluvial0
   c. Undefined
   d. Undefined

47. A _____ is an accumulation of alluvium or eluvium containing valuable minerals which is formed by deposition of dense mineral phases in a trap site.
   a. Placer0
   b. Thing
   c. Undefined
   d. Undefined

48. _____ is one of a number of channel types and has a channel that consists of a network of small channels separated by small and often temporary islands called braid bars or, in British usage, aits or eyots.
   a. Thing
   b. Braided stream0
   c. Undefined
   d. Undefined

49. A _____ is a natural or artificial slope or wall, usually earthen and often parallels the course of a river.

Chapter 10. Streams and Floods

a. Levee0
b. Thing
c. Undefined
d. Undefined

50. A _____ is a disturbance that propagates through space or spacetime, transferring energy and momentum and sometimes angular momentum.
   a. Wave0
   b. Thing
   c. Undefined
   d. Undefined

51. The _____ is defined as the part of the land adjoining or near the ocean. A coastline is properly a line on a map indicating the disposition of a _____, but the word is often used to refer to the _____ itself. The adjective coastal describes something as being on, near to, or associated with a _____.
   a. Coast0
   b. Place
   c. Undefined
   d. Undefined

52. Ocean _____ are any more or less continuous, directed movement of ocean water that flows in one of the Earth's oceans. They are rivers of hot or cold water within the ocean. They are generated from the forces acting upon the water like the earth's rotation, the wind, the temperature and salinity differences and the gravitation of the moon.
   a. Currents0
   b. Thing
   c. Undefined
   d. Undefined

53. _____ refers to the cyclic rizing and falling of Earth's ocean surface caused by the tidal forces of the Moon and the sun acting on the oceans. They cause changes in the depth of the marine and estuarine water bodies and produce oscillating currents known as tidal streams, making prediction of tides important for coastal navigation.
   a. Thing
   b. Tide0
   c. Undefined
   d. Undefined

54. _____ is an excavation activity or operation usually carried out at least partly underwater, in shallow seas or fresh water areas with the purpose of gathering up bottom sediments and disposing of them at a different location.
   a. Thing
   b. Dredging0
   c. Undefined
   d. Undefined

55. In geology, engineering, and surveying, _____ is the motion of a surface as it shifts downward relative to a datum such as sea-level. The opposite of _____ is uplift, which results in an increase in elevation. In meteorology, _____ refers to the downward movement of air.
   a. Thing
   b. Subsidence0
   c. Undefined
   d. Undefined

56. _____ is the process of a material being more closely packed together.
   a. Thing
   b. Compaction0
   c. Undefined
   d. Undefined

57. Mean _____ is the average height of the sea, with reference to a suitable reference surface.
   a. Sea level0
   b. Thing
   c. Undefined
   d. Undefined

Chapter 10. Streams and Floods

58. In geography, a _____ is a landscape form or region that receives very little precipitation. They are defined as areas that receive an average annual precipitation of less than 250 mm. A _____ where vegetation cover is exceedingly sparse correspond to the 'hyperarid' regions of the earth, where rainfall is exceedingly rare and infrequent.
   a. Desert0
   b. Place
   c. Undefined
   d. Undefined

59. _____ often refers to mudslides, mudflows, jökulhlaups, or debris avalanches. They consist primarily of geological material mixed with water. They may be generated when hillside colluvium or landslide material becomes rapidly saturated with water and flows into a channel.
   a. Thing
   b. Debris flow0
   c. Undefined
   d. Undefined

60. _____ is the ability of a substance to draw another substance into it. The standard reference is to a tube in plants but can be seen readily with porous paper. It occurs when the adhesive intermolecular forces between the liquid and a substance are stronger than the cohesive intermolecular forces inside the liquid. The effect causes a concave meniscus to form where the substance is touching a vertical surface. The same effect is what causes porous materials to soak up liquids.
   a. Capillary action0
   b. Thing
   c. Undefined
   d. Undefined

61. Most often, a _____ refers to an artificial lake, used to store water for various uses. Reservoirs are created first by building a sturdy dam, usually out of cement, earth, rock, or a mixture. Once the dam is completed, a stream is allowed to flow behind it and eventually fill it to capacity.
   a. Reservoir0
   b. Thing
   c. Undefined
   d. Undefined

62. _____ is rock or other material used to armor shorelines or stream banks against water erosion
   a. Thing
   b. Riprap0
   c. Undefined
   d. Undefined

63. _____ is a geological process that deepens the channel of a stream or valley by removing material from the stream's bed or the valley's floor. How fast _____ occurs depends on the stream's base level, which is the lowest point to which the stream can erode. Sea level is the ultimate base level, but many streams have a higher "temporary" base level because they empty into another body of water that is above sea level or encounter bedrock that resists erosion.
   a. Downcutting0
   b. Thing
   c. Undefined
   d. Undefined

64. The _____ of a river or stream is the lowest point to which it can flow, often referred to as the 'mouth' of the river. For large rivers, sea level is usually the _____, but a large river or lake is likewise the _____ for tributary streams.
   a. Thing
   b. Base level0
   c. Undefined
   d. Undefined

Chapter 10. Streams and Floods

65. The _____ on the geologic timescale had been intended to cover the world's recent period of repeated glaciations. The _____ follows the Pliocene and is followed by the Holocene. The _____ is the third epoch of the Neogene period or 6th epoch of the Cenozoic era. The end of the _____ corresponds with the end of the Paleolithic age used in archaeology. The _____ is divided into the Early _____, Middle _____ and Late _____, and numerous faunal stages.
   a. Thing
   c. Undefined
   b. Pleistocene0
   d. Undefined

66. _____ can refer to: a period of time; a distinctive historical period or era, a unit of the geologic time scale, less than a period and greater than an age, or a phase in the development of the universe with distinctive properties.
   a. Thing
   c. Undefined
   b. Epoch0
   d. Undefined

67. _____ is a fluvial process of erosion that lengthens a stream, a valley or a gully at its head and also enlarges its drainage basin. The stream erodes away at the rock and soil at its headwaters in the opposite direction that it flows. Once a stream has begun to cut back, the erosion is sped up by the steep gradient the water is flowing down.
   a. Headward erosion0
   c. Undefined
   b. Thing
   d. Undefined

68. In agriculture, a _____ is a leveled section of a hilly cultivated area, designed as a method of soil conservation to slow or prevent the rapid surface runoff of irrigation water
   a. Thing
   c. Undefined
   b. Terrace0
   d. Undefined

69. A _____ is a large, slow moving river of ice, formed from compacted layers of snow, that slowly deforms and flows in response to gravity. _____ ice is the largest reservoir of fresh water on Earth, and second only to oceans as the largest reservoir of total water. Glaciers cover vast areas of polar regions but are restricted to the highest mountains in the tropics.
   a. Thing
   c. Undefined
   b. Glacier0
   d. Undefined

70. _____ is the native consolidated rock underlying the Earth's surface. Above the _____ is usually an area of broken and weathered unconsolidated rock in the basal subsoil.
   a. Thing
   c. Undefined
   b. Bedrock0
   d. Undefined

71. A _____ is a bend in a river. A stream or river flowing through a wide valley or flat plain will tend to form a meandering stream course as it alternatively erodes and deposits sediments along its course. The result is a snaking pattern.
   a. Meander0
   c. Undefined
   b. Thing
   d. Undefined

72. A _____ is a group of mountains bordered by lowlands or separated from other mountain ranges by passes or rivers. Individual mountains within the same _____ do not necessarily have the same geology; they may be a mix of different orogeny, for example volcanoes, uplifted mountains or fold mountains and may, therefore, be of different rock.

a. Thing
b. Mountain range0
c. Undefined
d. Undefined

Chapter 11. Ground Water

1. _____ is any particulate matter that can be transported by fluid flow and which eventually is deposited as a layer of solid particles on the bed or bottom of a body of water or other liquid.
   a. Sediment0
   b. Thing
   c. Undefined
   d. Undefined

2. _____ is any product of the condensation of atmospheric water vapor that is deposited on the earth's surface. It occurs when the atmosphere becomes saturated with water vapour and the water condenses and falls out of solution. Air becomes saturated via two processes, cooling and adding moisture.
   a. Precipitation0
   b. Thing
   c. Undefined
   d. Undefined

3. The Earth's water is always in movement, and the _____, describes the continuous movement of water on, above, and below the surface of the Earth. Since the _____ is truly a "cycle," there is no beginning or end. Water can change states among liquid, vapor, and ice at various places in the _____, with these processes happening in the blink of an eye and over millions of years. Although the balance of water on Earth remains fairly constant over time, individual water molecules can come and go in a hurry.
   a. Hydrologic cycle0
   b. Thing
   c. Undefined
   d. Undefined

4. _____ is a measure of the void spaces in a material, and is measured as a fraction, between 0–1, or as a percentage between 0–100%.
   a. Thing
   b. Porosity0
   c. Undefined
   d. Undefined

5. _____ rock is one of the three main rock groups. Rock formed from these covers 75% of the Earth's land area, and includes common types such as chalk, limestone, dolomite, sandstone, and shale.
   a. Sedimentary0
   b. Thing
   c. Undefined
   d. Undefined

6. _____ is one of the three main rock groups. _____ covers 75% of the Earth's land area. Four basic processes are involved in the formation of a clastic _____: weathering caused mainly by friction of waves, transportation where the sediment is carried along by a current, deposition and compaction where the sediment is squashed together to form a rock of this kind.
   a. Thing
   b. Sedimentary rock0
   c. Undefined
   d. Undefined

7. _____ is a sedimentary rock composed mainly of sand-size mineral or rock grains. Most _____ is composed of quartz and/or feldspar because these are the most common minerals in the Earth's crust. Like sand, _____ may be any color, but the most common colors are tan, brown, yellow, red, gray and white.
   a. Sandstone0
   b. Thing
   c. Undefined
   d. Undefined

8. A _____ is a rock consisting of individual stones that have become cemented together. Conglomerates are sedimentary rocks consisting of rounded fragements and are thus differentiated from breccias, which consist of angular clasts. Both conglomerates and breccias are characterized by clasts larger than sand.

a. Thing b. Conglomerate0
c. Undefined d. Undefined

9. _____ is the process of a material being more closely packed together.
a. Compaction0 b. Thing
c. Undefined d. Undefined

10. _____ is the process of deposition of dissolved mineral components in the interstices of sediments. It is an important factor in the consolidation of coarse-grained clastic sedimentary rocks such as sandstones, conglomerates, or breccias during diagenesis or lithification. Cementing materials may include silica, carbonates, iron oxides, or clay minerals.
a. Cementation0 b. Thing
c. Undefined d. Undefined

11. _____ is a common and widely occurring type of intrusive, felsic, igneous rock. Granites are usually medium to coarsely crystalline, occasionally with some individual crystals larger than the groundmass forming a rock known as porphyry. Granites can be pink to dark gray or even black, depending on their chemistry and mineralogy.
a. Thing b. Granite0
c. Undefined d. Undefined

12. The _____ refers to a group of medium-grade metamorphic rocks, chiefly notable for the preponderance of lamellar minerals such as micas, chlorite, talc, hornblende, graphite, and others. Quartz often occurs in drawn-out grains to such an extent that a particular form called quartz _____ is produced.
a. Schist0 b. Thing
c. Undefined d. Undefined

13. _____ is a naturally occurring liquid found in formations in the Earth consisting of a complex mixture of hydrocarbons of various lengths.
a. Petroleum0 b. Thing
c. Undefined d. Undefined

14. In the earth sciences, _____ is a measure of the ability of a material to transmit fluids. It is of great importance in determining the flow characteristics of hydrocarbons in oil and gas reservoirs, and of groundwater in aquifers.
a. Thing b. Permeability0
c. Undefined d. Undefined

15. _____ is a fine-grained sedimentary rock whose original constituents were clays or muds. It is characterized by thin laminae breaking with an irregular curving fracture, often splintery and usually parallel to the often-indistinguishable bedding plane.
a. Shale0 b. Thing
c. Undefined d. Undefined

16. _____, in everyday life, is most familiar as the agency that endows objects with weight. _____ is responsible for keeping the Earth and the other planets in their orbits around the Sun; for the formation of tides; and for various other phenomena that we observe. _____ is also the reason for the very existence of the Earth, the Sun, and most macroscopic objects in the universe; without it, matter would not have coalesced into these large masses, and life, as we know it, would not exist.

a. Thing
c. Undefined
b. Gravitation0
d. Undefined

17. In geology, a _____ is the outermost layer of a planet, part of its lithosphere. They are generally composed of a less dense material than its deeper layers.Earths' is composed mainly of basalt and granite. It is cooler and more rigid than the deeper layers of the mantle and core.
   a. Crust0
   b. Thing
   c. Undefined
   d. Undefined

18. _____ can be defined as the solid state recrystallisation of pre-existing rocks due to changes in heat and/or pressure and/or introduction of fluids. There will be mineralogical, chemical and crystallographic changes. _____ produced with increasing pressure and temperature conditions is known as prograde _____. Conversely, decreasing temperatures and pressure characterize retrograde _____.
   a. Thing
   b. Metamorphism0
   c. Undefined
   d. Undefined

19. The _____ is defined as the part of the land adjoining or near the ocean. A coastline is properly a line on a map indicating the disposition of a _____, but the word is often used to refer to the _____ itself. The adjective coastal describes something as being on, near to, or associated with a _____.
   a. Coast0
   b. Place
   c. Undefined
   d. Undefined

20. The _____ is the surface where the water pressure is equal to atmospheric pressure. A large amount of water within a body of sand or rock below the _____ is called an aquifer, and the ability of rocks to store such groundwater is dependent on their porosity and permeability.
   a. Thing
   b. Water table0
   c. Undefined
   d. Undefined

21. The _____ is the portion of Earth between the land surface and the phreatic zone or zone of saturation.
   a. Vadose Zone0
   b. Thing
   c. Undefined
   d. Undefined

22. _____ is an effect within the surface layer of a liquid that causes that layer to behave as an elastic sheet. This effect allows insects to walk on water. It allows small metal objects such as needles, razor blades, or foil fragments to float on the surface of water, and causes capillary action.
   a. Thing
   b. Surface tension0
   c. Undefined
   d. Undefined

23. _____ is a reaction force applied by a stretched string, rope or a similar object on the objects which stretch it. The direction of the force of it is parallel to the string, towards the string.
   a. Thing
   b. Tension0
   c. Undefined
   d. Undefined

24. The _____ is the subsurface layer in which groundwater seeps up from a water table by capillary action to fill pores. Pores at the base of the _____ are filled with water due to tension saturation. This saturated portion of the _____ is less than total capillary rise because of the presence of a mix in pore size.

Chapter 11. Ground Water

a. Capillary fringe0
b. Thing
c. Undefined
d. Undefined

25. In seismology, the region between about 410 km and 660 km depth, the lower part of the upper mantle, is called the _____.

a. Transition zone0
b. Thing
c. Undefined
d. Undefined

26. _____ is rock that is of a certain particle size range. In geology, _____ is any loose rock that is at least two millimeters in its largest dimension and no more than 75 millimeters.

a. Gravel0
b. Thing
c. Undefined
d. Undefined

27. _____ is the amount of water present in the soil. It is equivalent to soil water content. _____ may be measured in situ with different instrument, such as Time Domain Reflectometry , neutron probe, frequency domain sensor, tensiometer, capacitance probe, etc. In the laboratory, it is measured gravimetrically; by weighing the moist volume of soil, drying it, and then weighing it again.

a. Soil moisture0
b. Thing
c. Undefined
d. Undefined

28. A _____ is a naturally occurring substance formed through geological processes that has a characteristic chemical composition, a highly ordered atomic structure and specific physical properties. A rock, by comparison, is an aggregate of minerals and need not have a specific chemical composition. Minerals range in composition from pure elements and simple salts to very complex silicates with thousands of known forms.

a. Thing
b. Mineral0
c. Undefined
d. Undefined

29. _____ is a term used to describe a group of hydrous aluminium phyllosilicate minerals, that are typically less than 2 micrometres in diameter. _____ consists of a variety of phyllosilicate minerals rich in silicon and aluminium oxides and hydroxides which include variable amounts of structural water. Clays are generally formed by the chemical weathering of silicate-bearing rocks by carbonic acid but some are formed by hydrothermal activity.

a. Thing
b. Clay0
c. Undefined
d. Undefined

30. _____ are hydrous aluminium phyllosilicates, sometimes with variable amounts of iron, magnesium, alkali metals, alkaline earths and other cations. Clays have structures similar to the micas and therefore form flat hexagonal sheets. _____ are common weathering products and low temperature hydrothermal alteration products.

a. Thing
b. Clay minerals0
c. Undefined
d. Undefined

31. _____ is water located beneath the ground surface in soil pore spaces and in the fractures of geologic formations. _____ is recharged from, and eventually flows to, the surface naturally; natural discharge often occurs at springs and seeps, streams and can often form oases or wetlands.

a. Thing
b. Groundwater0
c. Undefined
d. Undefined

Chapter 11. Ground Water

32. _____ is the study of Earth's surface features or those of other planets, moons, and asteroids
   a. Topography0
   b. Thing
   c. Undefined
   d. Undefined

33. _____, symbolically represented as K, is a property of vascular plants, soil or rock, that describes the ease with which water can move through pore spaces or fractures
   a. Thing
   b. Hydraulic Conductivity0
   c. Undefined
   d. Undefined

34. An _____ is an underground layer of water-bearing permeable rock or unconsolidated materials from which groundwater can be usefully extracted using a water well.
   a. Thing
   b. Aquifer0
   c. Undefined
   d. Undefined

35. _____ is a sedimentary rock composed largely of the mineral calcite. _____ often contains variable amounts of silica in the form of chert or flint, as well as varying amounts of clay, silt and sand as disseminations, nodules, or layers within the rock. The primary source of the calcite in _____ is most commonly marine organisms. These organisms secrete shells that settle out of the water column and are deposited on ocean floors as pelagic ooze or alternatively is conglomerated in a coral reef.
   a. Thing
   b. Limestone0
   c. Undefined
   d. Undefined

36. _____ is a common gray to black extrusive volcanic rock. It is usually fine-grained due to rapid cooling of lava on the Earth's surface. It may be porphyritic containing larger crystals in a fine matrix, or vesicular, or frothy scoria.
   a. Basalt0
   b. Thing
   c. Undefined
   d. Undefined

37. _____ is a dark, coarse-grained, intrusive igneous rock chemically equivalent to basalt. It is a plutonic rock, formed when molten magma is trapped beneath the Earth's surface and cools into a crystalline mass.
   a. Gabbro0
   b. Thing
   c. Undefined
   d. Undefined

38. _____ is a common and widely distributed type of rock formed by high-grade regional metamorphic processes from preexisting formations that were originally either igneous or sedimentary rocks. Gneissic rocks are usually medium to coarse foliated and largely recrystallized but do not carry large quantities of micas, chlorite or other platy minerals.
   a. Gneiss0
   b. Thing
   c. Undefined
   d. Undefined

39. An _____ is a zone within the earth that restricts the flow of groundwater from one aquifer to another.
   a. Aquitard0
   b. Thing
   c. Undefined
   d. Undefined

40. In geology, a _____ is a depression with predominant extent in one direction. The terms U-shaped and V-shaped are descriptive terms of geography to characterize the form of valleys. Most valleys belong to one of these two main types or a mixture of them, at least with respect of the cross section of the slopes or hillsides.

Chapter 11. Ground Water

    a. Valley0   b. Thing
    c. Undefined   d. Undefined

41. An _____ occurs in recharging aquifers, this happens because the water table at its recharge zone is at a higher elevation than the head of the well.
    a. Artesian well0   b. Thing
    c. Undefined   d. Undefined

42. A _____ is a body of water with a current, confined within a bed and banks. Streams are important as conduits in the water cycle, instruments in aquifer recharge, and corridors for fish and wildlife migration.
    a. Stream0   b. Thing
    c. Undefined   d. Undefined

43. In geography, a _____ is a landscape form or region that receives very little precipitation. They are defined as areas that receive an average annual precipitation of less than 250 mm. A _____ where vegetation cover is exceedingly sparse correspond to the 'hyperarid' regions of the earth, where rainfall is exceedingly rare and infrequent.
    a. Desert0   b. Place
    c. Undefined   d. Undefined

44. _____ technically refers to airborne solid particles or liquid droplets.
    a. Thing   b. Aerosol0
    c. Undefined   d. Undefined

45. _____ is the natural or artificial removal of surface and sub-surface water from a given area. Many agricultural soils need _____ to improve production or to manage water supplies.
    a. Thing   b. Drainage0
    c. Undefined   d. Undefined

46. _____ refers to the outflow of acidic water from abandoned metal mines. However, other areas where the earth has been disturbed may also contribute _____ to the environment
    a. Acid mine drainage0   b. Thing
    c. Undefined   d. Undefined

47. _____ is a fossil fuel formed in swamp ecosystems where plant remains were saved by water and mud from oxidization and biodegradation. It is a sedimentary rock, but the harder forms, such as anthracite _____, can be regarded as metamorphic rocks because of later exposure to elevated temperature and pressure. It is composed primarily of carbon along with assorted other elements, including sulfur.
    a. Coal0   b. Thing
    c. Undefined   d. Undefined

48. An _____ is a chemical compound containing an oxygen atom and other elements. Most of the earth's crust consists of them. They result when elements are oxidized by air.
    a. Oxide0   b. Thing
    c. Undefined   d. Undefined

Chapter 11. Ground Water

49. The term _____ refers to several types of chemical compounds containing sulfur in its lowest oxidation number of −2.
    a. Thing
    b. Sulfide0
    c. Undefined
    d. Undefined

50. A _____ is a landform that extends above the surrounding terrain in a limited area. A _____ is generally steeper than a hill, but there is no universally accepted standard definition for the height of a _____ or a hill although a _____ usually has an identifiable summit.
    a. Mountain0
    b. Place
    c. Undefined
    d. Undefined

51. An _____ is the result from the sudden release of stored energy in the Earth's crust that creates seismic waves. At the Earth's surface, earthquakes may manifest themselves by a shaking or displacement of the ground. An _____ is caused by tectonic plates getting stuck and putting a strain on the ground. The strain becomes so great that rocks give way by breaking and sliding along fault planes.
    a. Thing
    b. Earthquake0
    c. Undefined
    d. Undefined

52. _____ is soil composed of sand, silt, and clay in relatively even concentration. Loams are gritty, plastic when moist, and retain water easily. They generally contain more nutrients than sandy soils.
    a. Thing
    b. Loam0
    c. Undefined
    d. Undefined

53. An _____ is an atom or group of atoms which have lost or gained one or more electrons, making them negatively or positively charged.
    a. Thing
    b. Ion0
    c. Undefined
    d. Undefined

54. An _____ is a body of igneous rock that has crystallized from a molten magma below the surface of the Earth.
    a. Thing
    b. Intrusion0
    c. Undefined
    d. Undefined

55. In geology, engineering, and surveying, _____ is the motion of a surface as it shifts downward relative to a datum such as sea-level. The opposite of _____ is uplift, which results in an increase in elevation. In meteorology, _____ refers to the downward movement of air.
    a. Thing
    b. Subsidence0
    c. Undefined
    d. Undefined

56. _____ is the process by which water on the ground surface enters the soil.
    a. Thing
    b. Infiltration0
    c. Undefined
    d. Undefined

57. _____ is the process by which molecules in a liquid state become a gas.
    a. Thing
    b. Evaporation0
    c. Undefined
    d. Undefined

Chapter 11. Ground Water

58. _____ are where one sedimetary deposit ends and another one begins. The rock is prone to breakage at these points because of the weakness between the layers.
    a. Thing
    b. Bedding planes0
    c. Undefined
    d. Undefined

59. An _____ is a layer of gases that may surround a material body of sufficient mass. The gases are attracted by the gravity of the body, and are retained for a longer duration if gravity is high and the _____'s temperature is low. Some planets consist mainly of various gases, and thus have very deep atmospheres.
    a. Place
    b. Atmosphere0
    c. Undefined
    d. Undefined

60. A _____ is a natural underground void large enough for a human to enter. Some people suggest that the term '_____' should only apply to cavities that have some part which does not receive daylight; however, in popular usage, the term includes smaller spaces like a sea _____, rock shelters, and grottos.
    a. Cave0
    b. Place
    c. Undefined
    d. Undefined

61. A _____ is a type of speleothem that hangs from the ceiling or wall of limestone caves. Stalactites are formed by the deposition of calcium carbonate and other minerals, which is precipitated from mineralized water solutions. The corresponding formation on the floor underneath a _____ is known as a stalagmite.
    a. Stalactite0
    b. Thing
    c. Undefined
    d. Undefined

62. A _____ is a type of speleothem that rises from the floor of a limestone cave due to the dripping of mineralized solutions and the deposition of calcium carbonate. The corresponding formation on the ceiling of a cave is known as a stalactite. If these formations grow together, meeting in the middle, the result is known as a column.
    a. Thing
    b. Stalagmite0
    c. Undefined
    d. Undefined

63. _____ refers to composed sheetlike deposits of calcite formed where water flows down the walls or along the floors of a cave. They are typically found in "solution", or limestone caves, where they are the most common speleothem. However, they may form in any type of cave where water enters that has picked up dissolved minerals.
    a. Flowstone0
    b. Thing
    c. Undefined
    d. Undefined

64. _____ is the mineral form of sodium chloride. _____ forms isometric crystals. It commonly occurs with other evaporite deposit minerals such as several of the sulfates, halides and borates. _____ occurs in vast lakes of sedimentary evaporite minerals that result from the drying up of enclosed beds, playas, and seas.
    a. Halite0
    b. Thing
    c. Undefined
    d. Undefined

65. _____ is a three-dimensional landscape shaped by the dissolution of a soluble layer or layers of bedrock, usually carbonate rock such as limestone or dolomite. These landscapes display distinctive surface features and underground drainages, and in some examples there may be little or no surface drainage. Some areas of _____ are underlain by thousands of caves.

a. Thing
b. Karst topography0
c. Undefined
d. Undefined

66. _____ is a fossil wood, where all the organic materials have been replaced with minerals, while retaining the original structure of the wood. The petrifaction process occurs underground, when wood becomes buried under sediment. Mineral-rich water flowing through the sediment deposits minerals in the plant's cells and as the plant's lignin and cellulose decay away, a stone mould forms in its place.
a. Thing
b. Petrified wood0
c. Undefined
d. Undefined

67. _____ is the oxide of silicon, chemical formula SiO_2, and is known for its hardness as early as the 16th century. It is a principle component in most types of glass and substances such as concrete.
a. Thing
b. Silica0
c. Undefined
d. Undefined

68. A _____ is a volume of sedimentary rock in which a mineral cement fills the porosity. They are often ovoid or spherical in shape, although irregular shapes also occur. They form within layers of sedimentary strata that have already been deposited. They usually form early in the burial history of the sediment, before the rest of the sediment is hardened into rock.
a. Thing
b. Concretion0
c. Undefined
d. Undefined

69. Fossils are the mineralized or otherwise preserved remains or traces of animals, plants, and other organisms. The totality of fossils, both discovered and undiscovered, and their placement in fossiliferous rock formations and sedimentary layers is known as the _____ record.
a. Thing
b. Fossil0
c. Undefined
d. Undefined

70. An _____ solid is a solid in which there is no long-range order of the positions of the atoms. These materials are often prepared by rapidly cooling molten material, such as glass. The cooling reduces the mobility of the material's molecules before they can pack into a more thermodynamically favorable crystalline state.
a. Thing
b. Amorphous0
c. Undefined
d. Undefined

71. _____ is the second most common mineral in the Earth's continental crust. It is made up of a lattice of silica tetrahedra. _____ belongs to the rhombohedral crystal system. In nature _____ crystals are often twinned, distorted, or so intergrown with adjacent crystals of _____ or other minerals as to only show part of this shape, or to lack obvious crystal faces altogether and appear massive.
a. Thing
b. Quartz0
c. Undefined
d. Undefined

72. _____ is molten rock located beneath the surface of the Earth, and which often collects in a _____ chamber. _____ is a complex high-temperature fluid substance. Most are silicate solutions. It is capable of intrusion into adjacent rocks or of extrusion onto the surface as lava or ejected explosively as tephra to form pyroclastic rock. Environments of _____ formation include subduction zones, continental rift zones, mid-oceanic ridges, and hotspots, some of which are interpreted as mantle plumes.

Chapter 11. Ground Water

a. Magma0
c. Undefined
b. Thing
d. Undefined

73. A _____ is a large underground pool of molten rock lying under the surface of the earth's crust. The molten rock in such a chamber is under great pressure, and given enough time and pressure can gradually fracture the rock around it creating outlets for the magma.
   a. Thing
   b. Magma chamber0
   c. Undefined
   d. Undefined

74. _____ rocks form when molten rock, magma, cools and solidifies, with or without crystallization, either below the surface as intrusive, plutonic rocks or on the surface as extrusive, volcanic, rocks.
   a. Thing
   b. Igneous0
   c. Undefined
   d. Undefined

75. _____ forms when rock cools and solidifies either below the surface as intrusive rocks or on the surface as extrusive rocks. This magma can be derived from partial melts of pre-existing rocks in either the Earth's mantle or crust. Typically, the melting is caused by one or more of the following processes -- an increase in temperature, a decrease in pressure, or a change in composition.
   a. Thing
   b. Igneous rock0
   c. Undefined
   d. Undefined

76. A _____ is an opening, or rupture, in the Earth's surface or crust, which allows hot, molten rock, ash and gases to escape from deep below the surface.
   a. Thing
   b. Volcano0
   c. Undefined
   d. Undefined

77. In geology, _____ refers to heat sources within the planet. The planet's internal heat was originally generated during its accretion, due to gravitational binding energy, and since then additional heat has continued to be generated by the radioactive decay of elements such as uranium, thorium, and potassium.
   a. Thing
   b. Geothermal0
   c. Undefined
   d. Undefined

78. The _____ is the rate of increase in temperature per unit depth in the Earth. It varies with location and is typically measured by determining the bottom open-hole temperature after the drilling of a borehole.
   a. Geothermal gradient0
   b. Thing
   c. Undefined
   d. Undefined

79. A _____ is a type of hot spring that erupts periodically, ejecting a column of hot water and steam into the air.
   a. Geyser0
   b. Thing
   c. Undefined
   d. Undefined

80. A _____ is a spring that is produced by the emergence of geothermally-heated groundwater from the earth's crust. They are all over the earth, on every continent and even under the oceans and seas.
   a. Hot spring0
   b. Thing
   c. Undefined
   d. Undefined

Chapter 11. Ground Water

81. _____ is the gas phase component of a another state of matter which does not completely fill its container. It is distinguished from the pure gas phase by the presence of the same substance in another state of matter. Hence when a liquid has completely evaporated, it is said that the system has been completely transformed to the gas phase.
- a. Vapor0
- b. Thing
- c. Undefined
- d. Undefined

82. _____ is a sedimentary rock. _____ is a natural chemical precipitate of carbonate minerals; typically aragonite, but often recrystallized to or primarily calcite; which is deposited from the water of mineral springs or streams saturated with calcium carbonate.
- a. Travertine0
- b. Thing
- c. Undefined
- d. Undefined

83. _____ is a form of opaline silica that is often found around hot springs and geysers. Botryoidal _____ is known as fiorite.
- a. Thing
- b. Geyserite0
- c. Undefined
- d. Undefined

84. _____ is the process of breaking down rocks, soils and their minerals through direct contact with the atmosphere. _____ occurs without movement. Two main classifications of _____ processes exist. Mechanical or physical _____ involves the breakdown of rocks and soils through direct contact with atmospheric conditions. The second classification, chemical _____, involves the direct effect of atmospheric chemicals in the breakdown of rocks, soils and minerals.
- a. Thing
- b. Weathering0
- c. Undefined
- d. Undefined

85. _____ involves the change in the composition of rock, often leading to a 'break down' in its form.
- a. Chemical weathering0
- b. Thing
- c. Undefined
- d. Undefined

86. _____ is the use of geothermal heat to generate electricity.
- a. Geothermal power0
- b. Thing
- c. Undefined
- d. Undefined

87. _____ is a gaseous fossil fuel consisting primarily of methane but including significant quantities of ethane, butane, propane, carbon dioxide, nitrogen, helium and hydrogen sulfide.
- a. Thing
- b. Natural gas0
- c. Undefined
- d. Undefined

88. An _____ is a volume of rock containing components or minerals in a mode of occurrence that renders it valuable for mining.
- a. Ore0
- b. Thing
- c. Undefined
- d. Undefined

Chapter 12. Glaciers and Glaciation

1. A _____ is a large, slow moving river of ice, formed from compacted layers of snow, that slowly deforms and flows in response to gravity. _____ ice is the largest reservoir of fresh water on Earth, and second only to oceans as the largest reservoir of total water. Glaciers cover vast areas of polar regions but are restricted to the highest mountains in the tropics.
   a. Glacier0
   b. Thing
   c. Undefined
   d. Undefined

2. _____ climate is the average weather for a region above the tree line. The climate becomes colder at high elevations—this characteristic is described by the lapse rate of air: air will tend to get colder as it rises, since it expands.
   a. Alpine0
   b. Thing
   c. Undefined
   d. Undefined

3. A glacier is a large, slow moving river of ice, formed from compacted layers of snow, that slowly deforms and flows in response to gravity. Glacier ice is the largest reservoir of fresh water on Earth, and second only to oceans as the largest reservoir of total water. _____ cover vast areas of polar regions but are restricted to the highest mountains in the tropics.
   a. Glaciers0
   b. Thing
   c. Undefined
   d. Undefined

4. _____ occurs when snow falls on a glacier, is compressed, and becomes part of a glacier that winds its way toward a body of water.
   a. Thing
   b. Blue ice0
   c. Undefined
   d. Undefined

5. _____ refers to the principle that the same processes that shape the universe occurred in the past as they do now, and that the same laws of physics apply in all parts of the knowable universe.
   a. Uniformitarianism0
   b. Thing
   c. Undefined
   d. Undefined

6. _____ is displacement of solids by the agents of ocean currents, wind, water, or ice by downward or down-slope movement in response to gravity or by living organisms.
   a. Thing
   b. Erosion0
   c. Undefined
   d. Undefined

7. _____ is any particulate matter that can be transported by fluid flow and which eventually is deposited as a layer of solid particles on the bed or bottom of a body of water or other liquid.
   a. Thing
   b. Sediment0
   c. Undefined
   d. Undefined

8. In geology, a _____ is a depression with predominant extent in one direction. The terms U-shaped and V-shaped are descriptive terms of geography to characterize the form of valleys. Most valleys belong to one of these two main types or a mixture of them, at least with respect of the cross section of the slopes or hillsides.
   a. Valley0
   b. Thing
   c. Undefined
   d. Undefined

9. _____ is any product of the condensation of atmospheric water vapor that is deposited on the earth's surface. It occurs when the atmosphere becomes saturated with water vapour and the water condenses and falls out of solution. Air becomes saturated via two processes, cooling and adding moisture.

Chapter 12. Glaciers and Glaciation

    a. Precipitation0   b. Thing
    c. Undefined   d. Undefined

10. _____ is the average and variations of weather over long periods of time. _____ zones can be defined using parameters such as temperature and rainfall.
    a. Thing   b. Climate0
    c. Undefined   d. Undefined

11. Mean _____ is the average height of the sea, with reference to a suitable reference surface.
    a. Thing   b. Sea level0
    c. Undefined   d. Undefined

12. An _____ is a mass of glacier ice that covers surrounding terrain and is greater than 19,305 mile². The only current ice sheets are in Antarctica and Greenland. Ice sheets are bigger than ice shelves or glaciers. Masses of ice covering less than 50,000 km² are termed an ice cap. An ice cap will typically feed a series of glaciers around its periphery. Although the surface is cold, the base of an _____ is generally warmer. This process produces fast-flowing channels in the _____.
    a. Thing   b. Ice sheet0
    c. Undefined   d. Undefined

13. An _____ is a dome-shaped ice mass that covers less than 50,000 km² of land area. Masses of ice covering more than 50,000 km² are termed an ice sheet.
    a. Thing   b. Ice cap0
    c. Undefined   d. Undefined

14. A _____ is a landform that extends above the surrounding terrain in a limited area. A _____ is generally steeper than a hill, but there is no universally accepted standard definition for the height of a _____ or a hill although a _____ usually has an identifiable summit.
    a. Place   b. Mountain0
    c. Undefined   d. Undefined

15. _____ rock is one of the three main rock groups. Rock formed from these covers 75% of the Earth's land area, and includes common types such as chalk, limestone, dolomite, sandstone, and shale.
    a. Thing   b. Sedimentary0
    c. Undefined   d. Undefined

16. _____ is one of the three main rock groups. _____ covers 75% of the Earth's land area. Four basic processes are involved in the formation of a clastic _____: weathering caused mainly by friction of waves, transportation where the sediment is carried along by a current, deposition and compaction where the sediment is squashed together to form a rock of this kind.
    a. Sedimentary rock0   b. Thing
    c. Undefined   d. Undefined

17. _____ is the result of the transformation of a pre-existing rock type, the protolith, in a process called metamorphism, which means "change in form". The protolith is subjected to heat and extreme pressure causing profound physical and/or chemical change. The protolith may be sedimentary rock, igneous rock or another older rock.

Chapter 12. Glaciers and Glaciation 113

    a. Thing
    b. Metamorphic rock0
    c. Undefined
    d. Undefined

18. _____ can be defined as the solid state recrystallisation of pre-existing rocks due to changes in heat and/or pressure and/or introduction of fluids. There will be mineralogical, chemical and crystallographic changes. _____ produced with increasing pressure and temperature conditions is known as prograde _____. Conversely, decreasing temperatures and pressure characterize retrograde _____.
    a. Metamorphism0
    b. Thing
    c. Undefined
    d. Undefined

19. _____ is the process of a material being more closely packed together.
    a. Thing
    b. Compaction0
    c. Undefined
    d. Undefined

20. _____ is partially-compacted névé, a type of snow that has been left over from past seasons and has been recrystallized into a substance denser than névé. It is ice that is at an intermediate stage between snow and glacial ice.
    a. Firn0
    b. Thing
    c. Undefined
    d. Undefined

21. _____ is a sedimentary rock composed mainly of sand-size mineral or rock grains. Most _____ is composed of quartz and/or feldspar because these are the most common minerals in the Earth's crust. Like sand, _____ may be any color, but the most common colors are tan, brown, yellow, red, gray and white.
    a. Sandstone0
    b. Thing
    c. Undefined
    d. Undefined

22. _____ is an essentially physical process that has meanings in chemistry, metallurgy and geology. In geology, solid-state _____ is a metamorphic process that occurs under situations of intense temperature and pressure where grains, atoms or molecules of a rock or mineral are packed closer together, creating a new crystal structure.
    a. Recrystallization0
    b. Thing
    c. Undefined
    d. Undefined

23. _____ is a hard, metamorphic rock which was originally sandstone. Sandstone is converted into _____ through heating and pressure usually related to tectonic compression within orogenic belts.
    a. Thing
    b. Quartzite0
    c. Undefined
    d. Undefined

24. _____, in everyday life, is most familiar as the agency that endows objects with weight. _____ is responsible for keeping the Earth and the other planets in their orbits around the Sun; for the formation of tides; and for various other phenomena that we observe. _____ is also the reason for the very existence of the Earth, the Sun, and most macroscopic objects in the universe; without it, matter would not have coalesced into these large masses, and life, as we know it, would not exist.
    a. Thing
    b. Gravitation0
    c. Undefined
    d. Undefined

Chapter 12. Glaciers and Glaciation

25. _____ is the removal of material from the surface of an object by vaporization, chipping, or other erosive processes. The term occurs in space physics associated with atmospheric reentry, in glaciology, medicine and passive fire protection.
   a. Ablation0
   b. Thing
   c. Undefined
   d. Undefined

26. An _____ is a layer of gases that may surround a material body of sufficient mass. The gases are attracted by the gravity of the body, and are retained for a longer duration if gravity is high and the _____'s temperature is low. Some planets consist mainly of various gases, and thus have very deep atmospheres.
   a. Place
   b. Atmosphere0
   c. Undefined
   d. Undefined

27. _____ is the process by which molecules in a liquid state become a gas.
   a. Evaporation0
   b. Thing
   c. Undefined
   d. Undefined

28. The _____ is defined as the part of the land adjoining or near the ocean. A coastline is properly a line on a map indicating the disposition of a _____, but the word is often used to refer to the _____ itself. The adjective coastal describes something as being on, near to, or associated with a _____.
   a. Coast0
   b. Place
   c. Undefined
   d. Undefined

29. On a glacier, the _____ is the area in which annual loss of snow through melting, evaporation, iceberg calving and sublimation exceeds annual gain of snow and ice on the surface.
   a. Zone of wastage0
   b. Thing
   c. Undefined
   d. Undefined

30. _____ is the condition of a system in which competing influences are balanced.
   a. Equilibrium0
   b. Thing
   c. Undefined
   d. Undefined

31. An _____ is a period of long-term reduction in the temperature of Earth's climate, resulting in an expansion of the continental ice sheets, polar ice sheets and mountain glaciers.
   a. Ice Age0
   b. Thing
   c. Undefined
   d. Undefined

32. A _____ is a body of water with a current, confined within a bed and banks. Streams are important as conduits in the water cycle, instruments in aquifer recharge, and corridors for fish and wildlife migration.
   a. Thing
   b. Stream0
   c. Undefined
   d. Undefined

33. _____ is the act of a glacier sliding over the bed before it due to meltwater under the ice acting as a lubricant. This movement very much depends on the temperature of the area, the slope of the glacier, the bed's sediment size, the amount of meltwater from the glacier, and the overall glaciers size. The movement that happens to these glaciers as they slide is that of a jerky motion where any seismic events, especially at the base of glacier, can cause movement.

a. Thing
b. Basal sliding0
c. Undefined
d. Undefined

34. A _____ is a fracture in a glacier caused by large tensile stresses at or near the glacier's surface.
   a. Thing
   b. Crevasse0
   c. Undefined
   d. Undefined

35. On a glacier, the _____ is the area above the firn line, where snowfall accumulates and exceeds the losses from ablation.
   a. Thing
   b. Accumulation zone0
   c. Undefined
   d. Undefined

36. _____ is the native consolidated rock underlying the Earth's surface. Above the _____ is usually an area of broken and weathered unconsolidated rock in the basal subsoil.
   a. Thing
   b. Bedrock0
   c. Undefined
   d. Undefined

37. A _____ is an opening, or rupture, in the Earth's surface or crust, which allows hot, molten rock, ash and gases to escape from deep below the surface.
   a. Volcano0
   b. Thing
   c. Undefined
   d. Undefined

38. _____, in the sense relating to glaciers, is when a glacier erodes away chunks of bedrock to be later deposited as glacial erratics. Glacial _____ exploits pre-existing fractures in the bedrock. When the ice comes into contact with a joint, the friction on the ice results in melting of some of the ice.
   a. Plucking0
   b. Thing
   c. Undefined
   d. Undefined

39. _____ is mechanical scraping of a rock surface by friction between rocks and moving particles during their transport in wind, glacier, waves, gravity or running water.
   a. Thing
   b. Abrasion0
   c. Undefined
   d. Undefined

40. In geology, glacial _____ are grooves or lines inscribed on the surface of a rock, produced by a geological process such as glacial flow.
   a. Striations0
   b. Thing
   c. Undefined
   d. Undefined

41. _____ consists of clay-sized particles of rock, generated by glacial erosion or by artificial grinding to a similar size. Because the material is very small, it is suspended in river water making the water appear cloudy. If the river flows into a glacial lake, the lake may appear turquoise in color as a result.
   a. Rock flour0
   b. Thing
   c. Undefined
   d. Undefined

Chapter 12. Glaciers and Glaciation

42. _____ is the geomorphic process by which soil, regolith, and rock move downslope under the force of gravity. Types of _____ include creep, slides, flows, topples, and falls, each with their own characteristic features, and take place over timescales from seconds to years. _____ occurs on both terrestrial and submarine slopes, and has been observed on Earth, Mars, and Venus.
   a. Thing
   b. Mass wasting0
   c. Undefined
   d. Undefined

43. _____ is a geological process that deepens the channel of a stream or valley by removing material from the stream's bed or the valley's floor. How fast _____ occurs depends on the stream's base level, which is the lowest point to which the stream can erode. Sea level is the ultimate base level, but many streams have a higher "temporary" base level because they empty into another body of water that is above sea level or encounter bedrock that resists erosion.
   a. Thing
   b. Downcutting0
   c. Undefined
   d. Undefined

44. _____ is a solid deposition of water vapor from saturated air. If solid surfaces in contact with the air are chilled below the deposition point, then spicules of ice grow out from the solid surface. _____ is often observed around cracks in wooden sidewalks due to the moist air escaping from the ground below. Other objects on which _____ develops are those with low specific heat and high thermal emissivity, such as blackened metals.
   a. Frost0
   b. Thing
   c. Undefined
   d. Undefined

45. A _____ is a stream or river which flows into a mainstem river, and which does not flow directly into a sea. In orography, they are ordered from those nearest to the source of the river to those nearest to the mouth of the river.
   a. Thing
   b. Tributary0
   c. Undefined
   d. Undefined

46. A _____ occurs when the action of a glacier does not follow the original course of the river that wound round interlocking spurs, but, as the force of a glacier is much more powerful and cannot flow as freely around corners, it can carve its way though the rock cutting off the edges of interlocking spurs to form truncated spurs.
   a. Truncated spur0
   b. Thing
   c. Undefined
   d. Undefined

47. A _____ is a body of water or other liquid of considerable size contained on a body of land. A vast majority are fresh water, and lie in the Northern Hemisphere at higher latitudes. Most have a natural outflow in the form of a river or stream, but some do not, and lose water solely by evaporation and/or underground seepage.
   a. Lake0
   b. Thing
   c. Undefined
   d. Undefined

48. A _____ is an amphitheatre-like valley of glacial origin, formed by glacial erosion at the head of the glacier.
   a. Cirque0
   b. Place
   c. Undefined
   d. Undefined

Chapter 12. Glaciers and Glaciation

49. _____ is the process of breaking down rocks, soils and their minerals through direct contact with the atmosphere. _____ occurs without movement. Two main classifications of _____ processes exist. Mechanical or physical _____ involves the breakdown of rocks and soils through direct contact with atmospheric conditions. The second classification, chemical _____, involves the direct effect of atmospheric chemicals in the breakdown of rocks, soils and minerals.
   a. Thing
   b. Weathering0
   c. Undefined
   d. Undefined

50. _____ is the study of Earth's surface features or those of other planets, moons, and asteroids
   a. Topography0
   b. Thing
   c. Undefined
   d. Undefined

51. _____ refers to any glacially formed accumulation of unconsolidated debris which can occur in currently glaciated and formerly glaciated regions, such as those areas acted upon by a past ice age. This debris may have been plucked off the valley floor as a glacier advanced or fallen off the valley walls as a result of frost wedging. Moraines may be comprised of silt like glacial flour to large boulders. The debris is typically angular.
   a. Moraine0
   b. Thing
   c. Undefined
   d. Undefined

52. A _____ mark the maximum advance of the glacier. An is at the present boundary of the glacier. One famous is the Giant's Wall in Norway which, according to legend, was built by giants to keep intruders out of their realm.
   a. Terminal moraines0
   b. Thing
   c. Undefined
   d. Undefined

53. A _____ is an elongated whale-shaped hill formed by glacial action. Its long axis is parallel with the movement of the ice, with the blunter end facing into the glacial movement.
   a. Drumlin0
   b. Thing
   c. Undefined
   d. Undefined

54. An _____ is a long, winding ridge of stratified sand and gravel which occur in glaciated and formerly glaciated regions of Europe and North America.
   a. Esker0
   b. Thing
   c. Undefined
   d. Undefined

55. _____ in meteorology are large scale patterns in the atmospheric pressure field that are nearly stationary, effectively "blocking" or redirecting migratory cyclones. These _____ can remain in place for several days or even weeks, causing the areas affected by them to have the same kind of weather for an extended period of time.
   a. Thing
   b. Blocks0
   c. Undefined
   d. Undefined

56. A _____ is a fluvioglacial landform occurring as the result of blocks of ice calving from the front of a receding glacier and becoming partially to wholly buried by glacial outwash. Glacial outwash is generated when sediment laden streams of meltwater flow away from the glacier and are deposited to form broad outwash plains called sandurs. When the ice blocks melt, holes are left in the sandur. When the development of numerous _____ holes disrupt sandur surfaces, a jumbled assemblage of ridges and mounds form, resembling kame and _____ topography.

a. Kettle0
b. Thing
c. Undefined
d. Undefined

57. Among the classifications of soil types, _____, is a fine, silty, windblown type of unconsolidated deposit. It is derived from glacial deposits, where glacial activity has ground rocks very fine. After drying, these deposits are highly susceptible to wind erosion, and downwind deposits may become very deep. _____ deposits are geologically unstable by nature, and will erode even without being disturbed by humans.
   a. Thing
   b. Loess0
   c. Undefined
   d. Undefined

58. _____ is the geological process whereby material is added to a landform. This is the process by which wind and water create a sediment deposit, through the laying down of granular material that has been eroded and transported from another geographical location.
   a. Thing
   b. Deposition0
   c. Undefined
   d. Undefined

59. A _____ is an annual layer of sediment or sedimentary rock. The word _____ is derived from the Swedish word varv whose meanings and connotations include revolution, in layers, and circle.
   a. Thing
   b. Varve0
   c. Undefined
   d. Undefined

60. A _____ is a lake with origins in a melted glacier. They can be green in color, the result of ground up minerals supporting a large population of algae.
   a. Glacial Lake0
   b. Place
   c. Undefined
   d. Undefined

61. The _____ on the geologic timescale had been intended to cover the world's recent period of repeated glaciations. The _____ follows the Pliocene and is followed by the Holocene. The _____ is the third epoch of the Neogene period or 6th epoch of the Cenozoic era. The end of the _____ corresponds with the end of the Paleolithic age used in archaeology. The _____ is divided into the Early _____, Middle _____ and Late _____, and numerous faunal stages.
   a. Thing
   b. Pleistocene0
   c. Undefined
   d. Undefined

62. _____ can refer to: a period of time; a distinctive historical period or era, a unit of the geologic time scale, less than a period and greater than an age, or a phase in the development of the universe with distinctive properties.
   a. Epoch0
   b. Thing
   c. Undefined
   d. Undefined

63. A _____ lake is a lake which experiences significant increase in depth and extent as a result of increased precipitation and reduced evaporation.
   a. Pluvial0
   b. Thing
   c. Undefined
   d. Undefined

64. A _____ is a lake which experiences significant increase in depth and extent as a result of increased precipitation and reduced evaporation. Such lakes are likely endorheic.

Chapter 12. Glaciers and Glaciation

a. Thing
b. Pluvial lake0
c. Undefined
d. Undefined

65. The _____ is the extended perimeter of each continent and associated coastal plain, which is covered during interglacial periods such as the current epoch by relatively shallow seas and gulfs. The shelf usually ends at a point of increasing slope.
a. Continental shelf0
b. Thing
c. Undefined
d. Undefined

66. A _____ is a long, narrow estuary with steep sides, made when a glacial valley is flooded by the sea. The seeds of a _____ are laid when a glacier cuts a U-shaped valley through abrasion of the surrounding bedrock by the rocks and sediment it carries. Many such valleys were formed during recent ice ages when the sea was at a much lower level than it is today. At the end of such a period, the climate warms up again and glaciers retreat.
a. Thing
b. Fjord0
c. Undefined
d. Undefined

67. In geology, a _____ is the outermost layer of a planet, part of its lithosphere. They are generally composed of a less dense material than its deeper layers. Earths' is composed mainly of basalt and granite. It is cooler and more rigid than the deeper layers of the mantle and core.
a. Crust0
b. Thing
c. Undefined
d. Undefined

68. The _____ is used by geologists and other scientists to describe the timing and relationships between events that have occurred during the history of Earth.
a. Geological time scale0
b. Thing
c. Undefined
d. Undefined

69. An _____ is a long period of time with different technical and colloquial meanings, and usages in language. It begins with some beginning event known as an epoch, epochal date, epochal event or epochal moment.
a. Era0
b. Thing
c. Undefined
d. Undefined

70. The _____ Era meaning "new life", is the most recent of the three classic geological eras. It covers the 65.5 million years since the Cretaceous-Tertiary extinction event at the end of the Cretaceous that marked the demise of the last non-avian dinosaurs and the end of the Mesozoic Era. The _____ era is ongoing.
a. Thing
b. Cenozoic0
c. Undefined
d. Undefined

71. The _____ is the most recent of the three classic geological eras. It covers the 65.5 million years since the Cretaceous-Tertiary extinction event at the end of the Cretaceous that marked the demise of the last non-avian dinosaurs and the end of the Mesozoic Era.
a. Cenozoic era0
b. Thing
c. Undefined
d. Undefined

Chapter 12. Glaciers and Glaciation

72. The _____ is an informal name for the eons of the geologic timescale that came before the current Phanerozoic eon. It spans from the formation of Earth around 4500 Ma to the evolution of abundant macroscopic hard-shelled animals, which marked the beginning of the Cambrian, the first period of the first era of the Phanerozoic eon, some 542 Ma.
- a. Precambrian0
- b. Thing
- c. Undefined
- d. Undefined

73. _____ is a field of study within geology concerned generally with the structures within the crust of the Earth, or other planets, and particularly with the forces and movements that have operated in a region to create these structures.
- a. Thing
- b. Tectonics0
- c. Undefined
- d. Undefined

74. _____ is a theory of geology that has been developed to explain the observed evidence for large scale motions of the Earth's lithosphere. The theory encompassed and superseded the older theory of continental drift.
- a. Thing
- b. Plate tectonics0
- c. Undefined
- d. Undefined

Chapter 13. Deserts and Wind Action

1. _____ gives the location of a place on Earth north or south of the equator. Lines of _____ are the horizontal lines shown running east-to-west on maps. Technically, _____ is an angular measurement in degrees ranging from 0° at the Equator to 90° at the poles.
   a. Thing
   b. Latitude0
   c. Undefined
   d. Undefined

2. In geography, a _____ is a landscape form or region that receives very little precipitation. They are defined as areas that receive an average annual precipitation of less than 250 mm. A _____ where vegetation cover is exceedingly sparse correspond to the 'hyperarid' regions of the earth, where rainfall is exceedingly rare and infrequent.
   a. Desert0
   b. Place
   c. Undefined
   d. Undefined

3. _____ is the evaporation of water from aerial parts and of plants, especially leaves but also stems, flowers and fruits. _____ is a side effect of the plant needing to open its stomata in order to obtain carbon dioxide gas from the air for photosynthesis. _____ also cools plants and enables mass flow of mineral nutrients from roots to shoots.
   a. Transpiration0
   b. Thing
   c. Undefined
   d. Undefined

4. An _____ is a layer of gases that may surround a material body of sufficient mass. The gases are attracted by the gravity of the body, and are retained for a longer duration if gravity is high and the _____'s temperature is low. Some planets consist mainly of various gases, and thus have very deep atmospheres.
   a. Place
   b. Atmosphere0
   c. Undefined
   d. Undefined

5. _____ is the gas phase component of a another state of matter which does not completely fill its container. It is distinguished from the pure gas phase by the presence of the same substance in another state of matter. Hence when a liquid has completely evaporated, it is said that the system has been completely transformed to the gas phase.
   a. Vapor0
   b. Thing
   c. Undefined
   d. Undefined

6. _____ is the process by which molecules in a liquid state become a gas.
   a. Thing
   b. Evaporation0
   c. Undefined
   d. Undefined

7. _____ is any product of the condensation of atmospheric water vapor that is deposited on the earth's surface. It occurs when the atmosphere becomes saturated with water vapour and the water condenses and falls out of solution. Air becomes saturated via two processes, cooling and adding moisture.
   a. Thing
   b. Precipitation0
   c. Undefined
   d. Undefined

8. A _____ is a dry region on the surface of the Earth that is leeward or behind of a mountain with respect to the prevailing wind direction.
   a. Rain shadow0
   b. Thing
   c. Undefined
   d. Undefined

Chapter 13. Deserts and Wind Action

9. A _____ is a landform that extends above the surrounding terrain in a limited area. A _____ is generally steeper than a hill, but there is no universally accepted standard definition for the height of a _____ or a hill although a _____ usually has an identifiable summit.
   - a. Place
   - b. Mountain0
   - c. Undefined
   - d. Undefined

10. A _____ is a group of mountains bordered by lowlands or separated from other mountain ranges by passes or rivers. Individual mountains within the same _____ do not necessarily have the same geology; they may be a mix of different orogeny, for example volcanoes, uplifted mountains or fold mountains and may, therefore, be of different rock.
    - a. Mountain range0
    - b. Thing
    - c. Undefined
    - d. Undefined

11. _____ is the average and variations of weather over long periods of time. _____ zones can be defined using parameters such as temperature and rainfall.
    - a. Climate0
    - b. Thing
    - c. Undefined
    - d. Undefined

12. The _____ is defined as the part of the land adjoining or near the ocean. A coastline is properly a line on a map indicating the disposition of a _____, but the word is often used to refer to the _____ itself. The adjective coastal describes something as being on, near to, or associated with a _____.
    - a. Coast0
    - b. Place
    - c. Undefined
    - d. Undefined

13. _____ is the study of Earth's surface features or those of other planets, moons, and asteroids
    - a. Thing
    - b. Topography0
    - c. Undefined
    - d. Undefined

14. A _____ is a body of water with a current, confined within a bed and banks. Streams are important as conduits in the water cycle, instruments in aquifer recharge, and corridors for fish and wildlife migration.
    - a. Stream0
    - b. Thing
    - c. Undefined
    - d. Undefined

15. The _____ of a river or stream is the lowest point to which it can flow, often referred to as the 'mouth' of the river. For large rivers, sea level is usually the _____, but a large river or lake is likewise the _____ for tributary streams.
    - a. Base level0
    - b. Thing
    - c. Undefined
    - d. Undefined

16. _____ is any particulate matter that can be transported by fluid flow and which eventually is deposited as a layer of solid particles on the bed or bottom of a body of water or other liquid.
    - a. Thing
    - b. Sediment0
    - c. Undefined
    - d. Undefined

17. _____ is a hardened deposit of calcium carbonate. This calcium carbonate cements together other materials, including gravel, sand, clay, and silt. It is found in aridisol and mollisol soil orders. _____ occurs worldwide, generally in arid or semi-arid regions.

Chapter 13. Deserts and Wind Action

a. Caliche0
b. Thing
c. Undefined
d. Undefined

18. _____ is rock that is of a certain particle size range. In geology, _____ is any loose rock that is at least two millimeters in its largest dimension and no more than 75 millimeters.
a. Gravel0
b. Thing
c. Undefined
d. Undefined

19. _____ is a geological process that deepens the channel of a stream or valley by removing material from the stream's bed or the valley's floor. How fast _____ occurs depends on the stream's base level, which is the lowest point to which the stream can erode. Sea level is the ultimate base level, but many streams have a higher "temporary" base level because they empty into another body of water that is above sea level or encounter bedrock that resists erosion.
a. Thing
b. Downcutting0
c. Undefined
d. Undefined

20. _____ is the process of breaking down rocks, soils and their minerals through direct contact with the atmosphere. _____ occurs without movement. Two main classifications of _____ processes exist. Mechanical or physical _____ involves the breakdown of rocks and soils through direct contact with atmospheric conditions. The second classification, chemical _____, involves the direct effect of atmospheric chemicals in the breakdown of rocks, soils and minerals.
a. Weathering0
b. Thing
c. Undefined
d. Undefined

21. _____ is displacement of solids by the agents of ocean currents, wind, water, or ice by downward or down-slope movement in response to gravity or by living organisms.
a. Thing
b. Erosion0
c. Undefined
d. Undefined

22. _____ is a sedimentary rock composed largely of the mineral calcite. _____ often contains variable amounts of silica in the form of chert or flint, as well as varying amounts of clay, silt and sand as disseminations, nodules, or layers within the rock. The primary source of the calcite in _____ is most commonly marine organisms. These organisms secrete shells that settle out of the water column and are deposited on ocean floors as pelagic ooze or alternatively is conglomerated in a coral reef.
a. Limestone0
b. Thing
c. Undefined
d. Undefined

23. _____ is a sedimentary rock composed mainly of sand-size mineral or rock grains. Most _____ is composed of quartz and/or feldspar because these are the most common minerals in the Earth's crust. Like sand, _____ may be any color, but the most common colors are tan, brown, yellow, red, gray and white.
a. Sandstone0
b. Thing
c. Undefined
d. Undefined

24. A _____ is a rock consisting of individual stones that have become cemented together. Conglomerates are sedimentary rocks consisting of rounded fragments and are thus differentiated from breccias, which consist of angular clasts. Both conglomerates and breccias are characterized by clasts larger than sand.

Chapter 13. Deserts and Wind Action

  a. Thing
  b. Conglomerate0
  c. Undefined
  d. Undefined

25. _____ is molten rock expelled by a volcano during an eruption. When first extruded from a volcanic vent, it is a liquid at temperatures from 700 °C to 1,200 °C.
  a. Thing
  b. Lava0
  c. Undefined
  d. Undefined

26. _____ is the result of the transformation of a pre-existing rock type, the protolith, in a process called metamorphism, which means "change in form". The protolith is subjected to heat and extreme pressure causing profound physical and/or chemical change. The protolith may be sedimentary rock, igneous rock or another older rock.
  a. Thing
  b. Metamorphic rock0
  c. Undefined
  d. Undefined

27. _____ can be defined as the solid state recrystallisation of pre-existing rocks due to changes in heat and/or pressure and/or introduction of fluids. There will be mineralogical, chemical and crystallographic changes. _____ produced with increasing pressure and temperature conditions is known as prograde _____. Conversely, decreasing temperatures and pressure characterize retrograde _____.
  a. Thing
  b. Metamorphism0
  c. Undefined
  d. Undefined

28. _____ is a fine-grained sedimentary rock whose original constituents were clays or muds. It is characterized by thin laminae breaking with an irregular curving fracture, often splintery and usually parallel to the often-indistinguishable bedding plane.
  a. Shale0
  b. Thing
  c. Undefined
  d. Undefined

29. _____ involves the change in the composition of rock, often leading to a 'break down' in its form.
  a. Thing
  b. Chemical weathering0
  c. Undefined
  d. Undefined

30. A _____ is a naturally occurring substance formed through geological processes that has a characteristic chemical composition, a highly ordered atomic structure and specific physical properties. A rock, by comparison, is an aggregate of minerals and need not have a specific chemical composition. Minerals range in composition from pure elements and simple salts to very complex silicates with thousands of known forms.
  a. Thing
  b. Mineral0
  c. Undefined
  d. Undefined

31. _____ is a term used to describe a group of hydrous aluminium phyllosilicate minerals, that are typically less than 2 micrometres in diameter. _____ consists of a variety of phyllosilicate minerals rich in silicon and aluminium oxides and hydroxides which include variable amounts of structural water. Clays are generally formed by the chemical weathering of silicate-bearing rocks by carbonic acid but some are formed by hydrothermal activity.
  a. Thing
  b. Clay0
  c. Undefined
  d. Undefined

Chapter 13. Deserts and Wind Action

32. _____ are hydrous aluminium phyllosilicates, sometimes with variable amounts of iron, magnesium, alkali metals, alkaline earths and other cations. Clays have structures similar to the micas and therefore form flat hexagonal sheets. _____ are common weathering products and low temperature hydrothermal alteration products.
    a. Thing
    b. Clay minerals0
    c. Undefined
    d. Undefined

33. _____, is the slow downward progression of rock and soil down a low grade slope; it can also refer to slow deformation of such materials as a result of prolonged pressure and stress.
    a. Thing
    b. Creep0
    c. Undefined
    d. Undefined

34. A _____ is an area of highland, usually consisting of relatively flat rural area.
    a. Place
    b. Plateau0
    c. Undefined
    d. Undefined

35. _____ rock is one of the three main rock groups. Rock formed from these covers 75% of the Earth's land area, and includes common types such as chalk, limestone, dolomite, sandstone, and shale.
    a. Thing
    b. Sedimentary0
    c. Undefined
    d. Undefined

36. _____ is one of the three main rock groups. _____ covers 75% of the Earth's land area. Four basic processes are involved in the formation of a clastic _____: weathering caused mainly by friction of waves, transportation where the sediment is carried along by a current, deposition and compaction where the sediment is squashed together to form a rock of this kind.
    a. Sedimentary rock0
    b. Thing
    c. Undefined
    d. Undefined

37. Mean _____ is the average height of the sea, with reference to a suitable reference surface.
    a. Thing
    b. Sea level0
    c. Undefined
    d. Undefined

38. A _____ is an elevated area of land with a flat top and sides that are usually steep cliffs. It takes its name from its characteristic table-top shape. It is a characteristic landform of arid environments.
    a. Mesa0
    b. Thing
    c. Undefined
    d. Undefined

39. A _____ is an isolated hill with steep sides and a small flat top, smaller than mesas and plateaus. Buttes are prevalent in the western United States and on the Hawaiian Islands, especially around Honolulu.
    a. Butte0
    b. Place
    c. Undefined
    d. Undefined

40. A _____ is a linear ridge composed of steeply tilted hard and soft strata of rock that protrude out of the surrounding strata. The softer rock erodes quicker than the capping harder rock above. In some cases the two strata that compose a _____ are different types of sedimentary rock that have differing weathering rates.

Chapter 13. Deserts and Wind Action

    a. Hogback0
    c. Undefined
    b. Thing
    d. Undefined

41. In geology, a _____ is a depression with predominant extent in one direction. The terms U-shaped and V-shaped are descriptive terms of geography to characterize the form of valleys. Most valleys belong to one of these two main types or a mixture of them, at least with respect of the cross section of the slopes or hillsides.
    a. Thing
    c. Undefined
    b. Valley0
    d. Undefined

42. _____ is the geological process whereby material is added to a landform. This is the process by which wind and water create a sediment deposit, through the laying down of granular material that has been eroded and transported from another geographical location.
    a. Thing
    c. Undefined
    b. Deposition0
    d. Undefined

43. An _____ plain is a relatively flat and gently sloping landform found at the base of a range of hills or mountains, formed by the deposition of _____ soil over a long period of time by one or more rivers coming from the mountains.
    a. Alluvial0
    c. Undefined
    b. Thing
    d. Undefined

44. Playas are small, round depressions in the surface of the ground. A _____ is formed when rain fills this hole with water, creating a small lake. Playas are typically endorheic. Playas can also form when the water table intersects the surface and water seeps into them.
    a. Thing
    c. Undefined
    b. Playa0
    d. Undefined

45. A _____ is a body of water or other liquid of considerable size contained on a body of land. A vast majority are fresh water, and lie in the Northern Hemisphere at higher latitudes. Most have a natural outflow in the form of a river or stream, but some do not, and lose water solely by evaporation and/or underground seepage.
    a. Lake0
    c. Undefined
    b. Thing
    d. Undefined

46. A convergence of neighboring alluvial fans into a single apron of deposits against a slope is called a _____.
    a. Bajada0
    c. Undefined
    b. Thing
    d. Undefined

47. A _____ is a classical architectural element consisting of the triangular section found above the horizontal structure and supported by columns.
    a. Pediment0
    c. Undefined
    b. Thing
    d. Undefined

48. _____ consists of very fine rock and mineral particles less than 2 mm in diameter that are ejected from a volcanic vent. The very fine particles may be carried for many miles, settling out as a dust-like layer across the landscape
    a. Thing
    c. Undefined
    b. Ash fall0
    d. Undefined

Chapter 13. Deserts and Wind Action

49. A _____ is an opening, or rupture, in the Earth's surface or crust, which allows hot, molten rock, ash and gases to escape from deep below the surface.
    a. Volcano0
    b. Thing
    c. Undefined
    d. Undefined

50. _____ is a specific type of particle transport by fluids. It occurs when loose material is removed from a bed and carried by the fluid, before being transported back to the surface.
    a. Saltation0
    b. Thing
    c. Undefined
    d. Undefined

51. _____ is mechanical scraping of a rock surface by friction between rocks and moving particles during their transport in wind, glacier, waves, gravity or running water.
    a. Abrasion0
    b. Thing
    c. Undefined
    d. Undefined

52. _____ processes pertain to the activity of the winds and more specifically, to the winds' ability to shape the surface of the Earth and other planets.
    a. Eolian0
    b. Thing
    c. Undefined
    d. Undefined

53. The _____ is the surface where the water pressure is equal to atmospheric pressure. A large amount of water within a body of sand or rock below the _____ is called an aquifer, and the ability of rocks to store such groundwater is dependent on their porosity and permeability.
    a. Thing
    b. Water table0
    c. Undefined
    d. Undefined

54. Among the classifications of soil types, _____, is a fine, silty, windblown type of unconsolidated deposit. It is derived from glacial deposits, where glacial activity has ground rocks very fine. After drying, these deposits are highly susceptible to wind erosion, and downwind deposits may become very deep. _____ deposits are geologically unstable by nature, and will erode even without being disturbed by humans.
    a. Loess0
    b. Thing
    c. Undefined
    d. Undefined

55. _____ is the second most common mineral in the Earth's continental crust. It is made up of a lattice of silica tetrahedra. _____ belongs to the rhombohedral crystal system. In nature _____ crystals are often twinned, distorted, or so intergrown with adjacent crystals of _____ or other minerals as to only show part of this shape, or to lack obvious crystal faces altogether and appear massive.
    a. Thing
    b. Quartz0
    c. Undefined
    d. Undefined

56. _____ is a measure of the void spaces in a material, and is measured as a fraction, between 0–1, or as a percentage between 0–100%.
    a. Porosity0
    b. Thing
    c. Undefined
    d. Undefined

Chapter 13. Deserts and Wind Action

57. An _____ is the result from the sudden release of stored energy in the Earth's crust that creates seismic waves. At the Earth's surface, earthquakes may manifest themselves by a shaking or displacement of the ground. An _____ is caused by tectonic plates getting stuck and putting a strain on the ground. The strain becomes so great that rocks give way by breaking and sliding along fault planes.
   a. Thing
   b. Earthquake0
   c. Undefined
   d. Undefined

58. The _____ on the geologic timescale had been intended to cover the world's recent period of repeated glaciations. The _____ follows the Pliocene and is followed by the Holocene. The _____ is the third epoch of the Neogene period or 6th epoch of the Cenozoic era. The end of the _____ corresponds with the end of the Paleolithic age used in archaeology. The _____ is divided into the Early _____, Middle _____ and Late _____, and numerous faunal stages.
   a. Pleistocene0
   b. Thing
   c. Undefined
   d. Undefined

59. _____ can refer to: a period of time; a distinctive historical period or era, a unit of the geologic time scale, less than a period and greater than an age, or a phase in the development of the universe with distinctive properties.
   a. Epoch0
   b. Thing
   c. Undefined
   d. Undefined

60. _____ consists of clay-sized particles of rock, generated by glacial erosion or by artificial grinding to a similar size. Because the material is very small, it is suspended in river water making the water appear cloudy. If the river flows into a glacial lake, the lake may appear turquoise in color as a result.
   a. Thing
   b. Rock flour0
   c. Undefined
   d. Undefined

61. A _____ is a hill of sand built by eolian processes. Dunes are subject to different forms and sizes based on their interaction with the wind. Most kinds of _____ are longer on the windward side where the sand is pushed up the _____, and a shorter in the lee of the wind. The trough between dunes is called a slack. A "_____ field" is an area covered by extensive sand dunes. Large _____ fields are known as ergs.
   a. Thing
   b. Dune0
   c. Undefined
   d. Undefined

62. In organic chemistry, a _____ is a salt of carbonic acid.
   a. Thing
   b. Carbonate0
   c. Undefined
   d. Undefined

63. The _____ is an engineering property of granular materials. The _____ is the maximum angle of a stable slope determined by friction, cohesion and the shapes of the particles.
   a. Angle of repose0
   b. Thing
   c. Undefined
   d. Undefined

64. _____ are very large slides of snow or rock down a mountainside, caused when a buildup of snow is released down a slope, and is one of the major dangers faced in the mountains.

Chapter 13. Deserts and Wind Action

a. Thing
b. Avalanches0
c. Undefined
d. Undefined

65. The _____ is part of the Neogene and Quaternary periods. Human civilization dates entirely within the _____. The _____ was preceded by the Younger Dryas cold period, the final part of the Pleistocene epoch. The _____ starts late in the retreat of the Pleistocene glaciers. It can be considered an interglacial in the current ice age.

a. Thing
b. Holocene0
c. Undefined
d. Undefined

66. A _____ is an arc-shaped sand ridge, comprised of well-sorted sand. This type of dune possesses two "horns" that face downwind, with the slip face at the angle of repose, or approximately 32 degrees.

a. Thing
b. Barchan0
c. Undefined
d. Undefined

67. A _____ is a desert surface that is covered with closely packed, interlocking angular or rounded rock fragments of pebble and cobble size. It is thought that they are formed by the gradual removal of the sand, dust and other fine grained material by the wind and intermittent rain.

a. Desert pavement0
b. Thing
c. Undefined
d. Undefined

Chapter 14. Waves, Beaches and Coasts

1. _____ is displacement of solids by the agents of ocean currents, wind, water, or ice by downward or down-slope movement in response to gravity or by living organisms.
   a. Thing
   b. Erosion0
   c. Undefined
   d. Undefined

2. _____ is a term for the length of water over which a given wind has blown. It is used in geography and meteorology and is usually associated with coastal erosion. It plays a large part in longshore drift as well.
   a. Fetch0
   b. Thing
   c. Undefined
   d. Undefined

3. A _____ is a disturbance that propagates through space or spacetime, transferring energy and momentum and sometimes angular momentum.
   a. Thing
   b. Wave0
   c. Undefined
   d. Undefined

4. In geology, a _____ generally refers to a linear structural depression that extends laterally over a distance, while being less steep than a trench. It can be a narrow basin or a geologic rift. In meteorolology a _____ is an elongated region of relatively low atmospheric pressure, often associated with fronts.
   a. Thing
   b. Trough0
   c. Undefined
   d. Undefined

5. A _____ is a series of waves created when a body of water, such as an ocean, is rapidly displaced on a massive scale. Earthquakes, mass movements above or below water, volcanic eruptions and other underwater explosions, landslides, large meteorite impacts and testing with nuclear weapons at sea all have the potential to generate a _____. The effects of a _____ can range from unnoticeable to devastating.
   a. Thing
   b. Tsunami0
   c. Undefined
   d. Undefined

6. An _____ is the result from the sudden release of stored energy in the Earth's crust that creates seismic waves. At the Earth's surface, earthquakes may manifest themselves by a shaking or displacement of the ground. An _____ is caused by tectonic plates getting stuck and putting a strain on the ground. The strain becomes so great that rocks give way by breaking and sliding along fault planes.
   a. Earthquake0
   b. Thing
   c. Undefined
   d. Undefined

7. In physics, _____ is the distance between repeating units of a propagating wave of a given frequency. It is commonly designated by the Greek letter lambda. Examples of wave-like phenomena are light, water waves, and sound waves. _____ of a sine wave.In a wave, a property varies with the position.
   a. Thing
   b. Wavelength0
   c. Undefined
   d. Undefined

8. A _____ is the fringe of land at the edge of a large body of water, such as an ocean, sea, or lake. A strict definition is the strip of land along a water body that is alternately exposed and covered by waves and tides.
   a. Thing
   b. Shoreline0
   c. Undefined
   d. Undefined

Chapter 14. Waves, Beaches and Coasts

9. _____ is the change in direction of a wave due to a change in its speed. This is most commonly seen when a wave passes from one medium to another.
   a. Thing
   b. Refraction0
   c. Undefined
   d. Undefined

10. Ocean _____ are any more or less continuous, directed movement of ocean water that flows in one of the Earth's oceans. They are rivers of hot or cold water within the ocean. They are generated from the forces acting upon the water like the earth's rotation, the wind, the temperature and salinity differences and the gravitation of the moon.
    a. Currents0
    b. Thing
    c. Undefined
    d. Undefined

11. _____ is any particulate matter that can be transported by fluid flow and which eventually is deposited as a layer of solid particles on the bed or bottom of a body of water or other liquid.
    a. Sediment0
    b. Thing
    c. Undefined
    d. Undefined

12. A _____ is a strong flow of water returning seaward from the shore. Colloquially a _____ is known simply as a rip, or undertow. Although rip currents would exist even without the tides, tides can make an existing rip much more dangerous.
    a. Rip current0
    b. Thing
    c. Undefined
    d. Undefined

13. The term _____ signifyies something thrown out, is applied to a variety of structures employed in river, dock, and maritime works which are generally carried out in pairs from river banks, or in continuation of river channels at their outlets into deep water; or out into docks, and outside their entrances; or for forming basins along the sea-coast for ports in tideless seas.
    a. Thing
    b. Jetty0
    c. Undefined
    d. Undefined

14. _____ is rock that is of a certain particle size range. In geology, _____ is any loose rock that is at least two millimeters in its largest dimension and no more than 75 millimeters.
    a. Thing
    b. Gravel0
    c. Undefined
    d. Undefined

15. _____ refers to the cyclic rizing and falling of Earth's ocean surface caused by the tidal forces of the Moon and the sun acting on the oceans. They cause changes in the depth of the marine and estuarine water bodies and produce oscillating currents known as tidal streams, making prediction of tides important for coastal navigation.
    a. Tide0
    b. Thing
    c. Undefined
    d. Undefined

16. In agriculture, a _____ is a leveled section of a hilly cultivated area, designed as a method of soil conservation to slow or prevent the rapid surface runoff of irrigation water
    a. Terrace0
    b. Thing
    c. Undefined
    d. Undefined

Chapter 14. Waves, Beaches and Coasts

17. A _____ is the narrow flat area often seen at the base of a sea cliff caused by the action of the waves. It forms after destructive waves hit against the cliff face, causing undercutting between the high and low water marks creating a wave-cut notch. This notch then enlarges into a cave. The waves undermine this portion until the roof of the cave cannot hold due to the pressure and freeze-thaw weathering acting on it, and collapses, resulting in the cliff retreating landward.
    a. Marine terrace0
    b. Thing
    c. Undefined
    d. Undefined

18. _____ is the second most common mineral in the Earth's continental crust. It is made up of a lattice of silica tetrahedra. _____ belongs to the rhombohedral crystal system. In nature _____ crystals are often twinned, distorted, or so intergrown with adjacent crystals of _____ or other minerals as to only show part of this shape, or to lack obvious crystal faces altogether and appear massive.
    a. Quartz0
    b. Thing
    c. Undefined
    d. Undefined

19. _____ is the process of breaking down rocks, soils and their minerals through direct contact with the atmosphere. _____ occurs without movement. Two main classifications of _____ processes exist. Mechanical or physical _____ involves the breakdown of rocks and soils through direct contact with atmospheric conditions. The second classification, chemical _____, involves the direct effect of atmospheric chemicals in the breakdown of rocks, soils and minerals.
    a. Weathering0
    b. Thing
    c. Undefined
    d. Undefined

20. _____ involves the change in the composition of rock, often leading to a 'break down' in its form.
    a. Thing
    b. Chemical weathering0
    c. Undefined
    d. Undefined

21. In organic chemistry, a _____ is a salt of carbonic acid.
    a. Thing
    b. Carbonate0
    c. Undefined
    d. Undefined

22. _____ is a common gray to black extrusive volcanic rock. It is usually fine-grained due to rapid cooling of lava on the Earth's surface. It may be porphyritic containing larger crystals in a fine matrix, or vesicular, or frothy scoria.
    a. Basalt0
    b. Thing
    c. Undefined
    d. Undefined

23. _____ is the condition of a system in which competing influences are balanced.
    a. Equilibrium0
    b. Thing
    c. Undefined
    d. Undefined

24. The _____ is defined as the part of the land adjoining or near the ocean. A coastline is properly a line on a map indicating the disposition of a _____, but the word is often used to refer to the _____ itself. The adjective coastal describes something as being on, near to, or associated with a _____.
    a. Place
    b. Coast0
    c. Undefined
    d. Undefined

25. _____ is a geological process by which sediments such as sand or other materials, move along a beach shore.

Chapter 14. Waves, Beaches and Coasts

a. Longshore drift0
b. Thing
c. Undefined
d. Undefined

26. A _____ is a deposition landform found off coasts. A _____ is a type of bar or beach that develops where a re-entrant occurs, such as at a cove, bay, ria, or river mouth. A _____ is formed by the movement of sediment along a shore by a process known as longshore drift. Where the direction of the shore turns inland the longshore current spreads out or dissipates. No longer able to carry the full load, much of the sediment is dropped. This causes a bar to build out from the shore, eventually becoming a _____.
a. Thing
b. Spit0
c. Undefined
d. Undefined

27. A _____ is a depostional feature as a result of longshore drift. It is a spit that completely closes access to a bay, thus sealing it off from the main body of water.
a. Event
b. Baymouth bar0
c. Undefined
d. Undefined

28. A _____ is a deposition landform such as a spit or bar which forms a narrow piece of land between an island or offshore rock and a mainland shore, or between two islands or offshore rocks.
a. Thing
b. Tombolo0
c. Undefined
d. Undefined

29. _____ is the geological process whereby material is added to a landform. This is the process by which wind and water create a sediment deposit, through the laying down of granular material that has been eroded and transported from another geographical location.
a. Thing
b. Deposition0
c. Undefined
d. Undefined

30. Most often, a _____ refers to an artificial lake, used to store water for various uses. Reservoirs are created first by building a sturdy dam, usually out of cement, earth, rock, or a mixture. Once the dam is completed, a stream is allowed to flow behind it and eventually fill it to capacity.
a. Reservoir0
b. Thing
c. Undefined
d. Undefined

31. Mean _____ is the average height of the sea, with reference to a suitable reference surface.
a. Sea level0
b. Thing
c. Undefined
d. Undefined

32. The _____ on the geologic timescale had been intended to cover the world's recent period of repeated glaciations. The _____ follows the Pliocene and is followed by the Holocene. The _____ is the third epoch of the Neogene period or 6th epoch of the Cenozoic era. The end of the _____ corresponds with the end of the Paleolithic age used in archaeology. The _____ is divided into the Early _____, Middle _____ and Late _____, and numerous faunal stages.
a. Pleistocene0
b. Thing
c. Undefined
d. Undefined

Chapter 14. Waves, Beaches and Coasts

33. _____ is a field of study within geology concerned generally with the structures within the crust of the Earth, or other planets, and particularly with the forces and movements that have operated in a region to create these structures.
   a. Tectonics0
   b. Thing
   c. Undefined
   d. Undefined

34. _____ is a sedimentary rock composed largely of the mineral calcite. _____ often contains variable amounts of silica in the form of chert or flint, as well as varying amounts of clay, silt and sand as disseminations, nodules, or layers within the rock. The primary source of the calcite in _____ is most commonly marine organisms. These organisms secrete shells that settle out of the water column and are deposited on ocean floors as pelagic ooze or alternatively is conglomerated in a coral reef.
   a. Thing
   b. Limestone0
   c. Undefined
   d. Undefined

35. _____ is a common and widely occurring type of intrusive, felsic, igneous rock. Granites are usually medium to coarsely crystalline, occasionally with some individual crystals larger than the groundmass forming a rock known as porphyry. Granites can be pink to dark gray or even black, depending on their chemistry and mineralogy.
   a. Granite0
   b. Thing
   c. Undefined
   d. Undefined

36. _____ is the geomorphic process by which soil, regolith, and rock move downslope under the force of gravity. Types of _____ include creep, slides, flows, topples, and falls, each with their own characteristic features, and take place over timescales from seconds to years. _____ occurs on both terrestrial and submarine slopes, and has been observed on Earth, Mars, and Venus.
   a. Mass wasting0
   b. Thing
   c. Undefined
   d. Undefined

37. The _____ refers to a group of medium-grade metamorphic rocks, chiefly notable for the preponderance of lamellar minerals such as micas, chlorite, talc, hornblende, graphite, and others. Quartz often occurs in drawn-out grains to such an extent that a particular form called quartz _____ is produced.
   a. Schist0
   b. Thing
   c. Undefined
   d. Undefined

38. _____ is rock or other material used to armor shorelines or stream banks against water erosion
   a. Thing
   b. Riprap0
   c. Undefined
   d. Undefined

39. _____ are a form of hard coastal defense constructed on the inland part of a coast to reduce the effects of strong waves and to defend the coast around a town or harbor from erosion. The walls can be sloping, vertical or curved to reflect wave power.
   a. Thing
   b. Seawalls0
   c. Undefined
   d. Undefined

40. A _____ is a significant vertical, or near vertical, rock exposure. Cliffs are categorized as erosion landforms due to the processes of erosion and weathering that produce them. Cliffs are common on coasts, in mountainous areas, escarpments and along rivers. Cliffs are usually formed by rock that is resistant to erosion and weathering.

a. Thing
b. Cliff0
c. Undefined
d. Undefined

41. A _____ mark the maximum advance of the glacier. An is at the present boundary of the glacier. One famous is the Giant's Wall in Norway which, according to legend, was built by giants to keep intruders out of their realm.
a. Thing
b. Terminal moraines0
c. Undefined
d. Undefined

42. _____ refers to any glacially formed accumulation of unconsolidated debris which can occur in currently glaciated and formerly glaciated regions, such as those areas acted upon by a past ice age. This debris may have been plucked off the valley floor as a glacier advanced or fallen off the valley walls as a result of frost wedging. Moraines may be comprised of silt like glacial flour to large boulders. The debris is typically angular.
a. Moraine0
b. Thing
c. Undefined
d. Undefined

43. _____ occurs when snow falls on a glacier, is compressed, and becomes part of a glacier that winds its way toward a body of water.
a. Thing
b. Blue ice0
c. Undefined
d. Undefined

44. A _____ is a rock, sandbar, or other feature lying beneath the surface of the water yet shallow enough to be a hazard to ships. They result from abiotic processes—deposition of sand, wave erosion planning down rock outcrops, and other natural processes.
a. Thing
b. Reef0
c. Undefined
d. Undefined

45. _____ is an accumulation of partially decayed vegetation matter. It forms in wetlands.
a. Thing
b. Peat0
c. Undefined
d. Undefined

46. In geology, a _____ is a deformational feature consisting of symmetrically-dipping anticlines; their general outline on a geologic map is circular or oval.
a. Thing
b. Dome0
c. Undefined
d. Undefined

47. A _____ is any disturbed state of an astronomical body's atmosphere, especially affecting its surface, and strongly implying severe weather. It may be marked by strong wind, thunder and lightning, heavy precipitation, such as ice, or wind transporting some substance through the atmosphere.
a. Thing
b. Storm0
c. Undefined
d. Undefined

48. A _____ is an offshore rise of water associated with a low pressure weather system, typically a tropical cyclone. _____ is caused primarily by high winds pushing on the ocean's surface. The wind causes the water to pile up higher than the ordinary sea level. Low pressure at the center of a weather system also has a small secondary effect, as can the bathymetry of the body of water.

a. Thing
b. Storm surge0
c. Undefined
d. Undefined

49. An _____ is any piece of land that is completely surrounded by water, above high tide. There are two main types of islands: continental islands and oceanic islands. There are also artificial islands. A grouping of geographically and/or geologically related islands is called an archipelago.

a. Thing
b. Island0
c. Undefined
d. Undefined

Chapter 15. Geologic Structures

1. _____ is the study of the three dimensional distribution of rock bodies and their planar or folded surfaces, and their internal fabrics.
   a. Structural geology0
   b. Thing
   c. Undefined
   d. Undefined

2. _____ is the science and study of the solid matter that constitute the Earth. Encompassing such things as rocks, soil, and gemstones, _____ studies the composition, structure, physical properties, history, and the processes that shape Earth's components.
   a. Geology0
   b. Thing
   c. Undefined
   d. Undefined

3. In geology, a _____ is the outermost layer of a planet, part of its lithosphere. They are generally composed of a less dense material than its deeper layers. Earths' is composed mainly of basalt and granite. It is cooler and more rigid than the deeper layers of the mantle and core.
   a. Crust0
   b. Thing
   c. Undefined
   d. Undefined

4. _____ is the native consolidated rock underlying the Earth's surface. Above the _____ is usually an area of broken and weathered unconsolidated rock in the basal subsoil.
   a. Thing
   b. Bedrock0
   c. Undefined
   d. Undefined

5. _____ is a field of study within geology concerned generally with the structures within the crust of the Earth, or other planets, and particularly with the forces and movements that have operated in a region to create these structures.
   a. Tectonics0
   b. Thing
   c. Undefined
   d. Undefined

6. _____ is displacement of solids by the agents of ocean currents, wind, water, or ice by downward or down-slope movement in response to gravity or by living organisms.
   a. Erosion0
   b. Thing
   c. Undefined
   d. Undefined

7. _____ is the stress applied to materials resulting in their compaction, decrease of volume.
   a. Compression stress0
   b. Thing
   c. Undefined
   d. Undefined

8. _____ is a stress state where the stress is parallel or tangential to a face of the material, as opposed to normal stress when the stress is perpendicular to the face. The variable used to denote _____ is τ.
   a. Shear stress0
   b. Thing
   c. Undefined
   d. Undefined

9. Faults are planar rock fractures, which show evidence of relative movement. Large faults within the Earth's crust are the result of shear motion and active _____ zones are the causal locations of most earthquakes. Earthquakes are caused by energy release during rapid slippage along faults. The largest examples are at tectonic plate boundaries but many faults occur far from active plate boundaries. Since faults do not usually consist of a single, clean fracture, the term _____ zone is used when referring to the zone of complex deformation that is associated with the _____ plane.

Chapter 15. Geologic Structures

a. Fault0
b. Thing
c. Undefined
d. Undefined

10. _____ have the mechanical property of being capable of sustaining large plastic deformations due to tensile stress without fracture in metals, such as being drawn into a wire. It is characterized by the material flowing under shear stress. It is contrasted with brittleness.
   a. Ductile materials0
   b. Thing
   c. Undefined
   d. Undefined

11. _____ can be defined as the solid state recrystallisation of pre-existing rocks due to changes in heat and/or pressure and/or introduction of fluids. There will be mineralogical, chemical and crystallographic changes. _____ produced with increasing pressure and temperature conditions is known as prograde _____. Conversely, decreasing temperatures and pressure characterize retrograde _____.
   a. Thing
   b. Metamorphism0
   c. Undefined
   d. Undefined

12. _____ rock is one of the three main rock groups. Rock formed from these covers 75% of the Earth's land area, and includes common types such as chalk, limestone, dolomite, sandstone, and shale.
   a. Sedimentary0
   b. Thing
   c. Undefined
   d. Undefined

13. _____ is one of the three main rock groups. _____ covers 75% of the Earth's land area. Four basic processes are involved in the formation of a clastic _____: weathering caused mainly by friction of waves, transportation where the sediment is carried along by a current, deposition and compaction where the sediment is squashed together to form a rock of this kind.
   a. Sedimentary rock0
   b. Thing
   c. Undefined
   d. Undefined

14. The _____ is the solid outermost shell of a rocky planet. On the Earth, the _____ includes the crust and the uppermost mantle which is joined to the crust across the Mohorovièiæ discontinuity. _____ is underlain by asthenosphere, the weaker, hotter, and deeper part of the upper mantle.
   a. Lithosphere0
   b. Thing
   c. Undefined
   d. Undefined

15. A _____ is a landform that extends above the surrounding terrain in a limited area. A _____ is generally steeper than a hill, but there is no universally accepted standard definition for the height of a _____ or a hill although a _____ usually has an identifiable summit.
   a. Place
   b. Mountain0
   c. Undefined
   d. Undefined

16. The _____ is defined as the part of the land adjoining or near the ocean. A coastline is properly a line on a map indicating the disposition of a _____, but the word is often used to refer to the _____ itself. The adjective coastal describes something as being on, near to, or associated with a _____.
   a. Place
   b. Coast0
   c. Undefined
   d. Undefined

Chapter 15. Geologic Structures

17. An _____ is a long period of time with different technical and colloquial meanings, and usages in language. It begins with some beginning event known as an epoch, epochal date, epochal event or epochal moment.
   a. Thing
   b. Era0
   c. Undefined
   d. Undefined

18. The _____ Era meaning "new life", is the most recent of the three classic geological eras. It covers the 65.5 million years since the Cretaceous-Tertiary extinction event at the end of the Cretaceous that marked the demise of the last non-avian dinosaurs and the end of the Mesozoic Era. The _____ era is ongoing.
   a. Thing
   b. Cenozoic0
   c. Undefined
   d. Undefined

19. The _____ is the most recent of the three classic geological eras. It covers the 65.5 million years since the Cretaceous-Tertiary extinction event at the end of the Cretaceous that marked the demise of the last non-avian dinosaurs and the end of the Mesozoic Era.
   a. Cenozoic era0
   b. Thing
   c. Undefined
   d. Undefined

20. _____ is a naturally occurring liquid found in formations in the Earth consisting of a complex mixture of hydrocarbons of various lengths.
   a. Thing
   b. Petroleum0
   c. Undefined
   d. Undefined

21. An _____ is a volume of rock containing components or minerals in a mode of occurrence that renders it valuable for mining.
   a. Ore0
   b. Thing
   c. Undefined
   d. Undefined

22. A _____ is a special-purpose map made to show geological features. The stratigraphic contour lines are drawn on the surface of a selected deep stratum, so that they can show the topographic trends of the strata under the ground. It is not always possible to properly show this when the strata are extremely fractured, mixed, in some discontinuities, or where they are otherwise disturbed.
   a. Geologic map0
   b. Thing
   c. Undefined
   d. Undefined

23. _____ is molten rock expelled by a volcano during an eruption. When first extruded from a volcanic vent, it is a liquid at temperatures from 700 °C to 1,200 °C.
   a. Lava0
   b. Thing
   c. Undefined
   d. Undefined

24. _____ is the geological process whereby material is added to a landform. This is the process by which wind and water create a sediment deposit, through the laying down of granular material that has been eroded and transported from another geographical location.
   a. Deposition0
   b. Thing
   c. Undefined
   d. Undefined

Chapter 15. Geologic Structures

25. _____ is the process in which sediments compact under pressure, expel connate fluids, and gradually become solid rock.
    a. Thing
    b. Lithification0
    c. Undefined
    d. Undefined

26. _____ is the result of the transformation of a pre-existing rock type, the protolith, in a process called metamorphism, which means "change in form". The protolith is subjected to heat and extreme pressure causing profound physical and/or chemical change. The protolith may be sedimentary rock, igneous rock or another older rock.
    a. Metamorphic rock0
    b. Thing
    c. Undefined
    d. Undefined

27. A _____ is a naturally occurring substance formed through geological processes that has a characteristic chemical composition, a highly ordered atomic structure and specific physical properties. A rock, by comparison, is an aggregate of minerals and need not have a specific chemical composition. Minerals range in composition from pure elements and simple salts to very complex silicates with thousands of known forms.
    a. Thing
    b. Mineral0
    c. Undefined
    d. Undefined

28. An _____ is a fold that is convex up or to the youngest beds. Anticlines are usually recognized by a sequence of rock layers that are progressively older toward the center of the fold because the uplifted core of the fold is preferentially eroded to a deeper stratigraphic level relative to the topographically lower flanks. If an _____ plunges, the surface strata will form Vs that point in the direction of the plunge.
    a. Thing
    b. Anticline0
    c. Undefined
    d. Undefined

29. The term _____ is used in geology when one or a stack of originally flat and planar surfaces, such as sedimentary strata, are bent or curved as a result of plastic, i.e. permanent, deformation.
    a. Fold0
    b. Thing
    c. Undefined
    d. Undefined

30. In structural geology, a _____ is a downward-curving fold, with layers that dip toward the center of the structure. On a geologic map, synclines are recognized by a sequence of rock layers that grow progressively younger, followed by the youngest layer at the fold's center or hinge, and by a reverse sequence of the same rock layers on the opposite side of the hinge.
    a. Thing
    b. Syncline0
    c. Undefined
    d. Undefined

31. _____ is an igneous rock of volcanic origin. They often have a vesicular texture, which is the result voids left by volatiles escaping from the molten lava. Pumice is a rock, which is an example of explosive volcanic eruption. It is so vesicular that it floats in water.
    a. Thing
    b. Volcanic rock0
    c. Undefined
    d. Undefined

32. In geology, a _____ is a deformational feature consisting of symmetrically-dipping anticlines; their general outline on a geologic map is circular or oval.

Chapter 15. Geologic Structures

a. Dome0
c. Undefined
b. Thing
d. Undefined

33. The basic idea of this is that an object, event or entity can be spanned across multiple realities or universes. When combined, these multiple, unique, pan-dimensional segments of the object, consciousness or event, make up parts or constituents of its _____.
   a. Thing
   b. Superposition0
   c. Undefined
   d. Undefined

34. _____ is when long fractures form vertically in rock as it cools and contracts.
   a. Thing
   b. Columnar jointing0
   c. Undefined
   d. Undefined

35. _____ is a reaction force applied by a stretched string, rope or a similar object on the objects which stretch it. The direction of the force of it is parallel to the string, towards the string.
   a. Tension0
   b. Thing
   c. Undefined
   d. Undefined

36. _____ is the process of breaking down rocks, soils and their minerals through direct contact with the atmosphere. _____ occurs without movement. Two main classifications of _____ processes exist. Mechanical or physical _____ involves the breakdown of rocks and soils through direct contact with atmospheric conditions. The second classification, chemical _____, involves the direct effect of atmospheric chemicals in the breakdown of rocks, soils and minerals.
   a. Thing
   b. Weathering0
   c. Undefined
   d. Undefined

37. _____ is the second most common mineral in the Earth's continental crust. It is made up of a lattice of silica tetrahedra. _____ belongs to the rhombohedral crystal system. In nature _____ crystals are often twinned, distorted, or so intergrown with adjacent crystals of _____ or other minerals as to only show part of this shape, or to lack obvious crystal faces altogether and appear massive.
   a. Quartz0
   b. Thing
   c. Undefined
   d. Undefined

38. Most often, a _____ refers to an artificial lake, used to store water for various uses. Reservoirs are created first by building a sturdy dam, usually out of cement, earth, rock, or a mixture. Once the dam is completed, a stream is allowed to flow behind it and eventually fill it to capacity.
   a. Reservoir0
   b. Thing
   c. Undefined
   d. Undefined

39. _____ in meteorology are large scale patterns in the atmospheric pressure field that are nearly stationary, effectively "blocking" or redirecting migratory cyclones. These _____ can remain in place for several days or even weeks, causing the areas affected by them to have the same kind of weather for an extended period of time.
   a. Blocks0
   b. Thing
   c. Undefined
   d. Undefined

Chapter 15. Geologic Structures

40. A _____ is a depressed block of land bordered by parallel faults. A _____ is the result of a block of land being downthrown producing a valley with a distinct scarp on each side.
   a. Thing
   b. Graben0
   c. Undefined
   d. Undefined

41. A _____ is a geological feature that is also known as a Rip in the earth causing magma to flow out and forming an undersea volcano, it also has geological features, a continuous elevational crest for some distance. Ridges are usually termed hills or mountains as well, depending on size.
   a. Ridge0
   b. Thing
   c. Undefined
   d. Undefined

42. A _____ is a group of mountains bordered by lowlands or separated from other mountain ranges by passes or rivers. Individual mountains within the same _____ do not necessarily have the same geology; they may be a mix of different orogeny, for example volcanoes, uplifted mountains or fold mountains and may, therefore, be of different rock.
   a. Mountain range0
   b. Thing
   c. Undefined
   d. Undefined

43. In physical geography and geology, a _____ is the raised fault block bounded by normal faults. The raised block is a portion of the Earth's crust that has remained stationary while the land has sunk on either side of it or has been crushed by a mountain range against it.
   a. Horst0
   b. Thing
   c. Undefined
   d. Undefined

44. A _____ fault is a particular type of fault, or break in the fabric of the Earth's crust with resulting movement of each side against the other, in which a lower stratigraphic position is pushed up and over another. This is the result of compressional forces.
   a. Thing
   b. Thrust0
   c. Undefined
   d. Undefined

45. A _____ is a body of water with a current, confined within a bed and banks. Streams are important as conduits in the water cycle, instruments in aquifer recharge, and corridors for fish and wildlife migration.
   a. Stream0
   b. Thing
   c. Undefined
   d. Undefined

46. In geology, a _____ is a depression with predominant extent in one direction. The terms U-shaped and V-shaped are descriptive terms of geography to characterize the form of valleys. Most valleys belong to one of these two main types or a mixture of them, at least with respect of the cross section of the slopes or hillsides.
   a. Valley0
   b. Thing
   c. Undefined
   d. Undefined

47. A _____ is a geological fault that is a special case of strike-slip faulting which terminates abruptly, at both ends, at a major transverse geological feature. Also known as a conservative plate boundary.
   a. Thing
   b. Transform fault0
   c. Undefined
   d. Undefined

Chapter 16. Earthquakes

1. An _____ is the result from the sudden release of stored energy in the Earth's crust that creates seismic waves. At the Earth's surface, earthquakes may manifest themselves by a shaking or displacement of the ground. An _____ is caused by tectonic plates getting stuck and putting a strain on the ground. The strain becomes so great that rocks give way by breaking and sliding along fault planes.
   a. Earthquake0   b. Thing
   c. Undefined   d. Undefined

2. Faults are planar rock fractures, which show evidence of relative movement. Large faults within the Earth's crust are the result of shear motion and active _____ zones are the causal locations of most earthquakes. Earthquakes are caused by energy release during rapid slippage along faults. The largest examples are at tectonic plate boundaries but many faults occur far from active plate boundaries. Since faults do not usually consist of a single, clean fracture, the term _____ zone is used when referring to the zone of complex deformation that is associated with the _____ plane.
   a. Thing   b. Fault0
   c. Undefined   d. Undefined

3. _____ is any particulate matter that can be transported by fluid flow and which eventually is deposited as a layer of solid particles on the bed or bottom of a body of water or other liquid.
   a. Sediment0   b. Thing
   c. Undefined   d. Undefined

4. _____ in meteorology are large scale patterns in the atmospheric pressure field that are nearly stationary, effectively "blocking" or redirecting migratory cyclones. These _____ can remain in place for several days or even weeks, causing the areas affected by them to have the same kind of weather for an extended period of time.
   a. Thing   b. Blocks0
   c. Undefined   d. Undefined

5. A _____ is a series of waves created when a body of water, such as an ocean, is rapidly displaced on a massive scale. Earthquakes, mass movements above or below water, volcanic eruptions and other underwater explosions, landslides, large meteorite impacts and testing with nuclear weapons at sea all have the potential to generate a _____. The effects of a _____ can range from unnoticeable to devastating.
   a. Thing   b. Tsunami0
   c. Undefined   d. Undefined

6. In geology, a _____ is a depression with predominant extent in one direction. The terms U-shaped and V-shaped are descriptive terms of geography to characterize the form of valleys. Most valleys belong to one of these two main types or a mixture of them, at least with respect of the cross section of the slopes or hillsides.
   a. Thing   b. Valley0
   c. Undefined   d. Undefined

7. In geology, the _____ theory was the first theory to satisfactorily explain earthquakes. The theory is that earthquake are the result of the _____ of previously stored elastic strain energy in the rocks on either side of the fault. In an interseismic period the earth's plates move relative to each other except at most plate boundaries where they are locked.
   a. Thing   b. Elastic rebound0
   c. Undefined   d. Undefined

Chapter 16. Earthquakes

8. In geology, the _____ was the first theory to satisfactorily explain earthquakes. Previously it was thought that ruptures of the surface were the result of strong ground shaking rather than the converse suggested by this theory. An earthquake must have been the result of the elastic rebound of previously stored elastic strain energy in the rocks on either side of the fault. In an interseismic period the earth's plates move relative to each other except at most plate boundaries where they are locked.
   a. Elastic rebound theory0
   b. Thing
   c. Undefined
   d. Undefined

9. _____ is a field of study within geology concerned generally with the structures within the crust of the Earth, or other planets, and particularly with the forces and movements that have operated in a region to create these structures.
   a. Tectonics0
   b. Thing
   c. Undefined
   d. Undefined

10. _____ is molten rock located beneath the surface of the Earth, and which often collects in a _____ chamber. _____ is a complex high-temperature fluid substance. Most are silicate solutions. It is capable of intrusion into adjacent rocks or of extrusion onto the surface as lava or ejected explosively as tephra to form pyroclastic rock. Environments of _____ formation include subduction zones, continental rift zones, mid-oceanic ridges, and hotspots, some of which are interpreted as mantle plumes.
    a. Magma0
    b. Thing
    c. Undefined
    d. Undefined

11. Earth's _____ is a ~2,900 km thick rocky shell comprizing approximately 70% of Earth's volume. It is predominantly solid and overlies the Earth's iron-rich core, which occupies about 30% of Earth's volume. Past episodes of melting and volcanism at the shallower levels of the _____ have produced a very thin crust of crystallized melt products near the surface, upon which we live.
    a. Mantle0
    b. Thing
    c. Undefined
    d. Undefined

12. A _____ is a naturally occurring substance formed through geological processes that has a characteristic chemical composition, a highly ordered atomic structure and specific physical properties. A rock, by comparison, is an aggregate of minerals and need not have a specific chemical composition. Minerals range in composition from pure elements and simple salts to very complex silicates with thousands of known forms.
    a. Mineral0
    b. Thing
    c. Undefined
    d. Undefined

13. _____ is a group of common rock-forming hydrous magnesium iron phyllosilicate $|Mg, Fe|_3Si_2O_5|OH|_4$ minerals; it may contain minor amounts of other elements including chromium, manganese, cobalt and nickel. There are three important mineral polymorphs of _____: antigorite, chrysotile and lizardite.
    a. Thing
    b. Serpentine0
    c. Undefined
    d. Undefined

14. The _____ or hypocentre, may refer to the site of an earthquake or to that of a nuclear explosion. In the former, it is a synonym of the focus; in the latter of ground zero.
    a. Hypocenter0
    b. Thing
    c. Undefined
    d. Undefined

Chapter 16. Earthquakes

15. The _____ is the point on the Earth's surface that is directly above the point where an earthquake or other underground explosion originates or focus. It is directly above the hypocenter the actual location of the energy released inside the earth and usually suffers the maximum destruction.
    a. Epicenter0
    b. Thing
    c. Undefined
    d. Undefined

16. In physics, _____ can refer to a mechanical wave that propagates along the interface between differing media, usually two fluids with different densities. A _____ can also be an electromagnetic wave guided by a refractive index gradient.
    a. Thing
    b. Surface wave0
    c. Undefined
    d. Undefined

17. A _____ is a disturbance that propagates through space or spacetime, transferring energy and momentum and sometimes angular momentum.
    a. Thing
    b. Wave0
    c. Undefined
    d. Undefined

18. _____ are essentially horizontally polarized shear waves guided by an elastic layer, which is "welded" to an elastic half space on one side and borders vacuum on the other side.
    a. Love waves0
    b. Thing
    c. Undefined
    d. Undefined

19. _____ are a type of surface wave. They are associated on the Earth with earthquakes and subterranean movement of magma, or with any other source of seismic energy, such as an explosion or even a sledgehammer impact, and are also the form of ocean waves.
    a. Thing
    b. Rayleigh waves0
    c. Undefined
    d. Undefined

20. _____ is the property of an object to remain at constant velocity unless acted upon by an outside force. The principle of _____ is one of the fundamental principles of classical physics which are used to describe the motion of matter and how it is affected by applied forces.
    a. Inertia0
    b. Thing
    c. Undefined
    d. Undefined

21. A _____ is used by seismologists to measure and record the size and force of seismic waves.
    a. Seismograph0
    b. Thing
    c. Undefined
    d. Undefined

22. A _____ is a graph output by a seismograph. It is a record of the ground motion at a measuring station. The energy measured in a _____ may result from an earthquake or from some other source, such as an explosion.
    a. Seismogram0
    b. Thing
    c. Undefined
    d. Undefined

23. A _____ is a landform where the mouth of a river flows into an ocean, sea, desert, estuary or lake. It builds up sediment outwards into the flat area which the river's flow encounters transported by the water and set down as the currents slow.

Chapter 16. Earthquakes

 a. Thing
 b. Delta0
 c. Undefined
 d. Undefined

24. The _____ scale, or more correctly local magnitude ML scale, assigns a single number to quantify the amount of seismic energy released by an earthquake. It is a base-10 logarithmic scale obtained by calculating the logarithm of the combined horizontal amplitude of the largest displacement from zero on a seismometer output
 a. Thing
 b. Richter magnitude0
 c. Undefined
 d. Undefined

25. _____ is a quantity used by earthquake seismologists to measure the size of an earthquake.
 a. Thing
 b. Seismic moment0
 c. Undefined
 d. Undefined

26. _____ was introduced in 1979 by Tom Hanks and Hiroo Kanamori as a successor to the Richter scale and is used by seismologists to compare the energy released by earthquakes.
 a. Moment magnitude0
 b. Thing
 c. Undefined
 d. Undefined

27. In geology, a _____ is the outermost layer of a planet, part of its lithosphere. They are generally composed of a less dense material than its deeper layers.Earths' is composed mainly of basalt and granite. It is cooler and more rigid than the deeper layers of the mantle and core.
 a. Crust0
 b. Thing
 c. Undefined
 d. Undefined

28. In geology, engineering, and surveying, _____ is the motion of a surface as it shifts downward relative to a datum such as sea-level. The opposite of _____ is uplift, which results in an increase in elevation. In meteorology, _____ refers to the downward movement of air.
 a. Subsidence0
 b. Thing
 c. Undefined
 d. Undefined

29. Among the classifications of soil types, _____, is a fine, silty, windblown type of unconsolidated deposit. It is derived from glacial deposits, where glacial activity has ground rocks very fine. After drying, these deposits are highly susceptible to wind erosion, and downwind deposits may become very deep. _____ deposits are geologically unstable by nature, and will erode even without being disturbed by humans.
 a. Thing
 b. Loess0
 c. Undefined
 d. Undefined

30. _____ can be a change from a gas to a liquid through condensation, usually by cooling, or a change from a solid to a liquid through melting, usually by heating or by grinding and blending with another liquid to induce dissolution.
 a. Liquefaction0
 b. Thing
 c. Undefined
 d. Undefined

31. An _____ is a transition zone between different physiogeographic provinces that involves an elevation differential, often involving high cliffs. Most commonly, an _____, is a transition from one series of sedimentary rocks to another series of a different age and composition. In such cases, the _____ usually represents the line of erosional loss of the newer rock over the older.

Chapter 16. Earthquakes

    a. Thing
    b. Escarpment0
    c. Undefined
    d. Undefined

32. _____ are earthquakes in the same region of the central shock but of smaller magnitude and which occur with a pattern that follows Omori's law.
    a. Aftershocks0
    b. Thing
    c. Undefined
    d. Undefined

33. A _____ is a smaller earthquake preceding a much larger earthquake. Many scientists hope to use them to predict upcoming earthquakes.
    a. Foreshock0
    b. Thing
    c. Undefined
    d. Undefined

34. Mean _____ is the average height of the sea, with reference to a suitable reference surface.
    a. Sea level0
    b. Thing
    c. Undefined
    d. Undefined

35. In geology, a _____ zone is an area on Earth where two tectonic plates meet and move towards one another, with one sliding underneath the other and moving down into the mantle, at rates typically measured in centimeters per year. An oceanic plate ordinarily slides underneath a continental plate; this often creates an orogenic zone with many volcanoes and earthquakes.
    a. Subduction0
    b. Thing
    c. Undefined
    d. Undefined

36. A _____ is an area on Earth where two tectonic plates meet and move towards one another, with one sliding underneath the other and moving down into the mantle, at rates typically measured in centimeters per year. In a sense, subduction zones are the opposite of divergent boundaries, areas where material rises up from the mantle and plates are moving apart.
    a. Thing
    b. Subduction zone0
    c. Undefined
    d. Undefined

37. In physics, _____ is the distance between repeating units of a propagating wave of a given frequency. It is commonly designated by the Greek letter lambda. Examples of wave-like phenomena are light, water waves, and sound waves. _____ of a sine wave.In a wave, a property varies with the position.
    a. Wavelength0
    b. Thing
    c. Undefined
    d. Undefined

38. _____ is the study of Earth's surface features or those of other planets, moons, and asteroids
    a. Thing
    b. Topography0
    c. Undefined
    d. Undefined

39. The _____ is defined as the part of the land adjoining or near the ocean. A coastline is properly a line on a map indicating the disposition of a _____, but the word is often used to refer to the _____ itself. The adjective coastal describes something as being on, near to, or associated with a _____.

Chapter 16. Earthquakes

a. Place
b. Coast0
c. Undefined
d. Undefined

40. A _____ is a geological feature that is also known as a Rip in the earth causing magma to flow out and forming an undersea volcano, it also has geological features, a continuous elevational crest for some distance. Ridges are usually termed hills or mountains as well, depending on size.
a. Ridge0
b. Thing
c. Undefined
d. Undefined

41. A _____ is a landform that extends above the surrounding terrain in a limited area. A _____ is generally steeper than a hill, but there is no universally accepted standard definition for the height of a _____ or a hill although a _____ usually has an identifiable summit.
a. Mountain0
b. Place
c. Undefined
d. Undefined

42. A _____ is a group of mountains bordered by lowlands or separated from other mountain ranges by passes or rivers. Individual mountains within the same _____ do not necessarily have the same geology; they may be a mix of different orogeny, for example volcanoes, uplifted mountains or fold mountains and may, therefore, be of different rock.
a. Thing
b. Mountain range0
c. Undefined
d. Undefined

43. A _____ is a deep active seismic area in a subduction zone. Differential motion along the zone produces deep seated earthquakes, the foci of which may be as deep as about 435 miles. They develop beneath volcanic island arcs and continental margins above active subduction zones.
a. Thing
b. Benioff zone0
c. Undefined
d. Undefined

44. _____ is a theory of geology that has been developed to explain the observed evidence for large scale motions of the Earth's lithosphere. The theory encompassed and superseded the older theory of continental drift.
a. Thing
b. Plate tectonics0
c. Undefined
d. Undefined

45. A _____ is a type of excavation or depression in the ground. They are generally defined by being deeper than they are wide, and by being narrow compared to their length.
a. Thing
b. Trench0
c. Undefined
d. Undefined

46. In plate tectonics, a _____ a linear feature that exists between two tectonic plates that are moving away from each other. These areas can form in the middle of continents but eventually form ocean basins.
a. Thing
b. Divergent plate boundary0
c. Undefined
d. Undefined

47. In geology, a _____ is a place where the Earth's crust and lithosphere are being pulled apart.
a. Thing
b. Rift0
c. Undefined
d. Undefined

Chapter 16. Earthquakes

48. A _____ in geology is a valley created by the formation of a rift.
    a. Rift valley0
    b. Thing
    c. Undefined
    d. Undefined

49. In plate tectonics, a _____ is said to occur when tectonic plates slide and grind against each other along a transform fault. The relative motion of such plates is horizontal in either sinistral or dextral direction. Many transform boundaries are locked in tension before suddenly releasing, and causing earthquakes.
    a. Transform boundary0
    b. Thing
    c. Undefined
    d. Undefined

50. A _____ is a place where, through continental collision, two continental plates have joined together. The Himilayas and the Alps mark these zones as do other very high mountain ranges.
    a. Thing
    b. Suture zone0
    c. Undefined
    d. Undefined

51. _____ is a reaction force applied by a stretched string, rope or a similar object on the objects which stretch it. The direction of the force of it is parallel to the string, towards the string.
    a. Thing
    b. Tension0
    c. Undefined
    d. Undefined

52. The _____ is the solid outermost shell of a rocky planet. On the Earth, the _____ includes the crust and the uppermost mantle which is joined to the crust across the Mohorovièiæ discontinuity. _____ is underlain by asthenosphere, the weaker, hotter, and deeper part of the upper mantle.
    a. Thing
    b. Lithosphere0
    c. Undefined
    d. Undefined

53. In geology the term _____ refers to the system of forces that tend to decrease the volume of or shorten rocks. Compressive strength refers to the maximum compressive stress that can be applied to a material before failure occurs.
    a. Compression0
    b. Thing
    c. Undefined
    d. Undefined

54. The mineral _____ is a magnesium iron silicate. It is one of the most common minerals on Earth, and has also been identified on the Moon, Mars, and comet Wild 2.
    a. Thing
    b. Olivine0
    c. Undefined
    d. Undefined

55. _____ is the part of Earth's lithosphere that surfaces in the ocean basins. _____ is primarily composed of mafic rocks, or sima. It is thinner than continental crust, or sial, generally less than 10 kilometers thick, however it is more dense, having a mean density of about 3.3 grams per cubic centimeter.
    a. Oceanic crust0
    b. Thing
    c. Undefined
    d. Undefined

56. A _____ is an area of highland, usually consisting of relatively flat rural area.
    a. Plateau0
    b. Place
    c. Undefined
    d. Undefined

Chapter 16. Earthquakes

57. _____ is one of the phenomena by which materials exert attractive or repulsive forces on other materials. Some well known materials that exhibit easily detectable magnetic properties are nickel, iron, some steels, and the mineral magnetite; however, all materials are influenced to greater or lesser degree by the presence of a magnetic field.
   a. Magnetism0
   b. Thing
   c. Undefined
   d. Undefined

58. _____ is a measure of the void spaces in a material, and is measured as a fraction, between 0–1, or as a percentage between 0–100%.
   a. Porosity0
   b. Thing
   c. Undefined
   d. Undefined

59. _____ is the process in which an unstable atomic nucleus loses energy by emitting radiation in the form of particles or electromagnetic waves.
   a. Radioactive decay0
   b. Thing
   c. Undefined
   d. Undefined

60. A _____ is a type of hot spring that erupts periodically, ejecting a column of hot water and steam into the air.
   a. Geyser0
   b. Thing
   c. Undefined
   d. Undefined

61. _____ is the geomorphic process by which soil, regolith, and rock move downslope under the force of gravity. Types of _____ include creep, slides, flows, topples, and falls, each with their own characteristic features, and take place over timescales from seconds to years. _____ occurs on both terrestrial and submarine slopes, and has been observed on Earth, Mars, and Venus.
   a. Mass wasting0
   b. Thing
   c. Undefined
   d. Undefined

Chapter 17. Earth's Interior and Geophysical Properties

1. Earth's _____ is a ~2,900 km thick rocky shell comprizing approximately 70% of Earth's volume. It is predominantly solid and overlies the Earth's iron-rich core, which occupies about 30% of Earth's volume. Past episodes of melting and volcanism at the shallower levels of the _____ have produced a very thin crust of crystallized melt products near the surface, upon which we live.
   a. Mantle0
   b. Thing
   c. Undefined
   d. Undefined

2. _____ is a common gray to black extrusive volcanic rock. It is usually fine-grained due to rapid cooling of lava on the Earth's surface. It may be porphyritic containing larger crystals in a fine matrix, or vesicular, or frothy scoria.
   a. Basalt0
   b. Thing
   c. Undefined
   d. Undefined

3. An _____ is a body of igneous rock that has crystallized from a molten magma below the surface of the Earth.
   a. Intrusion0
   b. Thing
   c. Undefined
   d. Undefined

4. _____ is displacement of solids by the agents of ocean currents, wind, water, or ice by downward or down-slope movement in response to gravity or by living organisms.
   a. Erosion0
   b. Thing
   c. Undefined
   d. Undefined

5. The _____ is the solid outermost shell of a rocky planet. On the Earth, the _____ includes the crust and the uppermost mantle which is joined to the crust across the Mohorovièiæ discontinuity. _____ is underlain by asthenosphere, the weaker, hotter, and deeper part of the upper mantle.
   a. Thing
   b. Lithosphere0
   c. Undefined
   d. Undefined

6. The _____ is the layer of granitic, sedimentary, and metamorphic rocks which form the continents and the areas of shallow seabed close to their shores, known as continental shelves. It is less dense than the material of the Earth's mantle and thus "floats" on top of it. _____ is also less dense than oceanic crust, though it is considerably thicker. About 40% of the Earth's surface is now underlain by _____.
   a. Continental crust0
   b. Thing
   c. Undefined
   d. Undefined

7. In geology, a _____ is the outermost layer of a planet, part of its lithosphere. They are generally composed of a less dense material than its deeper layers. Earths' is composed mainly of basalt and granite. It is cooler and more rigid than the deeper layers of the mantle and core.
   a. Thing
   b. Crust0
   c. Undefined
   d. Undefined

8. _____ is a theory of geology that has been developed to explain the observed evidence for large scale motions of the Earth's lithosphere. The theory encompassed and superseded the older theory of continental drift.
   a. Plate tectonics0
   b. Thing
   c. Undefined
   d. Undefined

Chapter 17. Earth's Interior and Geophysical Properties

9. In plate tectonics, a _____ is an actively deforming region where two tectonic plates or fragments of lithosphere move towards one another. When two plates move toward one another, they form either a subduction zone or a continental collision.
   a. Convergent boundary0
   b. Thing
   c. Undefined
   d. Undefined

10. _____ is the science and study of the solid matter that constitute the Earth. Encompassing such things as rocks, soil, and gemstones, _____ studies the composition, structure, physical properties, history, and the processes that shape Earth's components.
    a. Geology0
    b. Thing
    c. Undefined
    d. Undefined

11. In physics, a _____ is a solenoidal vector field in the space surrounding moving electric charges and magnetic dipoles, such as those in electric currents and magnets.
    a. Magnetic field0
    b. Thing
    c. Undefined
    d. Undefined

12. _____ is one of the phenomena by which materials exert attractive or repulsive forces on other materials. Some well known materials that exhibit easily detectable magnetic properties are nickel, iron, some steels, and the mineral magnetite; however, all materials are influenced to greater or lesser degree by the presence of a magnetic field.
    a. Thing
    b. Magnetism0
    c. Undefined
    d. Undefined

13. _____, in everyday life, is most familiar as the agency that endows objects with weight. _____ is responsible for keeping the Earth and the other planets in their orbits around the Sun; for the formation of tides; and for various other phenomena that we observe. _____ is also the reason for the very existence of the Earth, the Sun, and most macroscopic objects in the universe; without it, matter would not have coalesced into these large masses, and life, as we know it, would not exist.
    a. Gravitation0
    b. Thing
    c. Undefined
    d. Undefined

14. An _____ is the result from the sudden release of stored energy in the Earth's crust that creates seismic waves. At the Earth's surface, earthquakes may manifest themselves by a shaking or displacement of the ground. An _____ is caused by tectonic plates getting stuck and putting a strain on the ground. The strain becomes so great that rocks give way by breaking and sliding along fault planes.
    a. Earthquake0
    b. Thing
    c. Undefined
    d. Undefined

15. _____ is a method of exploration geophysics that uses the principles of seismology to estimate the properties of the Earth's subsurface from reflected seismic waves. The method requires a controlled seismic source of energy, such as dynamite or a specialized air gun.
    a. Seismic reflection0
    b. Thing
    c. Undefined
    d. Undefined

16. A _____ is a graph output by a seismograph. It is a record of the ground motion at a measuring station. The energy measured in a _____ may result from an earthquake or from some other source, such as an explosion.

Chapter 17. Earth's Interior and Geophysical Properties

a. Thing
b. Seismogram0
c. Undefined
d. Undefined

17. _____ is the change in direction of a wave due to a change in its speed. This is most commonly seen when a wave passes from one medium to another.
a. Thing
b. Refraction0
c. Undefined
d. Undefined

18. A _____ travels through the Earth, most often as the result of a tectonic earthquake, sometimes from an explosion. They are also continually excited by the pounding of ocean waves and the wind.
a. Seismic wave0
b. Thing
c. Undefined
d. Undefined

19. A _____ is a disturbance that propagates through space or spacetime, transferring energy and momentum and sometimes angular momentum.
a. Thing
b. Wave0
c. Undefined
d. Undefined

20. A _____ is used by seismologists to measure and record the size and force of seismic waves.
a. Seismograph0
b. Thing
c. Undefined
d. Undefined

21. The _____ is the point on the Earth's surface that is directly above the point where an earthquake or other underground explosion originates or focus. It is directly above the hypocenter the actual location of the energy released inside the earth and usually suffers the maximum destruction.
a. Thing
b. Epicenter0
c. Undefined
d. Undefined

22. _____ is the part of Earth's lithosphere that surfaces in the ocean basins. _____ is primarily composed of mafic rocks, or sima. It is thinner than continental crust, or sial, generally less than 10 kilometers thick, however it is more dense, having a mean density of about 3.3 grams per cubic centimeter.
a. Thing
b. Oceanic crust0
c. Undefined
d. Undefined

23. _____ is a dark, coarse-grained, intrusive igneous rock chemically equivalent to basalt. It is a plutonic rock, formed when molten magma is trapped beneath the Earth's surface and cools into a crystalline mass.
a. Gabbro0
b. Thing
c. Undefined
d. Undefined

24. _____ is a common and widely occurring type of intrusive, felsic, igneous rock. Granites are usually medium to coarsely crystalline, occasionally with some individual crystals larger than the groundmass forming a rock known as porphyry. Granites can be pink to dark gray or even black, depending on their chemistry and mineralogy.
a. Thing
b. Granite0
c. Undefined
d. Undefined

Chapter 17. Earth's Interior and Geophysical Properties

25. _____ is a common and widely distributed type of rock formed by high-grade regional metamorphic processes from preexisting formations that were originally either igneous or sedimentary rocks. Gneissic rocks are usually medium to coarse foliated and largely recrystallized but do not carry large quantities of micas, chlorite or other platy minerals.
    a. Thing
    b. Gneiss0
    c. Undefined
    d. Undefined

26. _____ rock is one of the three main rock groups. Rock formed from these covers 75% of the Earth's land area, and includes common types such as chalk, limestone, dolomite, sandstone, and shale.
    a. Sedimentary0
    b. Thing
    c. Undefined
    d. Undefined

27. _____ is one of the three main rock groups. _____ covers 75% of the Earth's land area. Four basic processes are involved in the formation of a clastic _____: weathering caused mainly by friction of waves, transportation where the sediment is carried along by a current, deposition and compaction where the sediment is squashed together to form a rock of this kind.
    a. Thing
    b. Sedimentary rock0
    c. Undefined
    d. Undefined

28. _____ is a term used in geology to refer to silicate minerals, magmas, and rocks which are enriched in the lighter elements such as silica, oxygen, aluminium, sodium, and potassium. _____ minerals are usually light in color and have specific gravities less than 3. Common _____ minerals include quartz, muscovite, orthoclase, and the sodium rich plagioclase feldspars.
    a. Thing
    b. Felsic0
    c. Undefined
    d. Undefined

29. In geology, _____ minerals and rocks are silicate minerals, magmas, and volcanic and intrusive igneous rocks that have relatively high concentrations of the heavier elements. The term is a combination of "magnesium" and ferrum.
    a. Mafic0
    b. Thing
    c. Undefined
    d. Undefined

30. A _____ is a landform that extends above the surrounding terrain in a limited area. A _____ is generally steeper than a hill, but there is no universally accepted standard definition for the height of a _____ or a hill although a _____ usually has an identifiable summit.
    a. Place
    b. Mountain0
    c. Undefined
    d. Undefined

31. _____ is a field of study within geology concerned generally with the structures within the crust of the Earth, or other planets, and particularly with the forces and movements that have operated in a region to create these structures.
    a. Tectonics0
    b. Thing
    c. Undefined
    d. Undefined

32. The _____ is the boundary between the Earth's crust and the mantle. The _____ serves to separate both oceanic crust and continental crust from underlying mantle. It mostly lies entirely within the lithosphere; only beneath mid-ocean ridges does the _____ also define the mesosphere-asthenosphere boundary.

Chapter 17. Earth's Interior and Geophysical Properties

    a. Thing
    b. Mohorovicic Discontinuity0
    c. Undefined
    d. Undefined

33. _____ is molten rock located beneath the surface of the Earth, and which often collects in a _____ chamber. _____ is a complex high-temperature fluid substance. Most are silicate solutions. It is capable of intrusion into adjacent rocks or of extrusion onto the surface as lava or ejected explosively as tephra to form pyroclastic rock. Environments of _____ formation include subduction zones, continental rift zones, mid-oceanic ridges, and hotspots, some of which are interpreted as mantle plumes.
    a. Magma0
    b. Thing
    c. Undefined
    d. Undefined

34. _____ is a dense, coarse-grained igneous rock, consisting mostly of the minerals olivine and pyroxene. _____ is ultramafic and ultrabasic, as the rock contains less than 45% silica. This type of rock is derived from the Earth's mantle, either as solid blocks and fragments, or as crystals accumulated from magmas that formed in the mantle.
    a. Peridotite0
    b. Thing
    c. Undefined
    d. Undefined

35. _____ rocks form when molten rock, magma, cools and solidifies, with or without crystallization, either below the surface as intrusive, plutonic rocks or on the surface as extrusive, volcanic, rocks.
    a. Igneous0
    b. Thing
    c. Undefined
    d. Undefined

36. _____ forms when rock cools and solidifies either below the surface as intrusive rocks or on the surface as extrusive rocks. This magma can be derived from partial melts of pre-existing rocks in either the Earth's mantle or crust. Typically, the melting is caused by one or more of the following processes -- an increase in temperature, a decrease in pressure, or a change in composition.
    a. Igneous rock0
    b. Thing
    c. Undefined
    d. Undefined

37. The mineral _____ is a magnesium iron silicate. It is one of the most common minerals on Earth, and has also been identified on the Moon, Mars, and comet Wild 2.
    a. Thing
    b. Olivine0
    c. Undefined
    d. Undefined

38. The _____ is the region of the Earth between 100-200 km below the surface that is the weak or "soft" zone in the upper mantle. It lies just below the lithosphere, which is involved in plate movements and isostatic adjustments. In spite of its heat, pressures keep it plastic, and it has a relatively low density. Seismic waves pass relatively slowly through the _____.
    a. Asthenosphere0
    b. Thing
    c. Undefined
    d. Undefined

39. A _____ is a solid in which the constituent atoms, molecules, or ions are packed in a regularly ordered, repeating pattern extending in all three spatial dimensions. Most metals encountered in everyday life are polycrystals. Crystals are often symmetrically intergrown to form _____ twins.

a. Crystal0
b. Thing
c. Undefined
d. Undefined

40. _____ uses digital seismographic records to image the interior of the Earth. The basic scheme is to first localize and characterize a set of significant earthquakes. These earthquakes are then considered to "illuminate" the interior of the earth with seismic waves.
   a. Seismic tomography0
   b. Thing
   c. Undefined
   d. Undefined

41. _____ is imaging by sections or sectioning. A device used in _____ is called a tomograph, while the image produced is a tomogram. In most cases it is based on the mathematical procedure called tomographic reconstruction.
   a. Thing
   b. Tomography0
   c. Undefined
   d. Undefined

42. A _____ is a naturally occurring substance formed through geological processes that has a characteristic chemical composition, a highly ordered atomic structure and specific physical properties. A rock, by comparison, is an aggregate of minerals and need not have a specific chemical composition. Minerals range in composition from pure elements and simple salts to very complex silicates with thousands of known forms.
   a. Mineral0
   b. Thing
   c. Undefined
   d. Undefined

43. A _____ is an area in which an S-Wave or secondary seismic wave, is not detected due to it not being able to pass through the core of the earth.
   a. Shadow zone0
   b. Thing
   c. Undefined
   d. Undefined

44. The _____ is a primarily solid sphere about 1220 km in radius situated at Earth's center. The existence of an _____ that is different from the liquid outer core was discovered in 1936 by seismologist Inge Lehman using observations of earthquake-generated seismic waves that partly reflect from its boundary and can be detected by sensitive instruments at Earth's surface called seismographs.
   a. Thing
   b. Inner core0
   c. Undefined
   d. Undefined

45. In geology and astronomy, the term _____ is used to denote types of rock that consist predominantly of _____ minerals. Such rocks include a wide range of igneous, metamorphic and sedimentary types. Most of the Earth's mantle and crust are made up of _____ rocks. The same is true of the Moon and the other rocky planets.
   a. Silicate0
   b. Thing
   c. Undefined
   d. Undefined

46. An _____ is a type of atom that is defined by its atomic number; that is, by the number of protons in its nucleus.
   a. Thing
   b. Element0
   c. Undefined
   d. Undefined

47. A _____ is a natural object originating in outer space that survives an impact with the Earth's surface without being destroyed. While in space it is called a meteoroid. When it enters the atmosphere, air resistance causes the body to heat up and emit light, thus forming a fireball.

Chapter 17. Earth's Interior and Geophysical Properties

a. Thing
b. Meteorite0
c. Undefined
d. Undefined

48. In seismology, the region between about 410 km and 660 km depth, the lower part of the upper mantle, is called the _____.
a. Thing
b. Transition zone0
c. Undefined
d. Undefined

49. _____ is any particulate matter that can be transported by fluid flow and which eventually is deposited as a layer of solid particles on the bed or bottom of a body of water or other liquid.
a. Sediment0
b. Thing
c. Undefined
d. Undefined

50. A _____ is an upwelling of abnormally hot rock within the Earth's mantle. As the heads of mantle plumes can partly melt when they reach shallow depths, they are thought to be the cause of volcanic centers known as hotspots and probably also to have caused flood basalts.
a. Mantle plume0
b. Event
c. Undefined
d. Undefined

51. _____ is a term used in Geology to refer to the state of gravitational equilibrium between the Earth's lithosphere and asthenosphere such that the tectonic plates "float" at an elevation which depends on their thickness and density. It is invoked to explain how different topographic heights can exist at the Earth's surface.
a. Isostasy0
b. Thing
c. Undefined
d. Undefined

52. _____ is the condition of a system in which competing influences are balanced.
a. Equilibrium0
b. Thing
c. Undefined
d. Undefined

53. _____ in meteorology are large scale patterns in the atmospheric pressure field that are nearly stationary, effectively "blocking" or redirecting migratory cyclones. These _____ can remain in place for several days or even weeks, causing the areas affected by them to have the same kind of weather for an extended period of time.
a. Blocks0
b. Thing
c. Undefined
d. Undefined

54. _____ is the rise of land masses that were depressed by the huge weight of ice sheets during the last ice age, through a process known as isostatic depression. It affects northern Europe, especially Scotland and Scandinavia, Siberia, Canada, and the Great Lakes of Canada and the United States.
a. Thing
b. Post glacial rebound0
c. Undefined
d. Undefined

55. _____ is the rise of land masses that were depressed by the huge weight of ice sheets during the last ice age, through a process known as isostatic depression.
a. Thing
b. Post-glacial rebound0
c. Undefined
d. Undefined

Chapter 17. Earth's Interior and Geophysical Properties

56. A _____ is a group of mountains bordered by lowlands or separated from other mountain ranges by passes or rivers. Individual mountains within the same _____ do not necessarily have the same geology; they may be a mix of different orogeny, for example volcanoes, uplifted mountains or fold mountains and may, therefore, be of different rock.
  a. Thing
  b. Mountain range0
  c. Undefined
  d. Undefined

57. _____ is a measure of the resistance of a fluid to deform under shear stress. It is commonly perceived as "thickness", or resistance to flow. _____ describes a fluid's internal resistance to flow and may be thought of as a measure of fluid friction.
  a. Viscosity0
  b. Thing
  c. Undefined
  d. Undefined

58. The _____ on the geologic timescale had been intended to cover the world's recent period of repeated glaciations. The _____ follows the Pliocene and is followed by the Holocene. The _____ is the third epoch of the Neogene period or 6th epoch of the Cenozoic era. The end of the _____ corresponds with the end of the Paleolithic age used in archaeology. The _____ is divided into the Early _____, Middle _____ and Late _____, and numerous faunal stages.
  a. Thing
  b. Pleistocene0
  c. Undefined
  d. Undefined

59. _____ can refer to: a period of time; a distinctive historical period or era, a unit of the geologic time scale, less than a period and greater than an age, or a phase in the development of the universe with distinctive properties.
  a. Epoch0
  b. Thing
  c. Undefined
  d. Undefined

60. In geology, a _____ zone is an area on Earth where two tectonic plates meet and move towards one another, with one sliding underneath the other and moving down into the mantle, at rates typically measured in centimeters per year. An oceanic plate ordinarily slides underneath a continental plate; this often creates an orogenic zone with many volcanoes and earthquakes.
  a. Subduction0
  b. Thing
  c. Undefined
  d. Undefined

61. _____ is molten rock expelled by a volcano during an eruption. When first extruded from a volcanic vent, it is a liquid at temperatures from 700 °C to 1,200 °C.
  a. Thing
  b. Lava0
  c. Undefined
  d. Undefined

62. An _____ is a volume of rock containing components or minerals in a mode of occurrence that renders it valuable for mining.
  a. Ore0
  b. Thing
  c. Undefined
  d. Undefined

63. Mean _____ is the average height of the sea, with reference to a suitable reference surface.
  a. Sea level0
  b. Thing
  c. Undefined
  d. Undefined

64. An _____ phenomenon is an observed event which deviates from what is expected according to existing rules or scientific theory.
   a. Thing
   b. Anomalous0
   c. Undefined
   d. Undefined

65. The _____ is a term in physics and materials science and refers to a characteristic property of a ferromagnetic or piezoelectric material.
   a. Thing
   b. Curie point0
   c. Undefined
   d. Undefined

66. _____ is a ferrimagnetic mineral one of several iron oxides and a member of the spinel group. The chemical IUPAC name is iron oxide and the common chemical name ferrous-ferric oxide.
   a. Thing
   b. Magnetite0
   c. Undefined
   d. Undefined

67. _____ refers to the study of the record of the Earth's magnetic field preserved in various magnetic minerals through time. The study of _____ has demonstrated that the Earth's magnetic field varies substantially in both orientation and intensity through time.
   a. Paleomagnetism0
   b. Thing
   c. Undefined
   d. Undefined

68. _____ are a class of astronomical objects. The term is generally used to indicate a diverse group of small celestial bodies that drift in the solar system in orbit around the Sun.
   a. Asteroids0
   b. Thing
   c. Undefined
   d. Undefined

69. _____ are small bodies in the solar system that orbit the Sun and occasionally exhibit a coma or atmosphere and/or a tail — both primarily from the effects of solar radiation upon its nucleus, which itself is a minor body composed of rock, dust, and ice.
   a. Comets0
   b. Thing
   c. Undefined
   d. Undefined

70. A _____ is a scientific instrument used to measure the strength and/or direction of the magnetic field in the vicinity of the instrument.
   a. Thing
   b. Magnetometer0
   c. Undefined
   d. Undefined

71. _____ is a sedimentary rock composed largely of the mineral calcite. _____ often contains variable amounts of silica in the form of chert or flint, as well as varying amounts of clay, silt and sand as disseminations, nodules, or layers within the rock. The primary source of the calcite in _____ is most commonly marine organisms. These organisms secrete shells that settle out of the water column and are deposited on ocean floors as pelagic ooze or alternatively is conglomerated in a coral reef.
   a. Limestone0
   b. Thing
   c. Undefined
   d. Undefined

Chapter 17. Earth's Interior and Geophysical Properties

72. A _____ is an intrusion into a cross-cutting fissure, meaning a _____ cuts across other pre-existing layers or bodies of rock, this means that a _____ is always younger than the rocks that contain it. The thickness is usually much smaller than the other two dimensions. Thickness can vary from sub-centimeter scale to many meters in thickness and the lateral dimensions can extend over many kilometers.
   a. Thing
   b. Dike0
   c. Undefined
   d. Undefined

73. Faults are planar rock fractures, which show evidence of relative movement. Large faults within the Earth's crust are the result of shear motion and active _____ zones are the causal locations of most earthquakes. Earthquakes are caused by energy release during rapid slippage along faults. The largest examples are at tectonic plate boundaries but many faults occur far from active plate boundaries. Since faults do not usually consist of a single, clean fracture, the term _____ zone is used when referring to the zone of complex deformation that is associated with the _____ plane.
   a. Thing
   b. Fault0
   c. Undefined
   d. Undefined

74. A _____ is a depressed block of land bordered by parallel faults. A _____ is the result of a block of land being downthrown producing a valley with a distinct scarp on each side.
   a. Thing
   b. Graben0
   c. Undefined
   d. Undefined

75. In geology, _____ refers to heat sources within the planet. The planet's internal heat was originally generated during its accretion, due to gravitational binding energy, and since then additional heat has continued to be generated by the radioactive decay of elements such as uranium, thorium, and potassium.
   a. Thing
   b. Geothermal0
   c. Undefined
   d. Undefined

76. The _____ is the rate of increase in temperature per unit depth in the Earth. It varies with location and is typically measured by determining the bottom open-hole temperature after the drilling of a borehole.
   a. Thing
   b. Geothermal gradient0
   c. Undefined
   d. Undefined

77. _____ is the use of geothermal heat to generate electricity.
   a. Geothermal power0
   b. Thing
   c. Undefined
   d. Undefined

78. An _____ is a layer of gases that may surround a material body of sufficient mass. The gases are attracted by the gravity of the body, and are retained for a longer duration if gravity is high and the _____'s temperature is low. Some planets consist mainly of various gases, and thus have very deep atmospheres.
   a. Atmosphere0
   b. Place
   c. Undefined
   d. Undefined

79. _____ are any of the several different forms of an element each having different atomic mass. _____ of an element have nuclei with the same number of protons but different numbers of neutrons.
   a. Isotopes0
   b. Thing
   c. Undefined
   d. Undefined

Chapter 17. Earth's Interior and Geophysical Properties

80. _____ is the process in which an unstable atomic nucleus loses energy by emitting radiation in the form of particles or electromagnetic waves.
- a. Thing
- b. Radioactive decay0
- c. Undefined
- d. Undefined

81. A _____ in geology is an intrusive igneous rock body that crystallized from a magma below the surface of the Earth. Plutons include batholiths, dikes, sills, laccoliths, lopoliths, and other igneous bodies. In practice, "_____" usually refers to a distinctive mass of igneous rock, typically kilometers in dimension, without a tabular shape like those of dikes and sills.
- a. Thing
- b. Pluton0
- c. Undefined
- d. Undefined

82. A _____ is a geological feature that is also known as a Rip in the earth causing magma to flow out and forming an undersea volcano, it also has geological features, a continuous elevational crest for some distance. Ridges are usually termed hills or mountains as well, depending on size.
- a. Thing
- b. Ridge0
- c. Undefined
- d. Undefined

Chapter 18. The Sea Floor

1. _____ is any particulate matter that can be transported by fluid flow and which eventually is deposited as a layer of solid particles on the bed or bottom of a body of water or other liquid.
   a. Thing
   b. Sediment0
   c. Undefined
   d. Undefined

2. _____ is the study of Earth's surface features or those of other planets, moons, and asteroids
   a. Topography0
   b. Thing
   c. Undefined
   d. Undefined

3. _____ is a field of study within geology concerned generally with the structures within the crust of the Earth, or other planets, and particularly with the forces and movements that have operated in a region to create these structures.
   a. Tectonics0
   b. Thing
   c. Undefined
   d. Undefined

4. _____ is a theory of geology that has been developed to explain the observed evidence for large scale motions of the Earth's lithosphere. The theory encompassed and superseded the older theory of continental drift.
   a. Thing
   b. Plate tectonics0
   c. Undefined
   d. Undefined

5. _____ is the science and study of the solid matter that constitute the Earth. Encompassing such things as rocks, soil, and gemstones, _____ studies the composition, structure, physical properties, history, and the processes that shape Earth's components.
   a. Thing
   b. Geology0
   c. Undefined
   d. Undefined

6. _____ is the technique of using sound pulses directed from the surface or from a submarine vertically down to measure the distance to the bottom by means of sound waves.
   a. Thing
   b. Echo sounding0
   c. Undefined
   d. Undefined

7. _____ are where one sedimetary deposit ends and another one begins. The rock is prone to breakage at these points because of the weakness between the layers.
   a. Thing
   b. Bedding planes0
   c. Undefined
   d. Undefined

8. _____, in everyday life, is most familiar as the agency that endows objects with weight. _____ is responsible for keeping the Earth and the other planets in their orbits around the Sun; for the formation of tides; and for various other phenomena that we observe. _____ is also the reason for the very existence of the Earth, the Sun, and most macroscopic objects in the universe; without it, matter would not have coalesced into these large masses, and life, as we know it, would not exist.
   a. Thing
   b. Gravitation0
   c. Undefined
   d. Undefined

9. _____ is the change in direction of a wave due to a change in its speed. This is most commonly seen when a wave passes from one medium to another.

a. Thing
b. Refraction0
c. Undefined
d. Undefined

10. The _____ is defined as the part of the land adjoining or near the ocean. A coastline is properly a line on a map indicating the disposition of a _____, but the word is often used to refer to the _____ itself. The adjective coastal describes something as being on, near to, or associated with a _____.
   a. Coast0
   b. Place
   c. Undefined
   d. Undefined

11. The _____ is the extended perimeter of each continent and associated coastal plain, which is covered during interglacial periods such as the current epoch by relatively shallow seas and gulfs. The shelf usually ends at a point of increasing slope.
   a. Thing
   b. Continental shelf0
   c. Undefined
   d. Undefined

12. The sea floor below the break is the _____. Below the slope is the continental rise, which finally merges into the deep ocean floor, the abyssal plain. As the continental shelf and the slope are part of the continental margin, both are covered in this article.
   a. Continental slope0
   b. Thing
   c. Undefined
   d. Undefined

13. The continental shelf is the extended perimeter of each continent and associated coastal plain, which is covered during interglacial periods such as the current epoch by relatively shallow seas and gulfs. The shelf usually ends at a point of increasing slope. The sea floor below the break is the continental slope. Below the slope is the _____, which finally merges into the deep ocean floor, the abyssal plain. As the continental shelf and the slope are part of the continental margin, both are covered in this article.
   a. Thing
   b. Continental rise0
   c. Undefined
   d. Undefined

14. The _____ is the pelagic zone that contains the very deep benthic communities near the bottom of oceans.
   a. Thing
   b. Abyssal0
   c. Undefined
   d. Undefined

15. An _____ is a flat or very gently sloping area of the deep ocean basin floor. They are among the Earth's flattest and smoothest regions and the least explored. They cover approximately 40% of the ocean floor and generally lie between the foot of a continental rise and a mid-oceanic ridge.
   a. Abyssal plain0
   b. Thing
   c. Undefined
   d. Undefined

16. A _____ is a type of excavation or depression in the ground. They are generally defined by being deeper than they are wide, and by being narrow compared to their length.
   a. Thing
   b. Trench0
   c. Undefined
   d. Undefined

Chapter 18. The Sea Floor

17. The _____ are hemispheric-scale long but narrow topographic depressions of the sea floor. They are also the deepest parts of the ocean floor. Trenches define one of the most important natural boundaries on the Earth's solid surface, that between two lithospheric plates. There are three types of lithospheric plate boundaries: divergent, convergent, and transform. Trenches are the spectacular and distinctive morphological features of convergent plate boundaries.
   a. Thing
   b. Oceanic trenches0
   c. Undefined
   d. Undefined

18. A _____ is a geological feature that is also known as a Rip in the earth causing magma to flow out and forming an undersea volcano, it also has geological features, a continuous elevational crest for some distance. Ridges are usually termed hills or mountains as well, depending on size.
   a. Ridge0
   b. Thing
   c. Undefined
   d. Undefined

19. Mean _____ is the average height of the sea, with reference to a suitable reference surface.
   a. Thing
   b. Sea level0
   c. Undefined
   d. Undefined

20. The _____ on the geologic timescale had been intended to cover the world's recent period of repeated glaciations. The _____ follows the Pliocene and is followed by the Holocene. The _____ is the third epoch of the Neogene period or 6th epoch of the Cenozoic era. The end of the _____ corresponds with the end of the Paleolithic age used in archaeology. The _____ is divided into the Early _____, Middle _____ and Late _____, and numerous faunal stages.
   a. Pleistocene0
   b. Thing
   c. Undefined
   d. Undefined

21. _____ can refer to: a period of time; a distinctive historical period or era, a unit of the geologic time scale, less than a period and greater than an age, or a phase in the development of the universe with distinctive properties.
   a. Thing
   b. Epoch0
   c. Undefined
   d. Undefined

22. _____ is a sedimentary rock composed mainly of sand-size mineral or rock grains. Most _____ is composed of quartz and/or feldspar because these are the most common minerals in the Earth's crust. Like sand, _____ may be any color, but the most common colors are tan, brown, yellow, red, gray and white.
   a. Sandstone0
   b. Thing
   c. Undefined
   d. Undefined

23. _____ is a fine-grained sedimentary rock whose original constituents were clays or muds. It is characterized by thin laminae breaking with an irregular curving fracture, often splintery and usually parallel to the often-indistinguishable bedding plane.
   a. Thing
   b. Shale0
   c. Undefined
   d. Undefined

Chapter 18. The Sea Floor

24. _____ is a sedimentary rock composed largely of the mineral calcite. _____ often contains variable amounts of silica in the form of chert or flint, as well as varying amounts of clay, silt and sand as disseminations, nodules, or layers within the rock. The primary source of the calcite in _____ is most commonly marine organisms. These organisms secrete shells that settle out of the water column and are deposited on ocean floors as pelagic ooze or alternatively is conglomerated in a coral reef.
    a. Limestone0
    b. Thing
    c. Undefined
    d. Undefined

25. _____ rock is one of the three main rock groups. Rock formed from these covers 75% of the Earth's land area, and includes common types such as chalk, limestone, dolomite, sandstone, and shale.
    a. Sedimentary0
    b. Thing
    c. Undefined
    d. Undefined

26. _____ is one of the three main rock groups. _____ covers 75% of the Earth's land area. Four basic processes are involved in the formation of a clastic _____: weathering caused mainly by friction of waves, transportation where the sediment is carried along by a current, deposition and compaction where the sediment is squashed together to form a rock of this kind.
    a. Sedimentary rock0
    b. Thing
    c. Undefined
    d. Undefined

27. The _____ is the layer of granitic, sedimentary, and metamorphic rocks which form the continents and the areas of shallow seabed close to their shores, known as continental shelves. It is less dense than the material of the Earth's mantle and thus "floats" on top of it. _____ is also less dense than oceanic crust, though it is considerably thicker. About 40% of the Earth's surface is now underlain by _____.
    a. Thing
    b. Continental crust0
    c. Undefined
    d. Undefined

28. In geology, a _____ is the outermost layer of a planet, part of its lithosphere. They are generally composed of a less dense material than its deeper layers.Earths' is composed mainly of basalt and granite. It is cooler and more rigid than the deeper layers of the mantle and core.
    a. Thing
    b. Crust0
    c. Undefined
    d. Undefined

29. _____ is the part of Earth's lithosphere that surfaces in the ocean basins. _____ is primarily composed of mafic rocks, or sima. It is thinner than continental crust, or sial, generally less than 10 kilometers thick, however it is more dense, having a mean density of about 3.3 grams per cubic centimeter.
    a. Oceanic crust0
    b. Thing
    c. Undefined
    d. Undefined

30. _____ is displacement of solids by the agents of ocean currents, wind, water, or ice by downward or down-slope movement in response to gravity or by living organisms.
    a. Thing
    b. Erosion0
    c. Undefined
    d. Undefined

31. _____ is a geological process by which sediments such as sand or other materials, move along a beach shore.

Chapter 18. The Sea Floor

a. Thing
b. Longshore drift0
c. Undefined
d. Undefined

32. _____ is a cloudiness or haziness of water caused by individual particles that are generally invisible to the naked eye, thus being much like smoke in air. _____ is generally caused by phytoplankton. Measurement of _____ is a key test of water quality.
   a. Thing
   b. Turbidity0
   c. Undefined
   d. Undefined

33. A _____ is a current of rapidly moving, sediment-laden water moving down a slope through air, water, or another fluid. The current moves because it has a higher density and turbidity than the fluid through which it flows.
   a. Thing
   b. Turbidity current0
   c. Undefined
   d. Undefined

34. Ocean _____ are any more or less continuous, directed movement of ocean water that flows in one of the Earth's oceans. They are rivers of hot or cold water within the ocean. They are generated from the forces acting upon the water like the earth's rotation, the wind, the temperature and salinity differences and the gravitation of the moon.
   a. Thing
   b. Currents0
   c. Undefined
   d. Undefined

35. An _____ is the result from the sudden release of stored energy in the Earth's crust that creates seismic waves. At the Earth's surface, earthquakes may manifest themselves by a shaking or displacement of the ground. An _____ is caused by tectonic plates getting stuck and putting a strain on the ground. The strain becomes so great that rocks give way by breaking and sliding along fault planes.
   a. Earthquake0
   b. Thing
   c. Undefined
   d. Undefined

36. The _____ is the point on the Earth's surface that is directly above the point where an earthquake or other underground explosion originates or focus. It is directly above the hypocenter the actual location of the energy released inside the earth and usually suffers the maximum destruction.
   a. Thing
   b. Epicenter0
   c. Undefined
   d. Undefined

37. In plate tectonics, a _____ is the normally gently sloping continental shelf area located on the trailing edge of a drifting continent. The _____ is free of the seismic and volcanic activity associated with the subduction, rifting or transform faulting that is the result of plate tectonic activity.
   a. Thing
   b. Passive margin0
   c. Undefined
   d. Undefined

38. A _____ is a landform that extends above the surrounding terrain in a limited area. A _____ is generally steeper than a hill, but there is no universally accepted standard definition for the height of a _____ or a hill although a _____ usually has an identifiable summit.
   a. Mountain0
   b. Place
   c. Undefined
   d. Undefined

39. A _____ is a naturally occurring substance formed through geological processes that has a characteristic chemical composition, a highly ordered atomic structure and specific physical properties. A rock, by comparison, is an aggregate of minerals and need not have a specific chemical composition. Minerals range in composition from pure elements and simple salts to very complex silicates with thousands of known forms.
   a. Mineral0
   b. Thing
   c. Undefined
   d. Undefined

40. _____ is the geological process whereby material is added to a landform. This is the process by which wind and water create a sediment deposit, through the laying down of granular material that has been eroded and transported from another geographical location.
   a. Thing
   b. Deposition0
   c. Undefined
   d. Undefined

41. _____ is the third or vertical dimension of land surface. When _____ is described underwater, the term bathymetry is used.
   a. Terrain0
   b. Thing
   c. Undefined
   d. Undefined

42. In geology, a _____ generally refers to a linear structural depression that extends laterally over a distance, while being less steep than a trench. It can be a narrow basin or a geologic rift. In meteorolology a _____ is an elongated region of relatively low atmospheric pressure, often associated with fronts.
   a. Thing
   b. Trough0
   c. Undefined
   d. Undefined

43. _____ is an igneous, volcanic rock, of intermediate composition, with aphanitic to porphyritic texture.
   a. Andesite0
   b. Thing
   c. Undefined
   d. Undefined

44. _____ refers to the mode of igneous volcanic rock formation in which hot magma from inside the Earth flows out onto the surface as lava or explodes violently into the atmosphere to fall back as pyroclastics or tuff.
   a. Extrusive0
   b. Thing
   c. Undefined
   d. Undefined

45. _____ is the condition of a system in which competing influences are balanced.
   a. Equilibrium0
   b. Thing
   c. Undefined
   d. Undefined

46. A _____ is a group of mountains bordered by lowlands or separated from other mountain ranges by passes or rivers. Individual mountains within the same _____ do not necessarily have the same geology; they may be a mix of different orogeny, for example volcanoes, uplifted mountains or fold mountains and may, therefore, be of different rock.
   a. Mountain range0
   b. Thing
   c. Undefined
   d. Undefined

47. _____ is a common gray to black extrusive volcanic rock. It is usually fine-grained due to rapid cooling of lava on the Earth's surface. It may be porphyritic containing larger crystals in a fine matrix, or vesicular, or frothy scoria.

a. Thing
c. Undefined
b. Basalt0
d. Undefined

48. In geology, a _____ is a place where the Earth's crust and lithosphere are being pulled apart.
    a. Rift0
    b. Thing
    c. Undefined
    d. Undefined

49. A _____ in geology is a valley created by the formation of a rift.
    a. Rift valley0
    b. Thing
    c. Undefined
    d. Undefined

50. In geology, a _____ is a depression with predominant extent in one direction. The terms U-shaped and V-shaped are descriptive terms of geography to characterize the form of valleys. Most valleys belong to one of these two main types or a mixture of them, at least with respect of the cross section of the slopes or hillsides.
    a. Thing
    b. Valley0
    c. Undefined
    d. Undefined

51. _____ is molten rock located beneath the surface of the Earth, and which often collects in a _____ chamber. _____ is a complex high-temperature fluid substance. Most are silicate solutions. It is capable of intrusion into adjacent rocks or of extrusion onto the surface as lava or ejected explosively as tephra to form pyroclastic rock. Environments of _____ formation include subduction zones, continental rift zones, mid-oceanic ridges, and hotspots, some of which are interpreted as mantle plumes.
    a. Thing
    b. Magma0
    c. Undefined
    d. Undefined

52. The term _____ refers to several types of chemical compounds containing sulfur in its lowest oxidation number of −2.
    a. Thing
    b. Sulfide0
    c. Undefined
    d. Undefined

53. A _____ is a spring that is produced by the emergence of geothermally-heated groundwater from the earth's crust. They are all over the earth, on every continent and even under the oceans and seas.
    a. Hot spring0
    b. Thing
    c. Undefined
    d. Undefined

54. _____ is any product of the condensation of atmospheric water vapor that is deposited on the earth's surface. It occurs when the atmosphere becomes saturated with water vapour and the water condenses and falls out of solution. Air becomes saturated via two processes, cooling and adding moisture.
    a. Precipitation0
    b. Thing
    c. Undefined
    d. Undefined

55. A _____ linear oceanic feature--often hundreds, even thousands of kilometers long--resulting from the action of offset mid-ocean ridge axis segments; they are a consequence of plate tectonics.
    a. Fracture zone0
    b. Thing
    c. Undefined
    d. Undefined

Chapter 18. The Sea Floor

56. A _____ is a geological fault that is a special case of strike-slip faulting which terminates abruptly, at both ends, at a major transverse geological feature. Also known as a conservative plate boundary.
   a. Transform fault0
   b. Thing
   c. Undefined
   d. Undefined

57. Faults are planar rock fractures, which show evidence of relative movement. Large faults within the Earth's crust are the result of shear motion and active _____ zones are the causal locations of most earthquakes. Earthquakes are caused by energy release during rapid slippage along faults. The largest examples are at tectonic plate boundaries but many faults occur far from active plate boundaries. Since faults do not usually consist of a single, clean fracture, the term _____ zone is used when referring to the zone of complex deformation that is associated with the _____ plane.
   a. Thing
   b. Fault0
   c. Undefined
   d. Undefined

58. A _____ is a flat-topped seamount. Guyots show evidence of having been above the surface with gradual subsidence through stages from fringed reefed mountain, coral atoll, and finally a flat topped submerged mountain. Guyots are very commonly found in the Pacific Ocean, and are considered to be extinct volcanoes.
   a. Thing
   b. Guyot0
   c. Undefined
   d. Undefined

59. In geology, engineering, and surveying, _____ is the motion of a surface as it shifts downward relative to a datum such as sea-level. The opposite of _____ is uplift, which results in an increase in elevation. In meteorology, _____ refers to the downward movement of air.
   a. Subsidence0
   b. Thing
   c. Undefined
   d. Undefined

60. _____ is an excavation activity or operation usually carried out at least partly underwater, in shallow seas or fresh water areas with the purpose of gathering up bottom sediments and disposing of them at a different location.
   a. Thing
   b. Dredging0
   c. Undefined
   d. Undefined

61. A _____ is a rock, sandbar, or other feature lying beneath the surface of the water yet shallow enough to be a hazard to ships. They result from abiotic processes—deposition of sand, wave erosion planning down rock outcrops, and other natural processes.
   a. Thing
   b. Reef0
   c. Undefined
   d. Undefined

62. _____ refers to a sediment, sedimentary rock, or soil type which is formed from or contains a high proportion of calcium carbonate in the form of calcite or aragonite.
   a. Calcareous0
   b. Thing
   c. Undefined
   d. Undefined

63. A _____ is an opening, or rupture, in the Earth's surface or crust, which allows hot, molten rock, ash and gases to escape from deep below the surface.
   a. Thing
   b. Volcano0
   c. Undefined
   d. Undefined

64. An _____ is an oceanic reef formation, often having a characteristic ring-like shape surrounding a lagoon. Atolls are formed when coral reef grows around a volcanic island that later subsides into the ocean.
   a. Atoll0
   b. Thing
   c. Undefined
   d. Undefined

65. The _____ is the part of the open sea or ocean that is not near the coast or sea floor. In contrast, the demersal zone comprises the water that is near to, and is significantly affected by, the coast or the sea floor.
   a. Thing
   b. Pelagic0
   c. Undefined
   d. Undefined

66. _____ is an accumulate in the abyssal plain of the deep ocean, far away from terrestrial sources that provide terrigenous sediments; the latter are primarily limited to the continental shelf, and deposited by rivers.
   a. Thing
   b. Pelagic sediment0
   c. Undefined
   d. Undefined

67. _____ consists of very fine rock and mineral particles less than 2 mm in diameter that are ejected from a volcanic vent. The very fine particles may be carried for many miles, settling out as a dust-like layer across the landscape
   a. Thing
   b. Ash fall0
   c. Undefined
   d. Undefined

68. _____ is a method of exploration geophysics that uses the principles of seismology to estimate the properties of the Earth's subsurface from reflected seismic waves. The method requires a controlled seismic source of energy, such as dynamite or a specialized air gun.
   a. Thing
   b. Seismic reflection0
   c. Undefined
   d. Undefined

69. _____ is molten rock expelled by a volcano during an eruption. When first extruded from a volcanic vent, it is a liquid at temperatures from 700 °C to 1,200 °C.
   a. Thing
   b. Lava0
   c. Undefined
   d. Undefined

70. In geology, a _____ is a tabular pluton that has intruded between older layers of sedimentary rock, beds of volcanic lava or tuff, or even along the direction of foliation in metamorphic rock. The term _____ is synonymous with concordant intrusive sheet. This means that the _____ does not cut across preexisting rocks. Contrast this with dikes.
   a. Sill0
   b. Thing
   c. Undefined
   d. Undefined

71. _____ is a dark, coarse-grained, intrusive igneous rock chemically equivalent to basalt. It is a plutonic rock, formed when molten magma is trapped beneath the Earth's surface and cools into a crystalline mass.
   a. Gabbro0
   b. Thing
   c. Undefined
   d. Undefined

72. _____ refers to sections of the oceanic crust and the subjacent upper mantle that have been uplifted or emplaced to be exposed within continental crustal rocks.

Chapter 18. The Sea Floor

a. Ophiolite0
b. Thing
c. Undefined
d. Undefined

73. _____ is a fine-grained silica-rich cryptocrystalline sedimentary rock that may contain small fossils. It varies greatly in color from white to black, but most often manifests as gray, brown, grayish brown and light green to rusty red; its color is an expression of trace elements present in the rock, and both red and green are most often related to traces of iron.
    a. Thing
    b. Chert0
    c. Undefined
    d. Undefined

74. A _____ is an intrusion into a cross-cutting fissure, meaning a _____ cuts across other pre-existing layers or bodies of rock, this means that a _____ is always younger than the rocks that contain it. The thickness is usually much smaller than the other two dimensions. Thickness can vary from sub-centimeter scale to many meters in thickness and the lateral dimensions can extend over many kilometers.
    a. Thing
    b. Dike0
    c. Undefined
    d. Undefined

75. _____ is a dense, coarse-grained igneous rock, consisting mostly of the minerals olivine and pyroxene. _____ is ultramafic and ultrabasic, as the rock contains less than 45% silica. This type of rock is derived from the Earth's mantle, either as solid blocks and fragments, or as crystals accumulated from magmas that formed in the mantle.
    a. Peridotite0
    b. Thing
    c. Undefined
    d. Undefined

76. _____ is a group of common rock-forming hydrous magnesium iron phyllosilicate $(Mg, Fe)_3Si_2O_5(OH)_4$ minerals; it may contain minor amounts of other elements including chromium, manganese, cobalt and nickel. There are three important mineral polymorphs of _____: antigorite, chrysotile and lizardite.
    a. Thing
    b. Serpentine0
    c. Undefined
    d. Undefined

77. _____ can be defined as the solid state recrystallisation of pre-existing rocks due to changes in heat and/or pressure and/or introduction of fluids. There will be mineralogical, chemical and crystallographic changes. _____ produced with increasing pressure and temperature conditions is known as prograde _____. Conversely, decreasing temperatures and pressure characterize retrograde _____.
    a. Metamorphism0
    b. Thing
    c. Undefined
    d. Undefined

78. Earth's _____ is a ~2,900 km thick rocky shell comprizing approximately 70% of Earth's volume. It is predominantly solid and overlies the Earth's iron-rich core, which occupies about 30% of Earth's volume. Past episodes of melting and volcanism at the shallower levels of the _____ have produced a very thin crust of crystallized melt products near the surface, upon which we live.
    a. Thing
    b. Mantle0
    c. Undefined
    d. Undefined

79. The _____ is the earliest of three geologic eras of the Phanerozoic eon. The _____ is subdivided into six geologic periods; from oldest to youngest they are: the Cambrian, Ordovician, Silurian, Devonian, Carboniferous, and Permian.

Chapter 18. The Sea Floor

a. Paleozoic0
b. Thing
c. Undefined
d. Undefined

80. An _____ is a long period of time with different technical and colloquial meanings, and usages in language. It begins with some beginning event known as an epoch, epochal date, epochal event or epochal moment.
   a. Era0
   b. Thing
   c. Undefined
   d. Undefined

81. The _____ is an informal name for the eons of the geologic timescale that came before the current Phanerozoic eon. It spans from the formation of Earth around 4500 Ma to the evolution of abundant macroscopic hard-shelled animals, which marked the beginning of the Cambrian, the first period of the first era of the Phanerozoic eon, some 542 Ma.
   a. Thing
   b. Precambrian0
   c. Undefined
   d. Undefined

82. _____ is a body of techniques for investigating phenomena and acquiring new knowledge, as well as for correcting and integrating previous knowledge. It is based on gathering observable, empirical and measurable evidence subject to specific principles of reasoning,
   a. Scientific method0
   b. Thing
   c. Undefined
   d. Undefined

Chapter 19. Plate Tectonics

1. _____ is a field of study within geology concerned generally with the structures within the crust of the Earth, or other planets, and particularly with the forces and movements that have operated in a region to create these structures.
   - a. Thing
   - b. Tectonics0
   - c. Undefined
   - d. Undefined

2. A _____ is a landform that extends above the surrounding terrain in a limited area. A _____ is generally steeper than a hill, but there is no universally accepted standard definition for the height of a _____ or a hill although a _____ usually has an identifiable summit.
   - a. Place
   - b. Mountain0
   - c. Undefined
   - d. Undefined

3. An _____ is the result from the sudden release of stored energy in the Earth's crust that creates seismic waves. At the Earth's surface, earthquakes may manifest themselves by a shaking or displacement of the ground. An _____ is caused by tectonic plates getting stuck and putting a strain on the ground. The strain becomes so great that rocks give way by breaking and sliding along fault planes.
   - a. Earthquake0
   - b. Thing
   - c. Undefined
   - d. Undefined

4. _____ is a theory of geology that has been developed to explain the observed evidence for large scale motions of the Earth's lithosphere. The theory encompassed and superseded the older theory of continental drift.
   - a. Plate tectonics0
   - b. Thing
   - c. Undefined
   - d. Undefined

5. In geology, a _____ is the outermost layer of a planet, part of its lithosphere. They are generally composed of a less dense material than its deeper layers.Earths' is composed mainly of basalt and granite. It is cooler and more rigid than the deeper layers of the mantle and core.
   - a. Thing
   - b. Crust0
   - c. Undefined
   - d. Undefined

6. Earth's _____ is a ~2,900 km thick rocky shell comprizing approximately 70% of Earth's volume. It is predominantly solid and overlies the Earth's iron-rich core, which occupies about 30% of Earth's volume. Past episodes of melting and volcanism at the shallower levels of the _____ have produced a very thin crust of crystallized melt products near the surface, upon which we live.
   - a. Mantle0
   - b. Thing
   - c. Undefined
   - d. Undefined

7. _____ refers to the movement of the Earth's continents relative to each other. _____ is a concept that said the shapes of continents on either side of the Atlantic Ocean seem to fit together and the similarity of southern continent fossil faunae could mean that all the continents had once been joined into a supercontinent. It was suggested that the continents had been pulled apart by the centrifugal pseudoforce of the Earth's rotation.
   - a. Continental drift0
   - b. Thing
   - c. Undefined
   - d. Undefined

8. The _____ the bottom of the ocean. At the bottom of the continental slope is the continental rise, which is caused by sediment cascading down the continental slope.

a. Thing
b. Seafloor0
c. Undefined
d. Undefined

9. _____ occurs at mid-ocean ridges, where new oceanic crust is formed through volcanic activity and then gradually moves away from the ridge. _____ helps explain continental drift in the theory of plate tectonics.
   a. Thing
   b. Seafloor spreading0
   c. Undefined
   d. Undefined

10. A _____ is a geological feature that is also known as a Rip in the earth causing magma to flow out and forming an undersea volcano, it also has geological features, a continuous elevational crest for some distance. Ridges are usually termed hills or mountains as well, depending on size.
    a. Thing
    b. Ridge0
    c. Undefined
    d. Undefined

11. A _____ is a type of excavation or depression in the ground. They are generally defined by being deeper than they are wide, and by being narrow compared to their length.
    a. Trench0
    b. Thing
    c. Undefined
    d. Undefined

12. The _____ are hemispheric-scale long but narrow topographic depressions of the sea floor. They are also the deepest parts of the ocean floor. Trenches define one of the most important natural boundaries on the Earth's solid surface, that between two lithospheric plates. There are three types of lithospheric plate boundaries: divergent, convergent, and transform. Trenches are the spectacular and distinctive morphological features of convergent plate boundaries.
    a. Oceanic trenches0
    b. Thing
    c. Undefined
    d. Undefined

13. Fossils are the mineralized or otherwise preserved remains or traces of animals, plants, and other organisms. The totality of fossils, both discovered and undiscovered, and their placement in fossiliferous rock formations and sedimentary layers is known as the _____ record.
    a. Thing
    b. Fossil0
    c. Undefined
    d. Undefined

14. _____ is the supercontinent that existed during the Paleozoic and Mesozoic eras before each of the component continents were separated into their current configuration.
    a. Pangaea0
    b. Event
    c. Undefined
    d. Undefined

15. _____ was a supercontinent that most recently existed as a part of the split of the Pangaean supercontinent in the late Mesozoic era. It included most of the landmasses which make up today's continents of the northern hemisphere, chiefly Laurentia, Baltica, Siberia, Kazakhstania, and the North China and East China Cratons.
    a. Thing
    b. Laurasia0
    c. Undefined
    d. Undefined

16. The southern supercontinent _____ included most of the landmasses in today's southern hemisphere, including Antarctica, South America, Africa, Madagascar, Australia-New Guinea, and New Zealand, as well as Arabia and the Indian subcontinent, which are in the Northern Hemisphere.

Chapter 19. Plate Tectonics

a. Thing
b. Gondwana0
c. Undefined
d. Undefined

17. A _____ is a large, slow moving river of ice, formed from compacted layers of snow, that slowly deforms and flows in response to gravity. _____ ice is the largest reservoir of fresh water on Earth, and second only to oceans as the largest reservoir of total water. Glaciers cover vast areas of polar regions but are restricted to the highest mountains in the tropics.
a. Thing
b. Glacier0
c. Undefined
d. Undefined

18. _____ is a fossil fuel formed in swamp ecosystems where plant remains were saved by water and mud from oxidization and biodegradation. It is a sedimentary rock, but the harder forms, such as anthracite _____, can be regarded as metamorphic rocks because of later exposure to elevated temperature and pressure. It is composed primarily of carbon along with assorted other elements, including sulfur.
a. Thing
b. Coal0
c. Undefined
d. Undefined

19. In geology, glacial _____ are grooves or lines inscribed on the surface of a rock, produced by a geological process such as glacial flow.
a. Striations0
b. Thing
c. Undefined
d. Undefined

20. _____ gives the location of a place on Earth north or south of the equator. Lines of _____ are the horizontal lines shown running east-to-west on maps. Technically, _____ is an angular measurement in degrees ranging from 0° at the Equator to 90° at the poles.
a. Thing
b. Latitude0
c. Undefined
d. Undefined

21. _____ rock is one of the three main rock groups. Rock formed from these covers 75% of the Earth's land area, and includes common types such as chalk, limestone, dolomite, sandstone, and shale.
a. Thing
b. Sedimentary0
c. Undefined
d. Undefined

22. _____ is one of the three main rock groups. _____ covers 75% of the Earth's land area. Four basic processes are involved in the formation of a clastic _____: weathering caused mainly by friction of waves, transportation where the sediment is carried along by a current, deposition and compaction where the sediment is squashed together to form a rock of this kind.
a. Thing
b. Sedimentary rock0
c. Undefined
d. Undefined

23. _____ is the magnetic north pole is constantly shifting relative to the axis of rotation. This is responsible for the shifting magnetic declination required for compass work and orienteering.
a. Thing
b. Polar wandering0
c. Undefined
d. Undefined

24. _____ is the study of Earth's surface features or those of other planets, moons, and asteroids

Chapter 19. Plate Tectonics

  a. Thing
  b. Topography0
  c. Undefined
  d. Undefined

25. _____ is the part of Earth's lithosphere that surfaces in the ocean basins. _____ is primarily composed of mafic rocks, or sima. It is thinner than continental crust, or sial, generally less than 10 kilometers thick, however it is more dense, having a mean density of about 3.3 grams per cubic centimeter.
  a. Thing
  b. Oceanic crust0
  c. Undefined
  d. Undefined

26. In physics, a _____ is a solenoidal vector field in the space surrounding moving electric charges and magnetic dipoles, such as those in electric currents and magnets.
  a. Magnetic field0
  b. Thing
  c. Undefined
  d. Undefined

27. _____ is one of the phenomena by which materials exert attractive or repulsive forces on other materials. Some well known materials that exhibit easily detectable magnetic properties are nickel, iron, some steels, and the mineral magnetite; however, all materials are influenced to greater or lesser degree by the presence of a magnetic field.
  a. Thing
  b. Magnetism0
  c. Undefined
  d. Undefined

28. _____ is a ferrimagnetic mineral one of several iron oxides and a member of the spinel group. The chemical IUPAC name is iron oxide and the common chemical name ferrous-ferric oxide.
  a. Thing
  b. Magnetite0
  c. Undefined
  d. Undefined

29. _____ is molten rock expelled by a volcano during an eruption. When first extruded from a volcanic vent, it is a liquid at temperatures from 700 °C to 1,200 °C.
  a. Lava0
  b. Thing
  c. Undefined
  d. Undefined

30. The _____ is a term in physics and materials science and refers to a characteristic property of a ferromagnetic or piezoelectric material.
  a. Thing
  b. Curie point0
  c. Undefined
  d. Undefined

31. _____ is a fine-grained sedimentary rock whose original constituents were clays or muds. It is characterized by thin laminae breaking with an irregular curving fracture, often splintery and usually parallel to the often-indistinguishable bedding plane.
  a. Shale0
  b. Thing
  c. Undefined
  d. Undefined

32. _____ refers to the study of the record of the Earth's magnetic field preserved in various magnetic minerals through time. The study of _____ has demonstrated that the Earth's magnetic field varies substantially in both orientation and intensity through time.

a. Paleomagnetism0
b. Thing
c. Undefined
d. Undefined

33. The sea floor below the break is the _____. Below the slope is the continental rise, which finally merges into the deep ocean floor, the abyssal plain. As the continental shelf and the slope are part of the continental margin, both are covered in this article.
   a. Thing
   b. Continental slope0
   c. Undefined
   d. Undefined

34. A _____ is the fringe of land at the edge of a large body of water, such as an ocean, sea, or lake. A strict definition is the strip of land along a water body that is alternately exposed and covered by waves and tides.
   a. Thing
   b. Shoreline0
   c. Undefined
   d. Undefined

35. The _____ is the earliest of three geologic eras of the Phanerozoic eon. The _____ is subdivided into six geologic periods; from oldest to youngest they are: the Cambrian, Ordovician, Silurian, Devonian, Carboniferous, and Permian.
   a. Paleozoic0
   b. Thing
   c. Undefined
   d. Undefined

36. An _____ is a long period of time with different technical and colloquial meanings, and usages in language. It begins with some beginning event known as an epoch, epochal date, epochal event or epochal moment.
   a. Era0
   b. Thing
   c. Undefined
   d. Undefined

37. _____ can be defined as the solid state recrystallisation of pre-existing rocks due to changes in heat and/or pressure and/or introduction of fluids. There will be mineralogical, chemical and crystallographic changes. _____ produced with increasing pressure and temperature conditions is known as prograde _____. Conversely, decreasing temperatures and pressure characterize retrograde _____.
   a. Thing
   b. Metamorphism0
   c. Undefined
   d. Undefined

38. The _____ is an informal name for the eons of the geologic timescale that came before the current Phanerozoic eon. It spans from the formation of Earth around 4500 Ma to the evolution of abundant macroscopic hard-shelled animals, which marked the beginning of the Cambrian, the first period of the first era of the Phanerozoic eon, some 542 Ma.
   a. Precambrian0
   b. Thing
   c. Undefined
   d. Undefined

39. In geology, a _____ zone is an area on Earth where two tectonic plates meet and move towards one another, with one sliding underneath the other and moving down into the mantle, at rates typically measured in centimeters per year. An oceanic plate ordinarily slides underneath a continental plate; this often creates an orogenic zone with many volcanoes and earthquakes.
   a. Thing
   b. Subduction0
   c. Undefined
   d. Undefined

40. _____ are any of the several different forms of an element each having different atomic mass. _____ of an element have nuclei with the same number of protons but different numbers of neutrons.
   a. Thing
   b. Isotopes0
   c. Undefined
   d. Undefined

41. _____ is a common gray to black extrusive volcanic rock. It is usually fine-grained due to rapid cooling of lava on the Earth's surface. It may be porphyritic containing larger crystals in a fine matrix, or vesicular, or frothy scoria.
   a. Basalt0
   b. Thing
   c. Undefined
   d. Undefined

42. _____ is the process of heating a solid substance to a point where it turns into a liquid. An object that has melted is molten.
   a. Thing
   b. Melting0
   c. Undefined
   d. Undefined

43. _____ is a reaction force applied by a stretched string, rope or a similar object on the objects which stretch it. The direction of the force of it is parallel to the string, towards the string.
   a. Thing
   b. Tension0
   c. Undefined
   d. Undefined

44. In geology, a _____ is a place where the Earth's crust and lithosphere are being pulled apart.
   a. Thing
   b. Rift0
   c. Undefined
   d. Undefined

45. A _____ in geology is a valley created by the formation of a rift.
   a. Thing
   b. Rift valley0
   c. Undefined
   d. Undefined

46. In geology, a _____ is a depression with predominant extent in one direction. The terms U-shaped and V-shaped are descriptive terms of geography to characterize the form of valleys. Most valleys belong to one of these two main types or a mixture of them, at least with respect of the cross section of the slopes or hillsides.
   a. Valley0
   b. Thing
   c. Undefined
   d. Undefined

47. _____, in everyday life, is most familiar as the agency that endows objects with weight. _____ is responsible for keeping the Earth and the other planets in their orbits around the Sun; for the formation of tides; and for various other phenomena that we observe. _____ is also the reason for the very existence of the Earth, the Sun, and most macroscopic objects in the universe; without it, matter would not have coalesced into these large masses, and life, as we know it, would not exist.
   a. Gravitation0
   b. Thing
   c. Undefined
   d. Undefined

48. _____ is the condition of a system in which competing influences are balanced.
   a. Thing
   b. Equilibrium0
   c. Undefined
   d. Undefined

Chapter 19. Plate Tectonics

49. A _____ is an area on Earth where two tectonic plates meet and move towards one another, with one sliding underneath the other and moving down into the mantle, at rates typically measured in centimeters per year. In a sense, subduction zones are the opposite of divergent boundaries, areas where material rises up from the mantle and plates are moving apart.
   a. Subduction zone0
   b. Thing
   c. Undefined
   d. Undefined

50. A _____ is an opening, or rupture, in the Earth's surface or crust, which allows hot, molten rock, ash and gases to escape from deep below the surface.
   a. Volcano0
   b. Thing
   c. Undefined
   d. Undefined

51. The _____ is the part of the open sea or ocean that is not near the coast or sea floor. In contrast, the demersal zone comprises the water that is near to, and is significantly affected by, the coast or the sea floor.
   a. Pelagic0
   b. Thing
   c. Undefined
   d. Undefined

52. _____ is an accumulate in the abyssal plain of the deep ocean, far away from terrestrial sources that provide terrigenous sediments; the latter are primarily limited to the continental shelf, and deposited by rivers.
   a. Pelagic sediment0
   b. Thing
   c. Undefined
   d. Undefined

53. _____ is any particulate matter that can be transported by fluid flow and which eventually is deposited as a layer of solid particles on the bed or bottom of a body of water or other liquid.
   a. Sediment0
   b. Thing
   c. Undefined
   d. Undefined

54. _____ is the science and study of the solid matter that constitute the Earth. Encompassing such things as rocks, soil, and gemstones, _____ studies the composition, structure, physical properties, history, and the processes that shape Earth's components.
   a. Geology0
   b. Thing
   c. Undefined
   d. Undefined

55. The _____ is the solid outermost shell of a rocky planet. On the Earth, the _____ includes the crust and the uppermost mantle which is joined to the crust across the Mohorovièiæ discontinuity. _____ is underlain by asthenosphere, the weaker, hotter, and deeper part of the upper mantle.
   a. Thing
   b. Lithosphere0
   c. Undefined
   d. Undefined

56. The _____ is the region of the Earth between 100-200 km below the surface that is the weak or "soft" zone in the upper mantle. It lies just below the lithosphere, which is involved in plate movements and isostatic adjustments. In spite of its heat, pressures keep it plastic, and it has a relatively low density. Seismic waves pass relatively slowly through the _____.
   a. Asthenosphere0
   b. Thing
   c. Undefined
   d. Undefined

Chapter 19. Plate Tectonics

57. In plate tectonics, a _____ a linear feature that exists between two tectonic plates that are moving away from each other. These areas can form in the middle of continents but eventually form ocean basins.
    a. Divergent plate boundary0
    b. Thing
    c. Undefined
    d. Undefined

58. In plate tectonics, a _____ is said to occur when tectonic plates slide and grind against each other along a transform fault. The relative motion of such plates is horizontal in either sinistral or dextral direction. Many transform boundaries are locked in tension before suddenly releasing, and causing earthquakes.
    a. Thing
    b. Transform boundary0
    c. Undefined
    d. Undefined

59. A _____ is a scientific instrument used to measure the strength and/or direction of the magnetic field in the vicinity of the instrument.
    a. Thing
    b. Magnetometer0
    c. Undefined
    d. Undefined

60. _____ is molten rock located beneath the surface of the Earth, and which often collects in a _____ chamber. _____ is a complex high-temperature fluid substance. Most are silicate solutions. It is capable of intrusion into adjacent rocks or of extrusion onto the surface as lava or ejected explosively as tephra to form pyroclastic rock. Environments of _____ formation include subduction zones, continental rift zones, mid-oceanic ridges, and hotspots, some of which are interpreted as mantle plumes.
    a. Thing
    b. Magma0
    c. Undefined
    d. Undefined

61. A _____ is an intrusion into a cross-cutting fissure, meaning a _____ cuts across other pre-existing layers or bodies of rock, this means that a _____ is always younger than the rocks that contain it. The thickness is usually much smaller than the other two dimensions. Thickness can vary from sub-centimeter scale to many meters in thickness and the lateral dimensions can extend over many kilometers.
    a. Dike0
    b. Thing
    c. Undefined
    d. Undefined

62. An _____ phenomenon is an observed event which deviates from what is expected according to existing rules or scientific theory.
    a. Anomalous0
    b. Thing
    c. Undefined
    d. Undefined

63. _____ rocks form when molten rock, magma, cools and solidifies, with or without crystallization, either below the surface as intrusive, plutonic rocks or on the surface as extrusive, volcanic, rocks.
    a. Igneous0
    b. Thing
    c. Undefined
    d. Undefined

64. _____ forms when rock cools and solidifies either below the surface as intrusive rocks or on the surface as extrusive rocks. This magma can be derived from partial melts of pre-existing rocks in either the Earth's mantle or crust. Typically, the melting is caused by one or more of the following processes -- an increase in temperature, a decrease in pressure, or a change in composition.

Chapter 19. Plate Tectonics

a. Thing
b. Igneous rock0
c. Undefined
d. Undefined

65. _____ is a body of techniques for investigating phenomena and acquiring new knowledge, as well as for correcting and integrating previous knowledge. It is based on gathering observable, empirical and measurable evidence subject to specific principles of reasoning,
   a. Scientific method0
   b. Thing
   c. Undefined
   d. Undefined

66. A _____ linear oceanic feature--often hundreds, even thousands of kilometers long--resulting from the action of offset mid-ocean ridge axis segments; they are a consequence of plate tectonics.
   a. Thing
   b. Fracture zone0
   c. Undefined
   d. Undefined

67. A _____ is a geological fault that is a special case of strike-slip faulting which terminates abruptly, at both ends, at a major transverse geological feature. Also known as a conservative plate boundary.
   a. Transform fault0
   b. Thing
   c. Undefined
   d. Undefined

68. Faults are planar rock fractures, which show evidence of relative movement. Large faults within the Earth's crust are the result of shear motion and active _____ zones are the causal locations of most earthquakes. Earthquakes are caused by energy release during rapid slippage along faults. The largest examples are at tectonic plate boundaries but many faults occur far from active plate boundaries. Since faults do not usually consist of a single, clean fracture, the term _____ zone is used when referring to the zone of complex deformation that is associated with the _____ plane.
   a. Fault0
   b. Thing
   c. Undefined
   d. Undefined

69. The _____ is the layer of granitic, sedimentary, and metamorphic rocks which form the continents and the areas of shallow seabed close to their shores, known as continental shelves. It is less dense than the material of the Earth's mantle and thus "floats" on top of it. _____ is also less dense than oceanic crust, though it is considerably thicker. About 40% of the Earth's surface is now underlain by _____.
   a. Continental crust0
   b. Thing
   c. Undefined
   d. Undefined

70. A _____ is a depressed block of land bordered by parallel faults. A _____ is the result of a block of land being downthrown producing a valley with a distinct scarp on each side.
   a. Thing
   b. Graben0
   c. Undefined
   d. Undefined

71. _____ in meteorology are large scale patterns in the atmospheric pressure field that are nearly stationary, effectively "blocking" or redirecting migratory cyclones. These _____ can remain in place for several days or even weeks, causing the areas affected by them to have the same kind of weather for an extended period of time.
   a. Thing
   b. Blocks0
   c. Undefined
   d. Undefined

72. A _____ is a fragment of cooled pyroclastic material, lava or magma.

Chapter 19. Plate Tectonics

    a. Thing   b. Cinder0
    c. Undefined   d. Undefined

73. _____ is an oceanographic phenomenon that involves wind-driven motion of dense, cooler, and usually nutrient-rich water towards the ocean surface, replacing the warmer, usually nutrient-deplete surface water.
    a. Upwelling0   b. Thing
    c. Undefined   d. Undefined

74. A _____ column is a column of rizing air in the lower altitudes of the Earth's atmosphere. Thermals are created by the uneven heating of the Earth's surface from solar radiation, and are an example of convection. The Sun warms the ground, which in turn warms the air directly above it.
    a. Thing   b. Thermal0
    c. Undefined   d. Undefined

75. A _____ is an intrusion caused by buoyancy and pressure differentials. A _____ is any relatively mobile mass that intrudes into preexisting strata. Diapirs commonly intrude vertically upward along fractures or zones of structural weakness through more dense overlying rocks because of density contrast between a less dense, lower rock mass and overlying denser rocks. The density contrast manifests as a force of buoyancy.
    a. Diapir0   b. Thing
    c. Undefined   d. Undefined

76. _____ is the mineral form of sodium chloride. _____ forms isometric crystals. It commonly occurs with other evaporite deposit minerals such as several of the sulfates, halides and borates. _____ occurs in vast lakes of sedimentary evaporite minerals that result from the drying up of enclosed beds, playas, and seas.
    a. Halite0   b. Thing
    c. Undefined   d. Undefined

77. _____ is any product of the condensation of atmospheric water vapor that is deposited on the earth's surface. It occurs when the atmosphere becomes saturated with water vapour and the water condenses and falls out of solution. Air becomes saturated via two processes, cooling and adding moisture.
    a. Precipitation0   b. Thing
    c. Undefined   d. Undefined

78. In geography, a _____ is a landscape form or region that receives very little precipitation. They are defined as areas that receive an average annual precipitation of less than 250 mm. A _____ where vegetation cover is exceedingly sparse correspond to the 'hyperarid' regions of the earth, where rainfall is exceedingly rare and infrequent.
    a. Place   b. Desert0
    c. Undefined   d. Undefined

79. _____ is displacement of solids by the agents of ocean currents, wind, water, or ice by downward or down-slope movement in response to gravity or by living organisms.
    a. Erosion0   b. Thing
    c. Undefined   d. Undefined

Chapter 19. Plate Tectonics

80. The _____ is the extended perimeter of each continent and associated coastal plain, which is covered during interglacial periods such as the current epoch by relatively shallow seas and gulfs. The shelf usually ends at a point of increasing slope.
    a. Continental shelf0   b. Thing
    c. Undefined   d. Undefined

81. The continental shelf is the extended perimeter of each continent and associated coastal plain, which is covered during interglacial periods such as the current epoch by relatively shallow seas and gulfs. The shelf usually ends at a point of increasing slope. The sea floor below the break is the continental slope. Below the slope is the _____, which finally merges into the deep ocean floor, the abyssal plain. As the continental shelf and the slope are part of the continental margin, both are covered in this article.
    a. Thing   b. Continental rise0
    c. Undefined   d. Undefined

82. In plate tectonics, a _____ is an actively deforming region where two tectonic plates or fragments of lithosphere move towards one another. When two plates move toward one another, they form either a subduction zone or a continental collision.
    a. Thing   b. Convergent boundary0
    c. Undefined   d. Undefined

83. A _____ is a deep active seismic area in a subduction zone. Differential motion along the zone produces deep seated earthquakes, the foci of which may be as deep as about 435 miles. They develop beneath volcanic island arcs and continental margins above active subduction zones.
    a. Thing   b. Benioff zone0
    c. Undefined   d. Undefined

84. A _____ is a chain of volcanic islands or mountains formed by plate tectonics as an oceanic tectonic plate subducts under another tectonic plate and produces magma.
    a. Thing   b. Volcanic arc0
    c. Undefined   d. Undefined

85. _____ is an igneous, volcanic rock, of intermediate composition, with aphanitic to porphyritic texture.
    a. Thing   b. Andesite0
    c. Undefined   d. Undefined

86. A _____ is an old and stable part of the continental crust that has survived the merging and splitting of continents and supercontinents. Cratons are generally found in the interiors of continents and are characteristically composed of ancient crystalline basement crust of lightweight felsic igneous rock such as granite. They have a thick crust and deep roots that extend into the mantle beneath to depths of 200 km.
    a. Thing   b. Craton0
    c. Undefined   d. Undefined

87. The term _____ is used in geology when one or a stack of originally flat and planar surfaces, such as sedimentary strata, are bent or curved as a result of plastic, i.e. permanent, deformation.

a. Fold0
b. Thing
c. Undefined
d. Undefined

88. The term _____ is used to refer to any geographical feature exhibiting subsidence and consequent infilling by sedimentation. As the sediments are buried, they are subjected to increasing pressure and begin the process of lithification.
   a. Sedimentary basin0
   b. Thing
   c. Undefined
   d. Undefined

89. Mean _____ is the average height of the sea, with reference to a suitable reference surface.
   a. Thing
   b. Sea level0
   c. Undefined
   d. Undefined

90. The _____ is one of three geologic eras of the Phanerozoic eon. The _____ was a time of tectonic, climatic and evolutionary activity, shifting from a state of connectedness into their present configuration. The climate was exceptionally warm throughout the period, also playing an important role in the evolution and diversification of new animal species. By the end of the era, the basis of modern life was in place.
   a. Mesozoic0
   b. Thing
   c. Undefined
   d. Undefined

91. A _____ is a place where, through continental collision, two continental plates have joined together. The Himilayas and the Alps mark these zones as do other very high mountain ranges.
   a. Thing
   b. Suture zone0
   c. Undefined
   d. Undefined

92. A _____ is a group of mountains bordered by lowlands or separated from other mountain ranges by passes or rivers. Individual mountains within the same _____ do not necessarily have the same geology; they may be a mix of different orogeny, for example volcanoes, uplifted mountains or fold mountains and may, therefore, be of different rock.
   a. Mountain range0
   b. Thing
   c. Undefined
   d. Undefined

93. _____ are earthquakes in the same region of the central shock but of smaller magnitude and which occur with a pattern that follows Omori's law.
   a. Aftershocks0
   b. Thing
   c. Undefined
   d. Undefined

94. In geology the term _____ refers to the system of forces that tend to decrease the volume of or shorten rocks. Compressive strength refers to the maximum compressive stress that can be applied to a material before failure occurs.
   a. Thing
   b. Compression0
   c. Undefined
   d. Undefined

95. _____ uses digital seismographic records to image the interior of the Earth. The basic scheme is to first localize and characterize a set of significant earthquakes. These earthquakes are then considered to "illuminate" the interior of the earth with seismic waves.
   a. Thing
   b. Seismic tomography0
   c. Undefined
   d. Undefined

Chapter 19. Plate Tectonics

96. _____ is imaging by sections or sectioning. A device used in _____ is called a tomograph, while the image produced is a tomogram. In most cases it is based on the mathematical procedure called tomographic reconstruction.
   a. Thing
   b. Tomography0
   c. Undefined
   d. Undefined

97. In geology, engineering, and surveying, _____ is the motion of a surface as it shifts downward relative to a datum such as sea-level. The opposite of _____ is uplift, which results in an increase in elevation. In meteorology, _____ refers to the downward movement of air.
   a. Subsidence0
   b. Thing
   c. Undefined
   d. Undefined

98. _____ is the third or vertical dimension of land surface. When _____ is described underwater, the term bathymetry is used.
   a. Terrain0
   b. Thing
   c. Undefined
   d. Undefined

99. A _____ is the result of a giant volcanic eruption or series of eruptions that coats large stretches of land or the ocean floor with basalt lava. Flood basalts have erupted at random intervals throughout history and are clear evidence that the Earth undergoes periods of enhanced activity rather than being in a uniform steady state.
   a. Flood basalt0
   b. Thing
   c. Undefined
   d. Undefined

100. A _____ is an upwelling of abnormally hot rock within the Earth's mantle. As the heads of mantle plumes can partly melt when they reach shallow depths, they are thought to be the cause of volcanic centers known as hotspots and probably also to have caused flood basalts.
   a. Event
   b. Mantle plume0
   c. Undefined
   d. Undefined

101. In geology, a _____ is a deformational feature consisting of symmetrically-dipping anticlines; their general outline on a geologic map is circular or oval.
   a. Dome0
   b. Thing
   c. Undefined
   d. Undefined

102. A _____ is a spring that is produced by the emergence of geothermally-heated groundwater from the earth's crust. They are all over the earth, on every continent and even under the oceans and seas.
   a. Thing
   b. Hot spring0
   c. Undefined
   d. Undefined

103. A _____ is a type of hot spring that erupts periodically, ejecting a column of hot water and steam into the air.
   a. Thing
   b. Geyser0
   c. Undefined
   d. Undefined

104. An _____ is a volume of rock containing components or minerals in a mode of occurrence that renders it valuable for mining.

a. Ore0
b. Thing
c. Undefined
d. Undefined

105. The term _____ refers to several types of chemical compounds containing sulfur in its lowest oxidation number of −2.
   a. Thing
   b. Sulfide0
   c. Undefined
   d. Undefined

106. In geology, _____ refers to heat sources within the planet. The planet's internal heat was originally generated during its accretion, due to gravitational binding energy, and since then additional heat has continued to be generated by the radioactive decay of elements such as uranium, thorium, and potassium.
   a. Geothermal0
   b. Thing
   c. Undefined
   d. Undefined

107. _____ is the use of geothermal heat to generate electricity.
   a. Geothermal power0
   b. Thing
   c. Undefined
   d. Undefined

108. _____ refers to sections of the oceanic crust and the subjacent upper mantle that have been uplifted or emplaced to be exposed within continental crustal rocks.
   a. Ophiolite0
   b. Thing
   c. Undefined
   d. Undefined

109. _____ is an igneous rock of volcanic origin. They often have a vesicular texture, which is the result voids left by volatiles escaping from the molten lava. Pumice is a rock, which is an example of explosive volcanic eruption. It is so vesicular that it floats in water.
   a. Thing
   b. Volcanic rock0
   c. Undefined
   d. Undefined

110. The _____ is a large shield covered by a thin layer of soil that forms the nucleus of the North American craton. It has a deep, common, joined bedrock region in eastern and central Canada and stretches North from the Great Lakes to the Arctic Ocean, covering half the country.
   a. Canadian Shield0
   b. Thing
   c. Undefined
   d. Undefined

111. _____ is a sedimentary rock composed largely of the mineral calcite. _____ often contains variable amounts of silica in the form of chert or flint, as well as varying amounts of clay, silt and sand as disseminations, nodules, or layers within the rock. The primary source of the calcite in _____ is most commonly marine organisms. These organisms secrete shells that settle out of the water column and are deposited on ocean floors as pelagic ooze or alternatively is conglomerated in a coral reef.
   a. Limestone0
   b. Thing
   c. Undefined
   d. Undefined

Chapter 20. Mountain Belts and the Continental Crust

1. A _____ is a landform that extends above the surrounding terrain in a limited area. A _____ is generally steeper than a hill, but there is no universally accepted standard definition for the height of a _____ or a hill although a _____ usually has an identifiable summit.
   - a. Place
   - b. Mountain0
   - c. Undefined
   - d. Undefined

2. A _____ is a group of mountains bordered by lowlands or separated from other mountain ranges by passes or rivers. Individual mountains within the same _____ do not necessarily have the same geology; they may be a mix of different orogeny, for example volcanoes, uplifted mountains or fold mountains and may, therefore, be of different rock.
   - a. Thing
   - b. Mountain range0
   - c. Undefined
   - d. Undefined

3. _____ is the result of the transformation of a pre-existing rock type, the protolith, in a process called metamorphism, which means "change in form". The protolith is subjected to heat and extreme pressure causing profound physical and/or chemical change. The protolith may be sedimentary rock, igneous rock or another older rock.
   - a. Metamorphic rock0
   - b. Thing
   - c. Undefined
   - d. Undefined

4. Metamorphic rock is the result of the transformation of a pre-existing rock type, the protolith, in a process called metamorphism. The protolith is subjected to heat and extreme pressure causing profound physical and/or chemical change. _____ make up a large part of the Earth's crust. They are formed deep beneath the Earth's surface by great stresses from rocks above and high pressures and temperatures.
   - a. Metamorphic rocks0
   - b. Thing
   - c. Undefined
   - d. Undefined

5. _____ can be defined as the solid state recrystallisation of pre-existing rocks due to changes in heat and/or pressure and/or introduction of fluids. There will be mineralogical, chemical and crystallographic changes. _____ produced with increasing pressure and temperature conditions is known as prograde _____. Conversely, decreasing temperatures and pressure characterize retrograde _____.
   - a. Metamorphism0
   - b. Thing
   - c. Undefined
   - d. Undefined

6. _____ is the native consolidated rock underlying the Earth's surface. Above the _____ is usually an area of broken and weathered unconsolidated rock in the basal subsoil.
   - a. Bedrock0
   - b. Thing
   - c. Undefined
   - d. Undefined

7. _____ is the science and study of the solid matter that constitute the Earth. Encompassing such things as rocks, soil, and gemstones, _____ studies the composition, structure, physical properties, history, and the processes that shape Earth's components.
   - a. Geology0
   - b. Thing
   - c. Undefined
   - d. Undefined

8. _____ is a term given to broken rock that appears at the bottom of crags, mountain cliffs or valley shoulders, forming a _____ slope. The maximum inclination of such deposits corresponds to the angle of repose of the mean debris size.

Chapter 20. Mountain Belts and the Continental Crust

    a. Thing
    b. Scree0
    c. Undefined
    d. Undefined

9. Mean _____ is the average height of the sea, with reference to a suitable reference surface.
    a. Thing
    b. Sea level0
    c. Undefined
    d. Undefined

10. In geology, a _____ is the outermost layer of a planet, part of its lithosphere. They are generally composed of a less dense material than its deeper layers. Earths' is composed mainly of basalt and granite. It is cooler and more rigid than the deeper layers of the mantle and core.
    a. Crust0
    b. Thing
    c. Undefined
    d. Undefined

11. _____ is a term used in Geology to refer to the state of gravitational equilibrium between the Earth's lithosphere and asthenosphere such that the tectonic plates "float" at an elevation which depends on their thickness and density. It is invoked to explain how different topographic heights can exist at the Earth's surface.
    a. Isostasy0
    b. Thing
    c. Undefined
    d. Undefined

12. _____ is the rise of land masses that were depressed by the huge weight of ice sheets during the last ice age, through a process known as isostatic depression. It affects northern Europe, especially Scotland and Scandinavia, Siberia, Canada, and the Great Lakes of Canada and the United States.
    a. Thing
    b. Post glacial rebound0
    c. Undefined
    d. Undefined

13. _____ is the rise of land masses that were depressed by the huge weight of ice sheets during the last ice age, through a process known as isostatic depression.
    a. Post-glacial rebound0
    b. Thing
    c. Undefined
    d. Undefined

14. The _____ is the layer of granitic, sedimentary, and metamorphic rocks which form the continents and the areas of shallow seabed close to their shores, known as continental shelves. It is less dense than the material of the Earth's mantle and thus "floats" on top of it. _____ is also less dense than oceanic crust, though it is considerably thicker. About 40% of the Earth's surface is now underlain by _____.
    a. Continental crust0
    b. Thing
    c. Undefined
    d. Undefined

15. Earth's _____ is a ~2,900 km thick rocky shell comprizing approximately 70% of Earth's volume. It is predominantly solid and overlies the Earth's iron-rich core, which occupies about 30% of Earth's volume. Past episodes of melting and volcanism at the shallower levels of the _____ have produced a very thin crust of crystallized melt products near the surface, upon which we live.
    a. Mantle0
    b. Thing
    c. Undefined
    d. Undefined

16. _____ is a field of study within geology concerned generally with the structures within the crust of the Earth, or other planets, and particularly with the forces and movements that have operated in a region to create these structures.

Chapter 20. Mountain Belts and the Continental Crust

a. Thing
b. Tectonics0
c. Undefined
d. Undefined

17. _____ is a theory of geology that has been developed to explain the observed evidence for large scale motions of the Earth's lithosphere. The theory encompassed and superseded the older theory of continental drift.
a. Thing
b. Plate tectonics0
c. Undefined
d. Undefined

18. A _____ is a special-purpose map made to show geological features. The stratigraphic contour lines are drawn on the surface of a selected deep stratum, so that they can show the topographic trends of the strata under the ground. It is not always possible to properly show this when the strata are extremely fractured, mixed, in some discontinuities, or where they are otherwise disturbed.
a. Thing
b. Geologic map0
c. Undefined
d. Undefined

19. The _____ is defined as the part of the land adjoining or near the ocean. A coastline is properly a line on a map indicating the disposition of a _____, but the word is often used to refer to the _____ itself. The adjective coastal describes something as being on, near to, or associated with a _____.
a. Coast0
b. Place
c. Undefined
d. Undefined

20. _____ is displacement of solids by the agents of ocean currents, wind, water, or ice by downward or down-slope movement in response to gravity or by living organisms.
a. Thing
b. Erosion0
c. Undefined
d. Undefined

21. The _____ is an informal name for the eons of the geologic timescale that came before the current Phanerozoic eon. It spans from the formation of Earth around 4500 Ma to the evolution of abundant macroscopic hard-shelled animals, which marked the beginning of the Cambrian, the first period of the first era of the Phanerozoic eon, some 542 Ma.
a. Precambrian0
b. Thing
c. Undefined
d. Undefined

22. _____ rock is one of the three main rock groups. Rock formed from these covers 75% of the Earth's land area, and includes common types such as chalk, limestone, dolomite, sandstone, and shale.
a. Thing
b. Sedimentary0
c. Undefined
d. Undefined

23. _____ is one of the three main rock groups. _____ covers 75% of the Earth's land area. Four basic processes are involved in the formation of a clastic _____: weathering caused mainly by friction of waves, transportation where the sediment is carried along by a current, deposition and compaction where the sediment is squashed together to form a rock of this kind.
a. Sedimentary rock0
b. Thing
c. Undefined
d. Undefined

24. In geology, a _____ is a deformational feature consisting of symmetrically-dipping anticlines; their general outline on a geologic map is circular or oval.

Chapter 20. Mountain Belts and the Continental Crust

    a. Dome0
    c. Undefined
    b. Thing
    d. Undefined

25. A _____ is an old and stable part of the continental crust that has survived the merging and splitting of continents and supercontinents. Cratons are generally found in the interiors of continents and are characteristically composed of ancient crystalline basement crust of lightweight felsic igneous rock such as granite. They have a thick crust and deep roots that extend into the mantle beneath to depths of 200 km.
    a. Craton0
    c. Undefined
    b. Thing
    d. Undefined

26. _____ is any particulate matter that can be transported by fluid flow and which eventually is deposited as a layer of solid particles on the bed or bottom of a body of water or other liquid.
    a. Sediment0
    c. Undefined
    b. Thing
    d. Undefined

27. _____ is an igneous rock of volcanic origin. They often have a vesicular texture, which is the result voids left by volatiles escaping from the molten lava. Pumice is a rock, which is an example of explosive volcanic eruption. It is so vesicular that it floats in water.
    a. Thing
    c. Undefined
    b. Volcanic rock0
    d. Undefined

28. _____ is molten rock expelled by a volcano during an eruption. When first extruded from a volcanic vent, it is a liquid at temperatures from 700 °C to 1,200 °C.
    a. Lava0
    c. Undefined
    b. Thing
    d. Undefined

29. The term _____ is used in geology when one or a stack of originally flat and planar surfaces, such as sedimentary strata, are bent or curved as a result of plastic, i.e. permanent, deformation.
    a. Fold0
    c. Undefined
    b. Thing
    d. Undefined

30. Faults are planar rock fractures, which show evidence of relative movement. Large faults within the Earth's crust are the result of shear motion and active _____ zones are the causal locations of most earthquakes. Earthquakes are caused by energy release during rapid slippage along faults. The largest examples are at tectonic plate boundaries but many faults occur far from active plate boundaries. Since faults do not usually consist of a single, clean fracture, the term _____ zone is used when referring to the zone of complex deformation that is associated with the _____ plane.
    a. Fault0
    c. Undefined
    b. Thing
    d. Undefined

31. _____ is associated with large-scale lithospheric extensional tectonics. They often have very large displacement 10s of km and juxtapose unmetamorphosed hanging walls against medium to high-grade metamorphic footwalls.
    a. Detachment faulting0
    c. Undefined
    b. Thing
    d. Undefined

32. _____ is the process of heating a solid substance to a point where it turns into a liquid. An object that has melted is molten.

Chapter 20. Mountain Belts and the Continental Crust

a. Thing
b. Melting0
c. Undefined
d. Undefined

33. _____ is a common and widely occurring type of intrusive, felsic, igneous rock. Granites are usually medium to coarsely crystalline, occasionally with some individual crystals larger than the groundmass forming a rock known as porphyry. Granites can be pink to dark gray or even black, depending on their chemistry and mineralogy.
a. Granite0
b. Thing
c. Undefined
d. Undefined

34. _____ is molten rock located beneath the surface of the Earth, and which often collects in a _____ chamber. _____ is a complex high-temperature fluid substance. Most are silicate solutions. It is capable of intrusion into adjacent rocks or of extrusion onto the surface as lava or ejected explosively as tephra to form pyroclastic rock. Environments of _____ formation include subduction zones, continental rift zones, mid-oceanic ridges, and hotspots, some of which are interpreted as mantle plumes.
a. Magma0
b. Thing
c. Undefined
d. Undefined

35. _____, in everyday life, is most familiar as the agency that endows objects with weight. _____ is responsible for keeping the Earth and the other planets in their orbits around the Sun; for the formation of tides; and for various other phenomena that we observe. _____ is also the reason for the very existence of the Earth, the Sun, and most macroscopic objects in the universe; without it, matter would not have coalesced into these large masses, and life, as we know it, would not exist.
a. Thing
b. Gravitation0
c. Undefined
d. Undefined

36. _____ is the part of Earth's lithosphere that surfaces in the ocean basins. _____ is primarily composed of mafic rocks, or sima. It is thinner than continental crust, or sial, generally less than 10 kilometers thick, however it is more dense, having a mean density of about 3.3 grams per cubic centimeter.
a. Thing
b. Oceanic crust0
c. Undefined
d. Undefined

37. _____ in meteorology are large scale patterns in the atmospheric pressure field that are nearly stationary, effectively "blocking" or redirecting migratory cyclones. These _____ can remain in place for several days or even weeks, causing the areas affected by them to have the same kind of weather for an extended period of time.
a. Blocks0
b. Thing
c. Undefined
d. Undefined

38. An _____ is any piece of land that is completely surrounded by water, above high tide. There are two main types of islands: continental islands and oceanic islands. There are also artificial islands. A grouping of geographically and/or geologically related islands is called an archipelago.
a. Thing
b. Island0
c. Undefined
d. Undefined

39. A _____ is a chain of volcanic islands or mountains formed by plate tectonics as an oceanic tectonic plate subducts under another tectonic plate and produces magma.

Chapter 20. Mountain Belts and the Continental Crust

    a. Volcanic arc0   b. Thing
    c. Undefined   d. Undefined

40. _____ is a sedimentary rock composed mainly of sand-size mineral or rock grains. Most _____ is composed of quartz and/or feldspar because these are the most common minerals in the Earth's crust. Like sand, _____ may be any color, but the most common colors are tan, brown, yellow, red, gray and white.
    a. Thing   b. Sandstone0
    c. Undefined   d. Undefined

41. _____ is the second most common mineral in the Earth's continental crust. It is made up of a lattice of silica tetrahedra. _____ belongs to the rhombohedral crystal system. In nature _____ crystals are often twinned, distorted, or so intergrown with adjacent crystals of _____ or other minerals as to only show part of this shape, or to lack obvious crystal faces altogether and appear massive.
    a. Thing   b. Quartz0
    c. Undefined   d. Undefined

42. _____ is a fine-grained sedimentary rock whose original constituents were clays or muds. It is characterized by thin laminae breaking with an irregular curving fracture, often splintery and usually parallel to the often-indistinguishable bedding plane.
    a. Thing   b. Shale0
    c. Undefined   d. Undefined

43. _____ is a sedimentary rock composed largely of the mineral calcite. _____ often contains variable amounts of silica in the form of chert or flint, as well as varying amounts of clay, silt and sand as disseminations, nodules, or layers within the rock. The primary source of the calcite in _____ is most commonly marine organisms. These organisms secrete shells that settle out of the water column and are deposited on ocean floors as pelagic ooze or alternatively is conglomerated in a coral reef.
    a. Limestone0   b. Thing
    c. Undefined   d. Undefined

44. The _____ is the extended perimeter of each continent and associated coastal plain, which is covered during interglacial periods such as the current epoch by relatively shallow seas and gulfs. The shelf usually ends at a point of increasing slope.
    a. Thing   b. Continental shelf0
    c. Undefined   d. Undefined

45. In plate tectonics, a _____ is an actively deforming region where two tectonic plates or fragments of lithosphere move towards one another. When two plates move toward one another, they form either a subduction zone or a continental collision.
    a. Thing   b. Convergent boundary0
    c. Undefined   d. Undefined

46. _____ are clastic rocks composed solely or primarily of volcanic materials.
    a. Thing   b. Pyroclastics0
    c. Undefined   d. Undefined

Chapter 20. Mountain Belts and the Continental Crust

47. _____ is the process of building mountains, and may be studied as a tectonic structural event, as a geographical event and a chronological event, in that orogenic events cause distinctive structural phenomena and related tectonic activity, affect certain regions of rocks and crust and happen within a time frame.
    a. Thing
    b. Orogeny0
    c. Undefined
    d. Undefined

48. In geology, a _____ zone is an area on Earth where two tectonic plates meet and move towards one another, with one sliding underneath the other and moving down into the mantle, at rates typically measured in centimeters per year. An oceanic plate ordinarily slides underneath a continental plate; this often creates an orogenic zone with many volcanoes and earthquakes.
    a. Thing
    b. Subduction0
    c. Undefined
    d. Undefined

49. A _____ is an area on Earth where two tectonic plates meet and move towards one another, with one sliding underneath the other and moving down into the mantle, at rates typically measured in centimeters per year. In a sense, subduction zones are the opposite of divergent boundaries, areas where material rises up from the mantle and plates are moving apart.
    a. Thing
    b. Subduction zone0
    c. Undefined
    d. Undefined

50. A _____ fault is a particular type of fault, or break in the fabric of the Earth's crust with resulting movement of each side against the other, in which a lower stratigraphic position is pushed up and over another. This is the result of compressional forces.
    a. Thing
    b. Thrust0
    c. Undefined
    d. Undefined

51. In geology the term _____ refers to the system of forces that tend to decrease the volume of or shorten rocks. Compressive strength refers to the maximum compressive stress that can be applied to a material before failure occurs.
    a. Thing
    b. Compression0
    c. Undefined
    d. Undefined

52. A _____ is a type of excavation or depression in the ground. They are generally defined by being deeper than they are wide, and by being narrow compared to their length.
    a. Thing
    b. Trench0
    c. Undefined
    d. Undefined

53. A _____ is an area of highland, usually consisting of relatively flat rural area.
    a. Place
    b. Plateau0
    c. Undefined
    d. Undefined

54. _____ is the supercontinent that existed during the Paleozoic and Mesozoic eras before each of the component continents were separated into their current configuration.
    a. Event
    b. Pangaea0
    c. Undefined
    d. Undefined

Chapter 20. Mountain Belts and the Continental Crust

55. An _____ is a long period of time with different technical and colloquial meanings, and usages in language. It begins with some beginning event known as an epoch, epochal date, epochal event or epochal moment.
    a. Era0
    b. Thing
    c. Undefined
    d. Undefined

56. The _____ is one of three geologic eras of the Phanerozoic eon. The _____ was a time of tectonic, climatic and evolutionary activity, shifting from a state of connectedness into their present configuration. The climate was exceptionally warm throughout the period, also playing an important role in the evolution and diversification of new animal species. By the end of the era, the basis of modern life was in place.
    a. Mesozoic0
    b. Thing
    c. Undefined
    d. Undefined

57. A _____ is a place where, through continental collision, two continental plates have joined together. The Himilayas and the Alps mark these zones as do other very high mountain ranges.
    a. Suture zone0
    b. Thing
    c. Undefined
    d. Undefined

58. In plate tectonics, a _____ a linear feature that exists between two tectonic plates that are moving away from each other. These areas can form in the middle of continents but eventually form ocean basins.
    a. Thing
    b. Divergent plate boundary0
    c. Undefined
    d. Undefined

59. The _____ describes the periodic opening and closing of ocean basins.
    a. Thing
    b. Wilson cycle0
    c. Undefined
    d. Undefined

60. _____ rocks form when molten rock, magma, cools and solidifies, with or without crystallization, either below the surface as intrusive, plutonic rocks or on the surface as extrusive, volcanic, rocks.
    a. Thing
    b. Igneous0
    c. Undefined
    d. Undefined

61. _____ forms when rock cools and solidifies either below the surface as intrusive rocks or on the surface as extrusive rocks. This magma can be derived from partial melts of pre-existing rocks in either the Earth's mantle or crust. Typically, the melting is caused by one or more of the following processes -- an increase in temperature, a decrease in pressure, or a change in composition.
    a. Igneous rock0
    b. Thing
    c. Undefined
    d. Undefined

62. _____ is the stress applied to materials resulting in their compaction, decrease of volume.
    a. Thing
    b. Compression stress0
    c. Undefined
    d. Undefined

63. _____ is the study of Earth's surface features or those of other planets, moons, and asteroids
    a. Thing
    b. Topography0
    c. Undefined
    d. Undefined

Chapter 20. Mountain Belts and the Continental Crust

64. _____ is the condition of a system in which competing influences are balanced.
   a. Thing
   b. Equilibrium0
   c. Undefined
   d. Undefined

65. _____ is the process of breaking down rocks, soils and their minerals through direct contact with the atmosphere. _____ occurs without movement. Two main classifications of _____ processes exist. Mechanical or physical _____ involves the breakdown of rocks and soils through direct contact with atmospheric conditions. The second classification, chemical _____, involves the direct effect of atmospheric chemicals in the breakdown of rocks, soils and minerals.
   a. Weathering0
   b. Thing
   c. Undefined
   d. Undefined

66. _____ is any product of the condensation of atmospheric water vapor that is deposited on the earth's surface. It occurs when the atmosphere becomes saturated with water vapour and the water condenses and falls out of solution. Air becomes saturated via two processes, cooling and adding moisture.
   a. Precipitation0
   b. Thing
   c. Undefined
   d. Undefined

67. A _____ is a large, slow moving river of ice, formed from compacted layers of snow, that slowly deforms and flows in response to gravity. _____ ice is the largest reservoir of fresh water on Earth, and second only to oceans as the largest reservoir of total water. Glaciers cover vast areas of polar regions but are restricted to the highest mountains in the tropics.
   a. Glacier0
   b. Thing
   c. Undefined
   d. Undefined

68. A _____ travels through the Earth, most often as the result of a tectonic earthquake, sometimes from an explosion. They are also continually excited by the pounding of ocean waves and the wind.
   a. Thing
   b. Seismic wave0
   c. Undefined
   d. Undefined

69. A _____ is a disturbance that propagates through space or spacetime, transferring energy and momentum and sometimes angular momentum.
   a. Wave0
   b. Thing
   c. Undefined
   d. Undefined

70. The _____ is the region of the Earth between 100-200 km below the surface that is the weak or "soft" zone in the upper mantle. It lies just below the lithosphere, which is involved in plate movements and isostatic adjustments. In spite of its heat, pressures keep it plastic, and it has a relatively low density. Seismic waves pass relatively slowly through the _____.
   a. Asthenosphere0
   b. Thing
   c. Undefined
   d. Undefined

71. A _____ is a dry region on the surface of the Earth that is leeward or behind of a mountain with respect to the prevailing wind direction.

Chapter 20. Mountain Belts and the Continental Crust

    a. Thing
    b. Rain shadow0
    c. Undefined
    d. Undefined

72. _____ is a mode of failure of laminated composite materials. Repeated cyclic stresses, impact, and so on can cause layers to separate, forming a mica-like structure of separate layers, with significant loss of mechanical toughness. _____ is an insidious kind of failure as it develops inside of the material, without being obvious on the surface, much like metal fatigue.
    a. Thing
    b. Delamination0
    c. Undefined
    d. Undefined

73. The _____ is the solid outermost shell of a rocky planet. On the Earth, the _____ includes the crust and the uppermost mantle which is joined to the crust across the Mohorovièiæ discontinuity. _____ is underlain by asthenosphere, the weaker, hotter, and deeper part of the upper mantle.
    a. Thing
    b. Lithosphere0
    c. Undefined
    d. Undefined

74. _____ is an igneous, volcanic rock, of felsic composition. It may have any texture from aphanitic to porphyritic. The mineral assemblage is usually quartz, alkali feldspar and plagioclase. Biotite and pyroxene are common accessory minerals.
    a. Rhyolite0
    b. Thing
    c. Undefined
    d. Undefined

75. Fossils are the mineralized or otherwise preserved remains or traces of animals, plants, and other organisms. The totality of fossils, both discovered and undiscovered, and their placement in fossiliferous rock formations and sedimentary layers is known as the _____ record.
    a. Thing
    b. Fossil0
    c. Undefined
    d. Undefined

76. The _____ is the earliest of three geologic eras of the Phanerozoic eon. The _____ is subdivided into six geologic periods; from oldest to youngest they are: the Cambrian, Ordovician, Silurian, Devonian, Carboniferous, and Permian.
    a. Paleozoic0
    b. Thing
    c. Undefined
    d. Undefined

77. A _____ in paleogeography is an accretion that has collided with a continental nucleus, or "craton" but can be recognized by the foreign origin of its rock strata. The boundaries of a _____ are usually represented by crustal faults. In the lithospheric scheme of plate tectonics, a _____ is not a microplate, but a piece of crust "riding" atop another plate.
    a. Thing
    b. Terrane0
    c. Undefined
    d. Undefined

Chapter 21. Geologic Resources

1. _____ is the second most common mineral in the Earth's continental crust. It is made up of a lattice of silica tetrahedra. _____ belongs to the rhombohedral crystal system. In nature _____ crystals are often twinned, distorted, or so intergrown with adjacent crystals of _____ or other minerals as to only show part of this shape, or to lack obvious crystal faces altogether and appear massive.
   a. Quartz0
   b. Thing
   c. Undefined
   d. Undefined

2. _____ is a naturally occurring liquid found in formations in the Earth consisting of a complex mixture of hydrocarbons of various lengths.
   a. Thing
   b. Petroleum0
   c. Undefined
   d. Undefined

3. _____ is a gaseous fossil fuel consisting primarily of methane but including significant quantities of ethane, butane, propane, carbon dioxide, nitrogen, helium and hydrogen sulfide.
   a. Thing
   b. Natural gas0
   c. Undefined
   d. Undefined

4. _____ is a fossil fuel formed in swamp ecosystems where plant remains were saved by water and mud from oxidization and biodegradation. It is a sedimentary rock, but the harder forms, such as anthracite _____, can be regarded as metamorphic rocks because of later exposure to elevated temperature and pressure. It is composed primarily of carbon along with assorted other elements, including sulfur.
   a. Thing
   b. Coal0
   c. Undefined
   d. Undefined

5. _____ is rock that is of a certain particle size range. In geology, _____ is any loose rock that is at least two millimeters in its largest dimension and no more than 75 millimeters.
   a. Gravel0
   b. Thing
   c. Undefined
   d. Undefined

6. _____ is a sedimentary rock composed largely of the mineral calcite. _____ often contains variable amounts of silica in the form of chert or flint, as well as varying amounts of clay, silt and sand as disseminations, nodules, or layers within the rock. The primary source of the calcite in _____ is most commonly marine organisms. These organisms secrete shells that settle out of the water column and are deposited on ocean floors as pelagic ooze or alternatively is conglomerated in a coral reef.
   a. Limestone0
   b. Thing
   c. Undefined
   d. Undefined

7. A _____ is a naturally occurring substance formed through geological processes that has a characteristic chemical composition, a highly ordered atomic structure and specific physical properties. A rock, by comparison, is an aggregate of minerals and need not have a specific chemical composition. Minerals range in composition from pure elements and simple salts to very complex silicates with thousands of known forms.
   a. Mineral0
   b. Thing
   c. Undefined
   d. Undefined

8. Fossils are the mineralized or otherwise preserved remains or traces of animals, plants, and other organisms. The totality of fossils, both discovered and undiscovered, and their placement in fossiliferous rock formations and sedimentary layers is known as the _____ record.

Chapter 21. Geologic Resources

    a. Thing
    b. Fossil0
    c. Undefined
    d. Undefined

9. Fossil fuels are hydrocarbons, primarily coal and petroleum, formed from the fossilized remains of dead plants and animals. In common parlance, the term _____ also includes hydrocarbon-containing natural resources that are not derived from animal or plant sources. Fossil fuels have made large-scale industrial development possible and have largely supplanted water-driven mills, as well as the combustion of wood or peat for heat.
    a. Fossil fuel0
    b. Thing
    c. Undefined
    d. Undefined

10. _____ are hydrocarbons, primarily coal and petroleum, formed from the fossilized remains of dead plants and animals by exposure to heat and pressure in the Earth's crust over hundreds of millions of years. The burning of _____ by humans is the largest source of emissions of carbon dioxide, which is one of the greenhouse gases that enhances radiative forcing and contributes to global warming.
    a. Thing
    b. Fossil fuels0
    c. Undefined
    d. Undefined

11. _____ is any particulate matter that can be transported by fluid flow and which eventually is deposited as a layer of solid particles on the bed or bottom of a body of water or other liquid.
    a. Sediment0
    b. Thing
    c. Undefined
    d. Undefined

12. _____ rock is one of the three main rock groups. Rock formed from these covers 75% of the Earth's land area, and includes common types such as chalk, limestone, dolomite, sandstone, and shale.
    a. Sedimentary0
    b. Thing
    c. Undefined
    d. Undefined

13. _____ is one of the three main rock groups. _____ covers 75% of the Earth's land area. Four basic processes are involved in the formation of a clastic _____: weathering caused mainly by friction of waves, transportation where the sediment is carried along by a current, deposition and compaction where the sediment is squashed together to form a rock of this kind.
    a. Sedimentary rock0
    b. Thing
    c. Undefined
    d. Undefined

14. _____ is a fine-grained sedimentary rock whose original constituents were clays or muds. It is characterized by thin laminae breaking with an irregular curving fracture, often splintery and usually parallel to the often-indistinguishable bedding plane.
    a. Shale0
    b. Thing
    c. Undefined
    d. Undefined

15. Most often, a _____ refers to an artificial lake, used to store water for various uses. Reservoirs are created first by building a sturdy dam, usually out of cement, earth, rock, or a mixture. Once the dam is completed, a stream is allowed to flow behind it and eventually fill it to capacity.
    a. Thing
    b. Reservoir0
    c. Undefined
    d. Undefined

Chapter 21. Geologic Resources

16. _____ is a sedimentary rock composed mainly of sand-size mineral or rock grains. Most _____ is composed of quartz and/or feldspar because these are the most common minerals in the Earth's crust. Like sand, _____ may be any color, but the most common colors are tan, brown, yellow, red, gray and white.
    a. Thing
    b. Sandstone0
    c. Undefined
    d. Undefined

17. The term _____ is used in geology when one or a stack of originally flat and planar surfaces, such as sedimentary strata, are bent or curved as a result of plastic, i.e. permanent, deformation.
    a. Fold0
    b. Thing
    c. Undefined
    d. Undefined

18. In geology the term _____ refers to the system of forces that tend to decrease the volume of or shorten rocks. Compressive strength refers to the maximum compressive stress that can be applied to a material before failure occurs.
    a. Compression0
    b. Thing
    c. Undefined
    d. Undefined

19. A _____ is a landform that extends above the surrounding terrain in a limited area. A _____ is generally steeper than a hill, but there is no universally accepted standard definition for the height of a _____ or a hill although a _____ usually has an identifiable summit.
    a. Mountain0
    b. Place
    c. Undefined
    d. Undefined

20. _____, a branch of geology, studies rock layers and layering. It is primarily used in the study of sedimentary and layered volcanic rocks. _____ includes two related subfields: lithologic or lithostratigraphy and biologic _____ or biostratigraphy.
    a. Stratigraphy0
    b. Thing
    c. Undefined
    d. Undefined

21. A _____ is a rock, sandbar, or other feature lying beneath the surface of the water yet shallow enough to be a hazard to ships. They result from abiotic processes—deposition of sand, wave erosion planning down rock outcrops, and other natural processes.
    a. Reef0
    b. Thing
    c. Undefined
    d. Undefined

22. In geology, engineering, and surveying, _____ is the motion of a surface as it shifts downward relative to a datum such as sea-level. The opposite of _____ is uplift, which results in an increase in elevation. In meteorology, _____ refers to the downward movement of air.
    a. Thing
    b. Subsidence0
    c. Undefined
    d. Undefined

23. The _____ is a geologic period of the Paleozoic era. During the _____ the first fish evolved legs and started to walk on land as tetrapods and the first insects and spiders also started to colonize terrestrial habitats. The first seed-bearing plants spread across dry land, forming huge forests. In the oceans, Primitive sharks became more numerous. The first ammonite mollusks appeared, and trilobites as well as great coral reefs were still common.

a. Thing
b. Devonian0
c. Undefined
d. Undefined

24. The _____ is defined as the part of the land adjoining or near the ocean. A coastline is properly a line on a map indicating the disposition of a _____, but the word is often used to refer to the _____ itself. The adjective coastal describes something as being on, near to, or associated with a _____.
   a. Coast0
   b. Place
   c. Undefined
   d. Undefined

25. In geology, _____ is soil at or below the freezing point of water for two or more years. Ice is not always present, as may be in the case of nonporous bedrock, but it frequently occurs and it may be in amounts exceeding the potential hydraulic saturation of the ground material. Most _____ is located in high latitudes, but alpine _____ exists at high altitudes.
   a. Permafrost0
   b. Thing
   c. Undefined
   d. Undefined

26. _____ is a measure of the resistance of a fluid to deform under shear stress. It is commonly perceived as "thickness", or resistance to flow. _____ describes a fluid's internal resistance to flow and may be thought of as a measure of fluid friction.
   a. Viscosity0
   b. Thing
   c. Undefined
   d. Undefined

27. _____ is the process by which molecules in a liquid state become a gas.
   a. Thing
   b. Evaporation0
   c. Undefined
   d. Undefined

28. _____ is a general term applied to a fine-grained sedimentary rock containing significant traces of kerogen that have not been buried for sufficient time to produce conventional fossil fuels. When heated to a sufficiently high temperature a vapor is driven off which can be distilled to yield a petroleum.
   a. Thing
   b. Oil shale0
   c. Undefined
   d. Undefined

29. _____ is the process of a material being more closely packed together.
   a. Compaction0
   b. Thing
   c. Undefined
   d. Undefined

30. _____ is an accumulation of partially decayed vegetation matter. It forms in wetlands.
   a. Peat0
   b. Thing
   c. Undefined
   d. Undefined

31. _____ is the lowest rank of coal and used almost exclusively as fuel for steam-electric power generation.
   a. Lignite0
   b. Thing
   c. Undefined
   d. Undefined

32. _____ is a relatively hard coal containing a tar-like substance called bitumen. It is of higher quality than lignite coal but of poorer quality than anthracite coal.

Chapter 21. Geologic Resources

a. Bituminous coal0
b. Thing
c. Undefined
d. Undefined

33. _____ is a hard, compact variety of mineral coal that has a high luster. It has the highest carbon count and contains the fewest impurities of all coals, despite its lower calorific content.
   a. Anthracite0
   b. Thing
   c. Undefined
   d. Undefined

34. _____ is the result of the transformation of a pre-existing rock type, the protolith, in a process called metamorphism, which means "change in form". The protolith is subjected to heat and extreme pressure causing profound physical and/or chemical change. The protolith may be sedimentary rock, igneous rock or another older rock.
   a. Metamorphic rock0
   b. Thing
   c. Undefined
   d. Undefined

35. _____ can be defined as the solid state recrystallisation of pre-existing rocks due to changes in heat and/or pressure and/or introduction of fluids. There will be mineralogical, chemical and crystallographic changes. _____ produced with increasing pressure and temperature conditions is known as prograde _____. Conversely, decreasing temperatures and pressure characterize retrograde _____.
   a. Thing
   b. Metamorphism0
   c. Undefined
   d. Undefined

36. _____ is a term used in geology to denote the pressure imposed on a stratigraphic layer by the weight of overlying layers of material.
   a. Lithostatic pressure0
   b. Event
   c. Undefined
   d. Undefined

37. A _____ is a type of excavation or depression in the ground. They are generally defined by being deeper than they are wide, and by being narrow compared to their length.
   a. Thing
   b. Trench0
   c. Undefined
   d. Undefined

38. _____ is the process of building mountains, and may be studied as a tectonic structural event, as a geographical event and a chronological event, in that orogenic events cause distinctive structural phenomena and related tectonic activity, affect certain regions of rocks and crust and happen within a time frame.
   a. Orogeny0
   b. Thing
   c. Undefined
   d. Undefined

39. The _____ is the surface where the water pressure is equal to atmospheric pressure. A large amount of water within a body of sand or rock below the _____ is called an aquifer, and the ability of rocks to store such groundwater is dependent on their porosity and permeability.
   a. Thing
   b. Water table0
   c. Undefined
   d. Undefined

Chapter 21. Geologic Resources

40. _____ is the increase in the average temperature of the Earth's near-surface air and oceans in recent decades and its projected continuation. An increase in global temperatures can in turn cause other changes, including sea level rise, and changes in the amount and pattern of precipitation resulting in floods and drought. There may also be changes in the frequency and intensity of extreme weather events.
   a. Global warming0
   b. Thing
   c. Undefined
   d. Undefined

41. An _____ is a chemical compound containing an oxygen atom and other elements. Most of the earth's crust consists of them. They result when elements are oxidized by air.
   a. Oxide0
   b. Thing
   c. Undefined
   d. Undefined

42. _____ is a fossil wood, where all the organic materials have been replaced with minerals, while retaining the original structure of the wood. The petrifaction process occurs underground, when wood becomes buried under sediment. Mineral-rich water flowing through the sediment deposits minerals in the plant's cells and as the plant's lignin and cellulose decay away, a stone mould forms in its place.
   a. Petrified wood0
   b. Thing
   c. Undefined
   d. Undefined

43. The _____ is used by geologists and other scientists to describe the timing and relationships between events that have occurred during the history of Earth.
   a. Thing
   b. Geological time scale0
   c. Undefined
   d. Undefined

44. A _____ is a sequence of reactions where a reactive product or by-product causes additional reactions to take place.
   a. Chain reaction0
   b. Thing
   c. Undefined
   d. Undefined

45. _____ is electricity produced by hydropower. _____ now supplies about 715,000 MWe or 19% of world electricity. It is also the world's leading form of renewable energy, accounting for over 63% of the total in 2005.
   a. Hydroelectricity0
   b. Thing
   c. Undefined
   d. Undefined

46. In geology, _____ refers to heat sources within the planet. The planet's internal heat was originally generated during its accretion, due to gravitational binding energy, and since then additional heat has continued to be generated by the radioactive decay of elements such as uranium, thorium, and potassium.
   a. Geothermal0
   b. Thing
   c. Undefined
   d. Undefined

47. _____ is the use of geothermal heat to generate electricity.
   a. Thing
   b. Geothermal power0
   c. Undefined
   d. Undefined

48. _____ is Solar Radiation emitted from our sun. It has been used in many traditional technologies for centuries, and has come into widespread use where other power supplies are absent, such as in remote locations and in space.

Chapter 21. Geologic Resources

a. Solar power0
b. Thing
c. Undefined
d. Undefined

49. _____ is an ecological concept referring to the relative representation of a species in a particular ecosystem. It is usually measured as the mean number of individuals found per sample.
 a. Abundance0
 b. Thing
 c. Undefined
 d. Undefined

50. An _____ is a volume of rock containing components or minerals in a mode of occurrence that renders it valuable for mining.
 a. Thing
 b. Ore0
 c. Undefined
 d. Undefined

51. _____ is an ore consisting in a mixture of hydrated iron oxide-hydroxide of varying composition. It often contains a varying amount of oxide compared to hydroxide.
 a. Limonite0
 b. Thing
 c. Undefined
 d. Undefined

52. _____ is a very common mineral, colored black to steel or silver-gray, brown to reddish brown, or red. It is mined as the main ore of iron. Varieties include kidney ore, martite iron rose and specularite. While the forms of it vary, they all have a rust-red streak. it is harder than pure iron, but much more brittle.
 a. Thing
 b. Hematite0
 c. Undefined
 d. Undefined

53. A _____ is a solid in which the constituent atoms, molecules, or ions are packed in a regularly ordered, repeating pattern extending in all three spatial dimensions. Most metals encountered in everyday life are polycrystals. Crystals are often symmetrically intergrown to form _____ twins.
 a. Thing
 b. Crystal0
 c. Undefined
 d. Undefined

54. _____ is molten rock located beneath the surface of the Earth, and which often collects in a _____ chamber. _____ is a complex high-temperature fluid substance. Most are silicate solutions. It is capable of intrusion into adjacent rocks or of extrusion onto the surface as lava or ejected explosively as tephra to form pyroclastic rock. Environments of _____ formation include subduction zones, continental rift zones, mid-oceanic ridges, and hotspots, some of which are interpreted as mantle plumes.
 a. Magma0
 b. Thing
 c. Undefined
 d. Undefined

55. An _____ is a body of igneous rock that has crystallized from a molten magma below the surface of the Earth.
 a. Intrusion0
 b. Thing
 c. Undefined
 d. Undefined

56. The _____ is an informal name for the eons of the geologic timescale that came before the current Phanerozoic eon. It spans from the formation of Earth around 4500 Ma to the evolution of abundant macroscopic hard-shelled animals, which marked the beginning of the Cambrian, the first period of the first era of the Phanerozoic eon, some 542 Ma.

a. Precambrian0
b. Thing
c. Undefined
d. Undefined

57. A _____ in geology is an intrusive igneous rock body that crystallized from a magma below the surface of the Earth. Plutons include batholiths, dikes, sills, laccoliths, lopoliths, and other igneous bodies. In practice, "_____" usually refers to a distinctive mass of igneous rock, typically kilometers in dimension, without a tabular shape like those of dikes and sills.
a. Thing
b. Pluton0
c. Undefined
d. Undefined

58. _____ is the oxide of silicon, chemical formula SiO_2, and is known for its hardness as early as the 16th century. It is a principle component in most types of glass and substances such as concrete.
a. Thing
b. Silica0
c. Undefined
d. Undefined

59. The term _____ refers to several types of chemical compounds containing sulfur in its lowest oxidation number of −2.
a. Thing
b. Sulfide0
c. Undefined
d. Undefined

60. _____ is a variety of igneous rock consisting of large-grained crystals, such as feldspar or quartz, dispersed in a fine-grained feldspathic matrix or groundmass. The larger crystals are called phenocrysts.
a. Porphyry0
b. Thing
c. Undefined
d. Undefined

61. _____ is a ductile metal with excellent electrical conductivity, and finds extensive use as an electrical conductor, heat conductor, as a building material, and as a component of various alloys.
a. Thing
b. Copper0
c. Undefined
d. Undefined

62. _____ is a field of study within geology concerned generally with the structures within the crust of the Earth, or other planets, and particularly with the forces and movements that have operated in a region to create these structures.
a. Thing
b. Tectonics0
c. Undefined
d. Undefined

63. _____ is a theory of geology that has been developed to explain the observed evidence for large scale motions of the Earth's lithosphere. The theory encompassed and superseded the older theory of continental drift.
a. Thing
b. Plate tectonics0
c. Undefined
d. Undefined

64. _____ rocks form when molten rock, magma, cools and solidifies, with or without crystallization, either below the surface as intrusive, plutonic rocks or on the surface as extrusive, volcanic, rocks.
a. Igneous0
b. Thing
c. Undefined
d. Undefined

Chapter 21. Geologic Resources

65. _____ forms when rock cools and solidifies either below the surface as intrusive rocks or on the surface as extrusive rocks. This magma can be derived from partial melts of pre-existing rocks in either the Earth's mantle or crust. Typically, the melting is caused by one or more of the following processes -- an increase in temperature, a decrease in pressure, or a change in composition.
- a. Thing
- b. Igneous rock0
- c. Undefined
- d. Undefined

66. _____ is any product of the condensation of atmospheric water vapor that is deposited on the earth's surface. It occurs when the atmosphere becomes saturated with water vapour and the water condenses and falls out of solution. Air becomes saturated via two processes, cooling and adding moisture.
- a. Precipitation0
- b. Thing
- c. Undefined
- d. Undefined

67. _____ is a fine-grained silica-rich cryptocrystalline sedimentary rock that may contain small fossils. It varies greatly in color from white to black, but most often manifests as gray, brown, grayish brown and light green to rusty red; its color is an expression of trace elements present in the rock, and both red and green are most often related to traces of iron.
- a. Thing
- b. Chert0
- c. Undefined
- d. Undefined

68. _____ is the process of breaking down rocks, soils and their minerals through direct contact with the atmosphere. _____ occurs without movement. Two main classifications of _____ processes exist. Mechanical or physical _____ involves the breakdown of rocks and soils through direct contact with atmospheric conditions. The second classification, chemical _____, involves the direct effect of atmospheric chemicals in the breakdown of rocks, soils and minerals.
- a. Weathering0
- b. Thing
- c. Undefined
- d. Undefined

69. An _____ is a layer of gases that may surround a material body of sufficient mass. The gases are attracted by the gravity of the body, and are retained for a longer duration if gravity is high and the _____'s temperature is low. Some planets consist mainly of various gases, and thus have very deep atmospheres.
- a. Atmosphere0
- b. Place
- c. Undefined
- d. Undefined

70. A _____ is an accumulation of alluvium or eluvium containing valuable minerals which is formed by deposition of dense mineral phases in a trap site.
- a. Thing
- b. Placer0
- c. Undefined
- d. Undefined

71. _____ is an aluminium ore. It consists largely of the Al minerals gibbsite, boehmite and diaspore, together with the iron oxides goethite and hematite, the clay mineral kaolinite and small amounts of anatase.
- a. Bauxite0
- b. Thing
- c. Undefined
- d. Undefined

72. In geology, a _____ is a place where the Earth's crust and lithosphere are being pulled apart.

Chapter 21. Geologic Resources

a. Rift0
b. Thing
c. Undefined
d. Undefined

73. A _____ in geology is a valley created by the formation of a rift.
   a. Rift valley0
   b. Thing
   c. Undefined
   d. Undefined

74. In geology, a _____ is a depression with predominant extent in one direction. The terms U-shaped and V-shaped are descriptive terms of geography to characterize the form of valleys. Most valleys belong to one of these two main types or a mixture of them, at least with respect of the cross section of the slopes or hillsides.
   a. Thing
   b. Valley0
   c. Undefined
   d. Undefined

75. In plate tectonics, a _____ a linear feature that exists between two tectonic plates that are moving away from each other. These areas can form in the middle of continents but eventually form ocean basins.
   a. Thing
   b. Divergent plate boundary0
   c. Undefined
   d. Undefined

76. In geology, a _____ is the outermost layer of a planet, part of its lithosphere. They are generally composed of a less dense material than its deeper layers. Earths' is composed mainly of basalt and granite. It is cooler and more rigid than the deeper layers of the mantle and core.
   a. Thing
   b. Crust0
   c. Undefined
   d. Undefined

77. Earth's _____ is a ~2,900 km thick rocky shell comprizing approximately 70% of Earth's volume. It is predominantly solid and overlies the Earth's iron-rich core, which occupies about 30% of Earth's volume. Past episodes of melting and volcanism at the shallower levels of the _____ have produced a very thin crust of crystallized melt products near the surface, upon which we live.
   a. Thing
   b. Mantle0
   c. Undefined
   d. Undefined

78. In geology, a _____ zone is an area on Earth where two tectonic plates meet and move towards one another, with one sliding underneath the other and moving down into the mantle, at rates typically measured in centimeters per year. An oceanic plate ordinarily slides underneath a continental plate; this often creates an orogenic zone with many volcanoes and earthquakes.
   a. Subduction0
   b. Thing
   c. Undefined
   d. Undefined

79. A _____ is an area on Earth where two tectonic plates meet and move towards one another, with one sliding underneath the other and moving down into the mantle, at rates typically measured in centimeters per year. In a sense, subduction zones are the opposite of divergent boundaries, areas where material rises up from the mantle and plates are moving apart.
   a. Subduction zone0
   b. Thing
   c. Undefined
   d. Undefined

Chapter 21. Geologic Resources

80. The _____ is the layer of granitic, sedimentary, and metamorphic rocks which form the continents and the areas of shallow seabed close to their shores, known as continental shelves. It is less dense than the material of the Earth's mantle and thus "floats" on top of it. _____ is also less dense than oceanic crust, though it is considerably thicker. About 40% of the Earth's surface is now underlain by _____.
    a. Continental crust0
    b. Thing
    c. Undefined
    d. Undefined

81. A _____ is a body of water with a current, confined within a bed and banks. Streams are important as conduits in the water cycle, instruments in aquifer recharge, and corridors for fish and wildlife migration.
    a. Stream0
    b. Thing
    c. Undefined
    d. Undefined

82. _____ is a ferrimagnetic mineral one of several iron oxides and a member of the spinel group. The chemical IUPAC name is iron oxide and the common chemical name ferrous-ferric oxide.
    a. Magnetite0
    b. Thing
    c. Undefined
    d. Undefined

83. An _____ is a homogeneous mixture of two or more elements, at least one of which is a metal, and where the resulting material has metallic properties. The resulting metallic substance usually has different properties from those of its components.
    a. Alloy0
    b. Thing
    c. Undefined
    d. Undefined

84. A _____ is an isolated hill with steep sides and a small flat top, smaller than mesas and plateaus. Buttes are prevalent in the western United States and on the Hawaiian Islands, especially around Honolulu.
    a. Place
    b. Butte0
    c. Undefined
    d. Undefined

85. _____ is the extraction of valuable minerals or other geological materials from the earth, usually from an ore body, vein, or seam. Any material that cannot be grown from agricultural processes, or created artificially in a laboratory or factory, is usually extracted from the earth by this method.
    a. Mining0
    b. Thing
    c. Undefined
    d. Undefined

86. An _____ is a type of atom that is defined by its atomic number; that is, by the number of protons in its nucleus.
    a. Element0
    b. Thing
    c. Undefined
    d. Undefined

87. A _____ is a fragment of cooled pyroclastic material, lava or magma.
    a. Thing
    b. Cinder0
    c. Undefined
    d. Undefined

88. _____ is a common and widely occurring type of intrusive, felsic, igneous rock. Granites are usually medium to coarsely crystalline, occasionally with some individual crystals larger than the groundmass forming a rock known as porphyry. Granites can be pink to dark gray or even black, depending on their chemistry and mineralogy.

Chapter 21. Geologic Resources

   a. Thing
   c. Undefined
   b. Granite0
   d. Undefined

89. _____ refers to water-soluble, mineral sediments that result from the evaporation of bodies of surficial water.
   a. Thing
   c. Undefined
   b. Evaporite0
   d. Undefined

90. _____ is the mineral form of sodium chloride. _____ forms isometric crystals. It commonly occurs with other evaporite deposit minerals such as several of the sulfates, halides and borates. _____ occurs in vast lakes of sedimentary evaporite minerals that result from the drying up of enclosed beds, playas, and seas.
   a. Thing
   c. Undefined
   b. Halite0
   d. Undefined

91. _____ is the characteristic of a solid material expressing its resistance to permanent deformation.
   a. Thing
   c. Undefined
   b. Hardness0
   d. Undefined

92. _____ is a group of common rock-forming hydrous magnesium iron phyllosilicate $|Mg, Fe|_3Si_2O_5|OH|_4$ minerals; it may contain minor amounts of other elements including chromium, manganese, cobalt and nickel. There are three important mineral polymorphs of _____: antigorite, chrysotile and lizardite.
   a. Thing
   c. Undefined
   b. Serpentine0
   d. Undefined

93. In geology and astronomy, the term _____ is used to denote types of rock that consist predominantly of _____ minerals. Such rocks include a wide range of igneous, metamorphic and sedimentary types. Most of the Earth's mantle and crust are made up of _____ rocks. The same is true of the Moon and the other rocky planets.
   a. Silicate0
   c. Undefined
   b. Thing
   d. Undefined

94. _____, in everyday life, is most familiar as the agency that endows objects with weight. _____ is responsible for keeping the Earth and the other planets in their orbits around the Sun; for the formation of tides; and for various other phenomena that we observe. _____ is also the reason for the very existence of the Earth, the Sun, and most macroscopic objects in the universe; without it, matter would not have coalesced into these large masses, and life, as we know it, would not exist.
   a. Thing
   c. Undefined
   b. Gravitation0
   d. Undefined

95. _____ is a naturally occurring, soft, chalk-like sedimentary rock that is easily crumbled into a fine white to off-white powder. This powder has an abrasive feel, similar to pumice powder, and is very light, due to its high porosity.
   a. Thing
   c. Undefined
   b. Diatomaceous earth0
   d. Undefined

96. A _____ in petrology or mineralogy is an irregular rounded to spherical concretion. They are typically solid replacement bodies of chert or iron oxides formed during diagenesis of a sedimentary rock.

Chapter 21. Geologic Resources

a. Thing
b. Nodule0
c. Undefined
d. Undefined

97. _____ is a chemical element. Its ions are variously colored, and are used industrially as pigments and as oxidation chemicals. Its ions function as cofactors for a number of enzymes and the element is thus a required trace mineral for all known living organisms. It is a grey-white metal, resembling iron.
a. Manganese0
b. Thing
c. Undefined
d. Undefined

98. _____, are rock concretions on the sea bottom formed of concentric layers of iron and manganese hydroxides around a core.
a. Manganese nodules0
b. Thing
c. Undefined
d. Undefined

99. _____ is the science and study of the solid matter that constitute the Earth. Encompassing such things as rocks, soil, and gemstones, _____ studies the composition, structure, physical properties, history, and the processes that shape Earth's components.
a. Thing
b. Geology0
c. Undefined
d. Undefined

Chapter 1
1. a	2. b	3. a	4. b	5. b	6. b	7. b	8. a	9. a	10. a
11. a	12. a	13. b	14. b	15. b	16. a	17. a	18. b	19. a	20. b
21. a	22. b	23. b	24. b	25. a	26. a	27. a	28. a	29. a	30. a
31. b	32. a	33. b	34. a	35. b	36. a	37. b	38. b	39. a	40. b
41. a	42. a	43. b	44. a	45. a	46. a	47. b	48. a	49. a	50. b
51. b	52. a	53. a	54. a	55. a	56. b	57. b	58. b	59. b	60. a
61. b	62. a	63. b	64. b	65. a	66. a				

Chapter 2
1. b	2. a	3. a	4. a	5. b	6. a	7. a	8. b	9. b	10. a
11. b	12. a	13. a	14. a	15. a	16. b	17. b	18. b	19. a	20. b
21. a	22. a	23. b	24. b	25. b	26. b	27. a	28. b	29. b	30. b
31. a	32. a	33. b	34. b	35. b	36. b	37. a	38. b	39. a	40. b
41. b	42. a	43. a	44. a	45. b	46. a	47. a	48. a	49. b	50. a
51. a	52. a	53. a	54. b	55. a	56. a	57. b	58. b	59. a	60. b

Chapter 3
1. b	2. b	3. b	4. a	5. a	6. b	7. b	8. b	9. a	10. a
11. b	12. a	13. a	14. a	15. a	16. a	17. a	18. b	19. b	20. a
21. b	22. a	23. b	24. b	25. b	26. a	27. b	28. b	29. b	30. b
31. b	32. b	33. a	34. b	35. a	36. a	37. a	38. a	39. a	40. a
41. a	42. b	43. a	44. b	45. a	46. a	47. a	48. b	49. b	50. a
51. b	52. b	53. a	54. b	55. a	56. a	57. b	58. b	59. b	60. a
61. a	62. a	63. a	64. a	65. a	66. b	67. b	68. a	69. b	70. b
71. a	72. a	73. a	74. b	75. a	76. a	77. a	78. b	79. a	

Chapter 4
1. a	2. b	3. a	4. a	5. a	6. a	7. a	8. b	9. a	10. a
11. b	12. a	13. a	14. a	15. b	16. b	17. a	18. b	19. b	20. b
21. a	22. a	23. b	24. a	25. a	26. a	27. b	28. b	29. b	30. b
31. a	32. b	33. b	34. a	35. a	36. b	37. b	38. b	39. b	40. a
41. a	42. b	43. a	44. b	45. a	46. b	47. b	48. a	49. b	50. a
51. b	52. a	53. b	54. a	55. b	56. a	57. a	58. a	59. a	60. a
61. a	62. a	63. b	64. b	65. a	66. a	67. a			

Chapter 5
1. a	2. b	3. b	4. a	5. a	6. a	7. b	8. a	9. b	10. a
11. a	12. b	13. b	14. a	15. b	16. a	17. a	18. b	19. b	20. a
21. b	22. b	23. a	24. a	25. a	26. a	27. a	28. a	29. b	30. b
31. a	32. a	33. a	34. b	35. a	36. a	37. b	38. b	39. a	40. a
41. b	42. a	43. a	44. b	45. b	46. b	47. a	48. a	49. a	50. a
51. b	52. a	53. a	54. a	55. b	56. a	57. b	58. b	59. a	60. a
61. a	62. a	63. a	64. b	65. b	66. a	67. b	68. b	69. b	70. a
71. a	72. b								

ANSWER KEY

Chapter 6

1. b	2. b	3. a	4. b	5. a	6. b	7. a	8. a	9. a	10. a
11. a	12. b	13. b	14. a	15. b	16. a	17. a	18. a	19. a	20. a
21. b	22. a	23. a	24. a	25. a	26. a	27. a	28. a	29. a	30. a
31. a	32. a	33. b	34. a	35. a	36. b	37. a	38. a	39. a	40. a
41. b	42. b	43. a	44. b	45. b	46. b	47. b	48. b	49. a	50. a
51. b	52. a	53. a	54. a	55. b	56. a	57. a	58. a	59. a	60. a
61. a	62. a	63. a	64. a	65. a	66. a	67. b	68. a	69. b	70. b
71. a	72. a	73. a	74. a	75. a	76. a	77. b	78. b	79. b	80. a
81. a	82. b	83. a	84. b	85. b	86. a	87. b	88. a	89. a	90. b
91. a	92. b	93. b	94. b	95. b	96. a	97. a	98. b	99. b	100. b
101. a	102. a	103. a							

Chapter 7

1. a	2. b	3. a	4. b	5. a	6. b	7. b	8. a	9. a	10. b
11. b	12. a	13. a	14. b	15. b	16. a	17. b	18. b	19. b	20. b
21. b	22. a	23. a	24. b	25. b	26. b	27. a	28. b	29. a	30. b
31. a	32. a	33. b	34. a	35. b	36. a	37. a	38. b	39. a	40. b
41. b	42. a	43. b	44. a	45. b	46. a	47. b	48. b	49. a	50. a
51. a	52. b	53. b	54. b	55. b	56. b	57. a	58. b	59. b	60. a
61. b	62. b	63. b	64. a	65. a	66. a	67. a	68. a	69. a	70. a
71. a	72. b	73. b	74. a	75. b	76. b	77. a	78. a	79. b	80. b
81. b	82. a	83. a	84. a	85. b	86. b	87. a	88. a	89. a	90. b
91. a									

Chapter 8

1. b	2. a	3. b	4. b	5. a	6. b	7. a	8. b	9. a	10. a
11. b	12. a	13. a	14. b	15. a	16. a	17. a	18. a	19. b	20. a
21. b	22. b	23. a	24. b	25. a	26. a	27. a	28. b	29. a	30. a
31. b	32. a	33. a	34. b	35. a	36. b	37. b	38. a	39. a	40. a
41. a	42. b	43. a	44. a	45. a	46. b	47. b	48. a	49. a	50. a
51. b	52. b	53. a	54. a	55. a	56. b	57. b	58. a	59. a	60. b
61. a	62. b	63. a	64. b	65. a	66. a	67. b	68. a	69. a	70. a
71. b	72. b	73. a	74. a						

Chapter 9

1. b	2. a	3. a	4. a	5. b	6. b	7. b	8. b	9. a	10. b
11. a	12. a	13. a	14. b	15. a	16. b	17. b	18. b	19. b	20. b
21. b	22. a	23. a	24. b	25. a	26. b	27. a	28. a	29. b	30. b
31. a	32. b	33. b	34. a	35. a	36. a	37. a	38. a	39. a	40. b
41. a	42. a	43. a	44. a	45. b	46. a	47. b			

Chapter 10

1. a	2. a	3. a	4. a	5. a	6. b	7. a	8. a	9. b	10. a
11. a	12. a	13. b	14. a	15. a	16. a	17. a	18. a	19. b	20. a
21. a	22. a	23. a	24. a	25. a	26. a	27. b	28. a	29. a	30. b
31. a	32. b	33. b	34. a	35. a	36. a	37. a	38. a	39. b	40. a
41. a	42. b	43. b	44. b	45. b	46. b	47. a	48. b	49. a	50. a
51. a	52. a	53. b	54. b	55. b	56. b	57. a	58. a	59. b	60. a
61. a	62. b	63. a	64. b	65. b	66. b	67. a	68. b	69. b	70. b
71. a	72. b								

Chapter 11

1. a	2. a	3. a	4. b	5. a	6. b	7. a	8. b	9. a	10. a
11. b	12. a	13. a	14. b	15. a	16. b	17. a	18. b	19. a	20. b
21. a	22. b	23. b	24. a	25. a	26. a	27. a	28. b	29. b	30. b
31. b	32. a	33. b	34. b	35. b	36. a	37. a	38. a	39. a	40. a
41. a	42. a	43. a	44. b	45. b	46. a	47. a	48. a	49. b	50. a
51. b	52. b	53. b	54. b	55. b	56. b	57. b	58. b	59. b	60. a
61. a	62. b	63. a	64. a	65. b	66. b	67. b	68. b	69. b	70. b
71. b	72. a	73. b	74. b	75. b	76. b	77. b	78. a	79. a	80. a
81. a	82. a	83. b	84. b	85. a	86. a	87. b	88. a		

Chapter 12

1. a	2. a	3. a	4. b	5. a	6. b	7. b	8. a	9. a	10. b
11. b	12. b	13. b	14. b	15. b	16. a	17. b	18. a	19. b	20. a
21. a	22. a	23. b	24. b	25. a	26. b	27. a	28. a	29. a	30. a
31. a	32. b	33. b	34. b	35. b	36. b	37. a	38. a	39. b	40. a
41. a	42. b	43. b	44. a	45. b	46. a	47. a	48. a	49. b	50. a
51. a	52. a	53. a	54. a	55. b	56. a	57. b	58. b	59. b	60. a
61. b	62. a	63. a	64. b	65. a	66. b	67. a	68. a	69. a	70. b
71. a	72. a	73. b	74. b						

Chapter 13

1. b	2. a	3. a	4. b	5. a	6. b	7. b	8. a	9. b	10. a
11. a	12. a	13. b	14. a	15. a	16. b	17. a	18. a	19. b	20. a
21. b	22. a	23. a	24. b	25. b	26. b	27. b	28. a	29. b	30. b
31. b	32. b	33. b	34. b	35. b	36. a	37. b	38. a	39. a	40. b
41. b	42. b	43. a	44. b	45. a	46. a	47. a	48. b	49. a	50. a
51. a	52. a	53. b	54. a	55. b	56. a	57. b	58. a	59. a	60. b
61. b	62. b	63. a	64. b	65. b	66. b	67. a			

ANSWER KEY

Chapter 14
1. b   2. a   3. b   4. b   5. b   6. a   7. b   8. b   9. b   10. a
11. a   12. a   13. b   14. b   15. a   16. a   17. a   18. a   19. a   20. b
21. b   22. a   23. a   24. b   25. a   26. b   27. b   28. b   29. b   30. a
31. a   32. a   33. a   34. b   35. a   36. a   37. a   38. b   39. b   40. b
41. b   42. a   43. b   44. b   45. b   46. b   47. b   48. b   49. b

Chapter 15
1. a   2. a   3. a   4. b   5. a   6. a   7. a   8. a   9. a   10. a
11. b   12. a   13. a   14. a   15. b   16. b   17. b   18. b   19. a   20. b
21. a   22. a   23. a   24. a   25. b   26. a   27. b   28. b   29. a   30. b
31. b   32. a   33. b   34. b   35. a   36. b   37. a   38. a   39. a   40. b
41. a   42. a   43. a   44. b   45. a   46. a   47. b

Chapter 16
1. a   2. b   3. a   4. b   5. b   6. b   7. b   8. a   9. a   10. a
11. a   12. a   13. b   14. a   15. a   16. b   17. b   18. a   19. b   20. a
21. a   22. a   23. b   24. b   25. b   26. a   27. a   28. a   29. b   30. a
31. b   32. a   33. a   34. a   35. a   36. b   37. a   38. b   39. b   40. a
41. a   42. b   43. b   44. b   45. b   46. b   47. b   48. a   49. a   50. b
51. b   52. b   53. a   54. b   55. a   56. a   57. a   58. a   59. a   60. a
61. a

Chapter 17
1. a   2. a   3. a   4. a   5. b   6. a   7. b   8. a   9. a   10. a
11. a   12. b   13. a   14. a   15. a   16. b   17. b   18. a   19. b   20. a
21. b   22. b   23. a   24. b   25. b   26. a   27. b   28. b   29. a   30. b
31. a   32. b   33. a   34. a   35. a   36. a   37. b   38. a   39. a   40. a
41. b   42. a   43. a   44. b   45. a   46. b   47. b   48. b   49. a   50. a
51. a   52. a   53. a   54. b   55. b   56. b   57. a   58. b   59. a   60. a
61. b   62. a   63. a   64. b   65. b   66. b   67. a   68. a   69. a   70. b
71. a   72. b   73. b   74. b   75. b   76. b   77. a   78. a   79. a   80. b
81. b   82. b

Chapter 18
1. b   2. a   3. a   4. b   5. b   6. b   7. b   8. b   9. b   10. a
11. b   12. a   13. b   14. b   15. a   16. b   17. b   18. a   19. b   20. a
21. b   22. a   23. b   24. a   25. a   26. a   27. b   28. b   29. a   30. b
31. b   32. b   33. b   34. b   35. a   36. b   37. b   38. a   39. a   40. b
41. a   42. b   43. a   44. a   45. a   46. a   47. b   48. a   49. a   50. b
51. b   52. b   53. a   54. a   55. a   56. a   57. b   58. b   59. a   60. b
61. b   62. a   63. b   64. a   65. b   66. b   67. b   68. b   69. b   70. a
71. a   72. a   73. b   74. b   75. a   76. b   77. a   78. b   79. a   80. a
81. b   82. a

Chapter 19

1. b	2. b	3. a	4. a	5. b	6. a	7. a	8. b	9. b	10. b
11. a	12. a	13. b	14. a	15. b	16. b	17. b	18. b	19. a	20. b
21. b	22. b	23. b	24. b	25. b	26. a	27. b	28. b	29. a	30. b
31. a	32. a	33. b	34. b	35. a	36. a	37. b	38. a	39. b	40. b
41. a	42. b	43. b	44. b	45. b	46. a	47. a	48. b	49. a	50. a
51. a	52. a	53. a	54. a	55. b	56. a	57. a	58. b	59. b	60. b
61. a	62. a	63. a	64. b	65. a	66. b	67. a	68. a	69. a	70. b
71. b	72. b	73. a	74. b	75. a	76. a	77. a	78. b	79. a	80. a
81. b	82. b	83. b	84. b	85. b	86. b	87. a	88. a	89. b	90. a
91. b	92. a	93. a	94. b	95. b	96. b	97. a	98. a	99. a	100. b
101. a	102. b	103. b	104. a	105. b	106. a	107. a	108. a	109. b	110. a
111. a									

Chapter 20

1. b	2. b	3. a	4. a	5. a	6. a	7. a	8. b	9. b	10. a
11. a	12. b	13. a	14. a	15. a	16. b	17. b	18. b	19. a	20. b
21. a	22. b	23. a	24. a	25. a	26. a	27. b	28. a	29. a	30. a
31. a	32. b	33. a	34. a	35. b	36. b	37. a	38. b	39. a	40. b
41. b	42. b	43. a	44. b	45. b	46. b	47. a	48. b	49. b	50. b
51. b	52. b	53. b	54. b	55. a	56. a	57. a	58. b	59. b	60. b
61. a	62. b	63. b	64. b	65. a	66. a	67. a	68. b	69. a	70. a
71. b	72. b	73. b	74. a	75. b	76. a	77. b			

Chapter 21

1. a	2. b	3. b	4. b	5. a	6. a	7. a	8. b	9. a	10. b
11. a	12. a	13. a	14. a	15. b	16. b	17. a	18. a	19. a	20. a
21. a	22. b	23. b	24. a	25. a	26. a	27. b	28. b	29. a	30. a
31. a	32. a	33. a	34. a	35. b	36. a	37. b	38. a	39. b	40. a
41. a	42. a	43. b	44. a	45. a	46. a	47. b	48. a	49. a	50. b
51. a	52. b	53. b	54. a	55. a	56. a	57. b	58. b	59. b	60. a
61. b	62. b	63. b	64. a	65. b	66. a	67. b	68. a	69. a	70. b
71. a	72. a	73. a	74. b	75. b	76. b	77. b	78. a	79. a	80. a
81. a	82. a	83. a	84. b	85. a	86. a	87. b	88. b	89. b	90. b
91. b	92. b	93. a	94. b	95. b	96. b	97. a	98. a	99. b	

www.ingramcontent.com/pod-product-compliance
Lightning Source LLC
Chambersburg PA
CBHW081351230426
43667CB00017B/2793